Japan
and
Korea

Regional Studies Series

The Regional Studies Series

Africa
China
Europe
The Subcontinent of India
Japan and Korea
Latin America
The Middle East and North Africa
Russia and the Commonwealth

Japan
and
Korea

Regional Studies Series

Consultant

Robert L. Clark

GLOBE FEARON

Pearson Learning Group

Robert L. Clark

Robert L. Clark has a master's degree in history from the University of Pennsylvania. He has traveled in Korea and has participated in seminars on Korean history and culture sponsored by the Korean Ministry of Education. He specializes in developing instructional materials in social studies and has written textbook materials in world history, U.S. history, and world geography.

Area Specialist: Burton F. Beers is professor of history at North Carolina State University. He is the coauthor of *The Far East* and author of *China in Old Photographs*. He is also the author of a high school world history textbook. He served as a consultant to the North Carolina Department of Education for many years and also planned and directed numerous workshops for social studies teachers.

Executive Editor: Stephen Lewin
Project Editor: Robert Rahtz
Art Director: Nancy Sharkey
Cover Designer: Armando Baez
Production Manager: Winston Sukhnanand
Photo Research: Jenifer Hixson
Marketing Manager: Elmer Ildefonso

Cover Image: The picture on the cover shows an ancient temple in Kyoto, with modern buildings in the distance.
Maps: Mapping Specialists, Ltd.
Graphs, Diagrams, and Charts: Keithley & Associates

Acknowledgments for illustrations appear on page 274.

ISBN 0-8359-0421-0
Printed in the United States of America
6 7 8 9 10   05 04

1-800-321-3106
www.pearsonlearning.com

CONTENTS

Maps

Graphs, Charts, and Diagrams

Japan has imported and digested the Western way of living and mechanical civilization to such a degree that travellers from abroad seeking [particularly "Japanese" characteristics] are often disappointed when they arrive in Tokyo. Yet if the stranger takes a little time to look beneath the surface he will find that the outwardly Western city actually is dominated inwardly by old Japanese customs and thoughts.

—Hisamitsu Noguchi,
This Is Japan: A Nation Re-shaped but Unchanged

We have been born into this land [Korea], charged with the historic mission of regenerating [reviving] the nation. This is the time for us to establish a self-reliant posture within and contribute to the common prosperity of [humankind] without, by revitalizing the illustrious [distinguished] spirit of our forefathers. We do hereby state the proper course to follow and set it up as the aim of our education.

—from the South Korean Charter of National Education

Introduction:
Japan and the Two Koreas

Japan and the two Koreas—North Korea and South Korea—have much in common as well as much that makes them different. As you can see from the map on page xii, these three East Asian nations lie in the shadow of the largest nation of all of Asia, China. In fact, the land of the two Koreas is a peninsula that juts south from China, while Japan's four main islands sit off the coast of China, with its southernmost island only about 100 miles (160 kilometers) off South Korea.

The closeness of Japan and the two Koreas to China has had a profound effect on the history and culture of these lands. As you read about these nations in this book, you will notice how often the influence of China on them is mentioned. From the perspective of the early Japanese and Koreans, the Chinese, with their rich civilization, had much to offer. It was, in fact, the only civilization near enough from which they could borrow to enrich their cultures.

The writing systems used by the Korean and Japanese people originated in China. China also was the home of some of the religious beliefs of these people and other aspects of their way of living. Even today, the way family members relate to one another in Japan and the Koreas shows the strong influence of China, especially as it reflects the teach-

The past, represented by the traditional ancient religions of the people of Japan and Korea, still plays an important part in their lives.

ings of China's great philospher, Confucius. Yet, as strong as the influence of China was, Japan and the Koreas developed individual cultures that were different from China's and special in their own way.

Japan and the Koreas are three highly industrialized countries. In less than a hundred years between the 1870s and the 1950s, Japan became one of the most highly industrialized nations in the world. Now it sends its manufactured products to nations all over the world. South Korea became an industrial nation more recently and in a much shorter period, but it also is a leading exporter of manufactured goods. North Korea lags behind Japan and South Korea in industry, but it too is on the road to becoming an industrial power.

There are, however, significant differences among these nations that set them apart from one another. Japan and South Korea both have democratic political systems, while North Korea is a communist country with an economy that is tightly controlled by the government. South Korea and North Korea have been separate countries for less than half a century, while Japan has been an independent country for several thousand years. Although the people of Japan and the Koreas face each other across a narrow body of water, they are not friendly neighbors. The Koreans have not forgotten that Japan conquered their peninsula in the early years of the 20th century and occupied it for 35 years.

With each passing year, Japan, South Korea, and North Korea as East Asian nations become increasingly important on the world scene. For the United States in particular they offer challenges that make knowing more about them both interesting and essential.

Computer-driven industries, in which many people work, represent the modern side of life in Japan and the two Koreas.

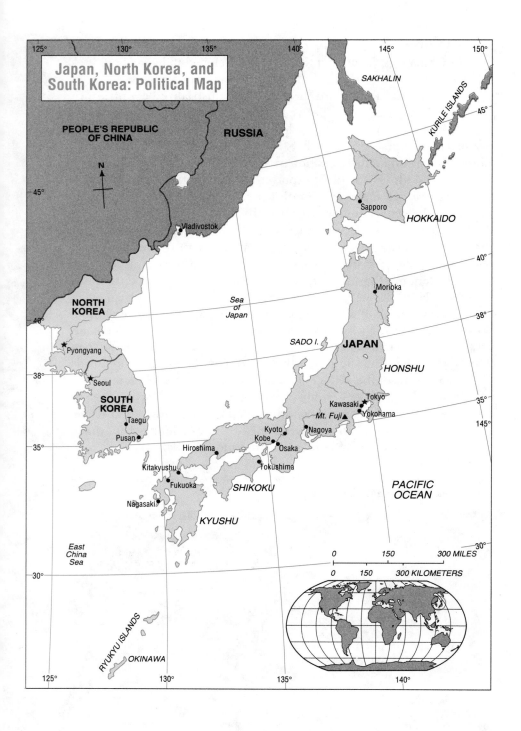

Japan, North Korea, and
South Korea: Political Map

PEOPLE'S REPUBLIC
OF CHINA

RUSSIA

SAKHALIN

KURILE ISLANDS

N

Vladivostok

Sapporo

HOKKAIDO

Morioka

NORTH
KOREA

Sea
of
Japan

SADO I.

JAPAN

HONSHU

Pyongyang

Seoul

SOUTH
KOREA

Taegu

Pusan

Tokyo
Kawasaki
Mt. Fuji▲
Yokohama

Kyoto
Kobe
Osaka

Nagoya

Hiroshima

Kitakyushu

Fukuoka

Tokushima

SHIKOKU

PACIFIC
OCEAN

Nagasaki

KYUSHU

East
China
Sea

0   150   300 MILES

0   150   300 KILOMETERS

RYUKYU ISLANDS

OKINAWA

1 Japan: An Island Nation and Its People

The attendants at the subway station at a Tokyo suburb, in their neat uniforms, watch carefully as the train rolls to a halt. Then, after the swarm of people have entered the cars, the attendants quickly move forward to push still more passengers onto the jammed train. Those who are standing are so tightly squeezed together that it seems they can scarcely breathe. Yet the passengers are polite and seldom shove or push one another. They ride patiently on the two- or three-hour trip that will take them into the distant city.

Most of the passengers are men in business suits. The rest are well-dressed women and young students in school uniforms. Those on board are headed for jobs, school, and the shopping they must complete before their children return from school. Most of them have just left apartments where they and their families live in two or three tiny rooms—not much larger than this subway car.

Scenes like this take place throughout Japan each workday morning, and again each evening. The long trip to and from work or school is not unusual. Crowding and lack of space are a major feature of much of present-day Japanese life. Yet the people of Japan have successfully adapted their lives to these conditions of their island nation. At the same time, they have achieved one of the highest standards of living in the world today.

THE LAND OF JAPAN

The ancestors of the people who commute to and from Japan's crowded cities first began arriving in Japan about 11,000 years ago from the Asian mainland. From that time to the present day, the special nature of the Japanese land has helped determine where the Japanese live, how they

1

earn their living, and what their ways of life are. Its mountains, hills, plains, rivers, and surrounding seas and oceans are the geographic heritage of the Japanese people.

A Chain of Islands. Japan consists of a group of islands located off the coast of Asia, separated from the Asian mainland by the Sea of Japan and the Korea Strait. Almost all of the Japanese people live on the country's four main islands—Honshu (HAHN-shoo), Shikoku (SHEE-koh-koo), Kyushu (kyoo-shoo), and Hokkaido (hoh-KEYE-doh). In addition, the country includes the small Ryukyu (ryoo-kyoo) Islands and more than 3,000 other, tiny islands. Japan thus forms an **archipelago** (ahr-kuh-PEL-uh-goh), or chain of islands, shaped like a crescent curving from north to southwest for nearly 1,400 miles (2,253 kilometers).

Japan's four main islands cover a land area of about 142,000 square miles (367,638 square kilometers). In size, Japan is slightly smaller than the state of California, although it is larger than such nations as Great Britain and Italy. It is dwarfed, however, by China, its giant neighbor on the East Asian mainland, which is 25 times as large as Japan.

Honshu is the nation's largest and most populous island. It has 60 percent of the total land area in Japan. It also is the home of nearly three quarters of the Japanese population and is the site of most of Japan's largest cities. To the south of Honshu is Kyushu, the Japanese island closest to Asia. Kyushu is separated from Korea by the Korea Strait, which is just over 100 miles (161 kilometers) wide. To the east of Kyushu is Shikoku, the smallest of the four islands. Hokkaido, the northernmost island, is the most isolated and sparsely populated of Japan's four main islands.

Japan's Isolation and Development. Japan's location in East Asia has been the most important factor in its history and culture. Separated from the Asian mainland, Japan was never conquered by other peoples in the years of its early development. Thus it was able to shape its own unique culture without being forced to accept the beliefs and ways of living of other peoples. This fact has distinguished Japan from most other nations of the world, who have been subjected to foreign rule at various times in their history. Yet, equally important, Japan was not very far from the Asian mainland, so it was not cut off from contacts with China, Korea, and other Asian lands. Indeed, as you will read, ancient Japan accepted many of the ideals and beliefs of those cultures, especially China. However, it usually adapted these religious, political, and

A bullet train speeds along near Mount Fuji, Japan's tallest mountain. The Japanese consider Fuji sacred, and thousands of pilgrims climb to the summit each year.

other cultural traditions to suit the temperament and special needs of the Japanese people.

A Mountainous Land.   Japan is a land of great beauty, in which nature provides spectacular scenery. The dominant feature of Japan's landscape is its mountains and hills, which cover four fifths of all the land area. These mountains form the backbone of the four main islands, consisting of rugged terrain with deeply wooded slopes and narrow valleys that extend almost to the sea. Of the four main islands, only Honshu has a group of mountains of impressive height. They are tall enough to justify their name as "the Japanese Alps." The tallest and most majestic peak among them is Mount Fuji, which soars 12,385 feet (3,775 meters) high. This extinct volcano is one of the most famous sites in Japan. The rest of the peaks are not as tall. But in the centuries before engineers could build tunnels or bridges across deep valleys, people had great difficulty traveling through Japan's interior.

Japan's islands have experienced severe earthquakes and volcanic eruptions since earliest times. Japan lies along the **Pacific Ring of Fire**, an area of deep trenches beneath the ocean. There, movements of the earth's crust produce sudden earthquakes and volcanic activity. In fact,

3

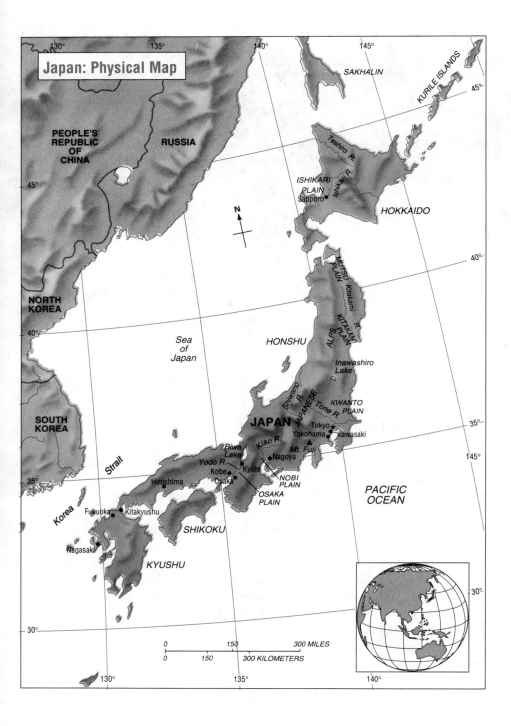

Japan: Physical Map

130°   135°   140°   145°

SAKHALIN

45°

KURILE ISLANDS

PEOPLE'S
REPUBLIC
OF
CHINA

RUSSIA

Teshio R.

45°

ISHIKARI
PLAIN
Sapporo   Ishikari R.

HOKKAIDO

N

40°

MUTSU
PLAIN

NORTH
KOREA

Kitakami

40°

Sea
of
Japan

HONSHU

KITAKAMI
PLAIN

ALPS   Kitakami R.

Inawashiro
Lake

KWANTO
PLAIN

SOUTH
KOREA

JAPAN

Shinano R.   JAPANESE   Tone R.

Tokyo   35°

Yokohama   Kawasaki

Biwa
Lake   Kiso R.   Mt. Fuji

Yodo R.   Nagoya

145°

Strait   Kobe   Kyoto

35°   Hiroshima   Osaka   NOBI
PLAIN

PACIFIC
OCEAN

OSAKA
PLAIN

Korea   Fukuoka   Kitakyushu

SHIKOKU

Nagasaki

KYUSHU

30°

30°

0   150   300 MILES

0   150   300 KILOMETERS

130°   135°   140°

4

much of Japan's land was formed by the peaks of great undersea mountains created millions of years ago by violent motions in the earth's crust. Today, there are 200 volcanoes in Japan, but only about 30 of them are still active, and they are remote from settled areas. However, earthquakes still are common occurrences, and Japan is rocked by 1,500 shocks and tremors each year. The last great earthquake, in 1923, destroyed large parts of Tokyo and killed 130,000 people.

Japan's mountainous terrain has greatly influenced the pattern of Japanese settlement and development. The rugged landscape could support only a few small isolated villages. Most of its steep mountain slopes were unsuited to agriculture. Frequent landslides and volcanic activity were added dangers that made life there extremely difficult.

The fact that Japan is divided into small sections of land that were isolated from one another was important in the country's early history. It led to the development of local communities with strong leaders. Each local area was independent of the others. Almost in spite of this, the Japanese people thought of themselves as belonging to a single united nation. This feeling has persisted to this day to a greater extent than in almost any other nation.

Japan's Plains. Because of the difficulty of living in the mountainous regions, from earliest times, most of the people settled along Japan's few river valleys and on the level, low-lying land found in several coastal plains. These plains are all fairly small in size. Together they make up only one eighth of the total land area. Despite the limited space offered by these coastal plains, the Japanese have settled there in ever-increasing numbers. Much of the interior of the islands is sparsely populated. The plains offer the most productive farm land and easy access to seas around the islands. Nearly 90 percent of the population now lives on the coastal plains. Japan's major cities are located there.

The Kanto Plain on the island of Honshu is the largest of Japan's coastal plains. Covering an area of 5,000 square miles (12,950 square kilometers) it surrounds Tokyo, Japan's capital city, and the nearby city of Yokohama. The Kanto Plain is Japan's most densely populated region and its largest industrial center, as well as one of its richest agricultural areas. The Nobi Plain, another major coastal plain on Honshu, borders Nagoya (nuh-GOY-uh), Japan's leading textile center. The Nobi Plain is also a major farming area. Farther south on Honshu is the Osaka (oh-SAH-kuh) Plain, another fairly large area of level land. The important ports and manufacturing cities of Kobe (KOH-bee), Osaka, and Kyoto (KYOH-toh) developed there.

5

These three coastal plains are the home of Japan's eight largest cities. More than 40 million people, or nearly one third of Japan's total population of 125 million, live in the **megalopolis** on Honshu called Tokaido (toh-KEYE-doh). A megalopolis is an area of nearly continuous cities. Tokaido forms a corridor of very densely populated land that extends for about 350 miles (545 kilometers) from Tokyo to Osaka. In addition, other coastal plains on the islands of Hokkaido and Kyushu are the sites of the major cities of Sapporo (suh-POHR-oh) and Fukuoka (foo-kuh-WOH-kuh) as well as farming areas on those islands.

A Maritime Nation. Since no part of Japan is more than 70 miles (112 kilometers) from the sea, the ocean is ever present in the people's minds. Rocky capes, steep cliffs, hillsides shrouded in fog, half-hidden inlets, and endless waves pounding against the coast—these provide unforgettable scenes that are greatly admired by the Japanese.

Surrounded by the Pacific Ocean on the east and the Sea of Japan on the west, Japan used its strategic location over time to help it overcome its isolation as an island nation. In time it became one of the world's leading **maritime**, or sea-oriented, nations. The long coastline of its four main islands stretches for 4,628 miles (7,448 kilometers) and is indented by many good natural harbors. From earliest times, fishing villages sprang up in many places along the coast, as fishers harvested an abundant food supply from the sea. Important seaports and ocean trading centers grew up along the deep harbors that dot the eastern coasts along the Pacific Ocean and border the Inland Sea. Today, Osaka and Kobe are among the world's largest seaports.

The Inland Sea that borders Honshu, Kyushu, and Shikoku also forms an important water highway within Japan. Throughout the country's history, this sea has helped the Japanese people reduce their isolation. The people, living on their separate islands, have used the Inland Sea to trade and exchange ideas with people on the other islands and develop a common culture. Today, the Inland Sea as a unifying roadway is less important than it once was. Hokkaido and Honshu are joined by the world's longest tunnel, while Shikoku is linked to Honshu by three bridges. Of course, all the islands are now also linked by airplane.

THE CLIMATE OF JAPAN

Japan has a generally moderate climate that has helped the Japanese make the best use of its mostly mountainous terrain. Most parts of

Japan enjoy fairly mild weather throughout the year, especially in the regions where most Japanese live.

A Temperate Climate.   Japan's four main islands extend from 31° to 45° north latitude, giving Japan a wide range of different climates. Japan's climate is often compared to that of the east coast of the United States. Winters are coldest in the northern island of Hokkaido and warmest in southern Kyushu. Winter temperatures in Tokyo and the other large cities of Honshu are similar to those in the state of Virginia. However, Japan receives more precipitation and has somewhat warmer temperatures than the east coast of the United States. Warm ocean currents in the Sea of Japan help moderate the nation's winter climate.

Most of Japan, in fact, has a fairly mild climate throughout the year, with moderate seasonal changes that favor agriculture. In the central and southern part of Japan, winters rarely fall below freezing. Summers there are warm, ranging from 77° to 80° degrees Fahrenheit (25° to 27° Celsius). Abundant rainfall arrives in late spring and during the summer. These seasonal winds, called **monsoons**, blow from the southeast, carrying moist, warm air from the Pacific Ocean. Downpours occur again in September and October, sometimes accompanied by **typhoons**, or

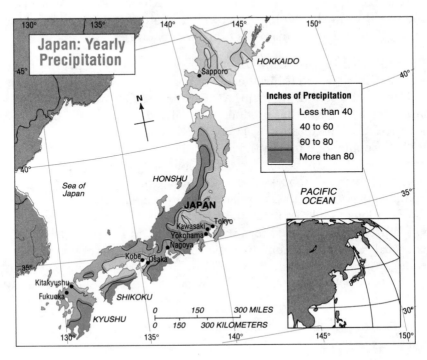

violent tropical winds, of great destructive force. In the winter, monsoons blow from the northwest, bringing cold air and snows of 5 or 6 feet (1.65 to 1.86 meters) to northwestern Honshu.

Climate and Agriculture. Japan's moderate climate makes possible a long growing season for farming, ranging from 215 days in central Honshu to 250 days in most of southern Honshu, Kyushu, and Shikoku. In central and southern Japan, where most farms are located, farmers are able to plant two crops each year. Usually a crop of rice is grown, and then a second crop, of barley, wheat, or a vegetable, is planted. In this way, Japan's climate has made it possible for the island nation, from earliest times, to support a large population despite the shortage of land that can be cultivated.

ECONOMIC RESOURCES

Compared with other modern industrialized nations, Japan has few of the resources and raw materials in sufficient quantities for developing an advanced economy. Yet Japan has been able to grow into the second-largest trading nation in the world, after the United States. It has used the wealth gained from the exports of its manufactured goods to buy minerals, fuel, and raw materials from other countries.

Pre-Industrial Japan. Until the mid-1800s, Japan was primarily a farming and fishing nation. Thus the lack of mineral resources and raw materials was not a serious problem. At that time, the manufacture of iron and steel as well as other products was carried on in small workshops. Further, until the mid-1800s, Japan had a population of only about 30 million people, one fourth the size of the present population. It had enough resources to support a society composed not only of people who produced their own food, shelter, and clothing but also merchants, small manufacturers, and a class of rulers and government officials. The steep slopes of Japan's hills and mountains were covered with forests that provided the lumber needed for building homes and the wood fuel and charcoal for heating them. Supplies of coal and iron ore were large enough to support an iron industry. The many swift-flowing mountain streams and several rivers helped provide power for the nation's early factories.

The Geography of Industrial Japan. In the latter part of the 1800s, the rulers of Japan decided to make it a modern, industrial nation. It did this despite the fact that it had only very limited quantities of the natural resources required for industrialization. Unlike the industrial giants of the time—the United States, Great Britain, and Germany—it had limited amounts of coal to power its manufacturing plants. Iron, zinc, and lead were in equally short supply. Then, in the second half of the 1900s, when oil became a major source of energy, it had to face the fact that it had only a trickle of this vital resource as well.

To become a truly first-rate industrial nation, Japan had to find the means to acquire these essentials. It tried to do so in two ways. One way was to conquer lands that had these resources. In the early 1900s, as you will read in Chapter 3, it set about acquiring an empire, without much success. The other, more successful, way was to import what it needed from nations that were well supplied with these products. Today, Japan has achieved its goal and is one of the world's leading industrial nations, buying almost all of its raw materials and energy resources from abroad. At the same time, it sells a major portion of its industrial output to markets beyond its horizons. A veteran analyst of Japan's history and culture has summed up the country's economy this way: "Japan's dependence on global trade for its very survival is the most important single fact about its economic geography and the chief determinant [deciding factor] of its relationship with the outside world."

Nevertheless, in its drive to become an international trading nation, Japan had certain geographic advantages. As an island nation, Japan was surrounded by seas that provided a ready transportation route. On the coastal plains, near such port cities as Kobe and Osaka, were existing cities. These were enlarged and new ones built where the imports could be turned into manufactured products. People by the thousands flocked to cities like Tokyo, Osaka, Yokohama, Kawasaki, and Nagoya to find work in the new industries. Today, an almost unbroken line of factories and houses stretches along the coastal plain from Tokyo down through Nagoya to northern Kyushu (see the map on page 4). Of Japan's major cities, only Kyoto is an inland city. A system of roads and railroads connects the cities, and, as noted earlier, bridges and a tunnel now help link the islands into a compact economic unit.

Cities and City Living. The economic transformation of Japan changed not only what the people do for a living but also how they have come to live in the great crowded urban centers. More than 90 percent of Japan's people live in cities, many of them in very large cities. Tokyo and Yokohama together form one of the world's largest metropolitan areas, with a population of over 23 million. Osaka, Japan's second-

CASE STUDY:

Japan and the Persian Gulf Crisis

In August 1990, Saddam Hussein, the leader of Iraq, invaded the oil-rich Persian Gulf country of Kuwait. The United Nations then placed an embargo on Iraq, in which Japan only reluctantly joined. For this attitude Japan was widely criticized in the West. This excerpt from an article in a U.S. magazine explains Japan's position.

> The notion that the Japanese have the most at stake in the gulf "is not a rational argument but an argument based on emotion," says Tomoharu Washio, [of a] Tokyo think tank. . . .Any rational analysis leads to the opposite conclusion: that it can cope economically with almost any oil-price scenario better than the United States can. . . . Japan's confidence is rooted in three fundamental facts. . . :
> • Oil reserves, no matter how vast, are worthless unless brought to market. . . . Most [Japanese leaders] would agree with . . . Tokyo business consultant James C. Abegglen: "If [Saddam] doesn't sell [oil], what's he going to do, drink it?. . . ."
> • Energy efficiency matters as much as dependency. . . . Since 1973 [Japan] has relentlessly [deliberately] implemented conservation policies that have paid off. During the first Arab embargo [in 1973], oil provided nearly 80 percent of Japan's energy. By 1986, that had fallen to 56 percent. Today, Japan's economy produces 81 percent more real output for the same amount of energy than it did in 1973 . . . . Overall, the Japanese economy is twice as energy efficient as America's.
> • While a war-induced oil-price hike . . . will almost certainly deepen and prolong the slump in the United States, in Japan the worst that's expected is slower growth.
> "The gulf crisis," said a 34-year-old Tokyo [woman worker] . . . "is like looking at a fire on the other side of the river."

From *Newsweek*, January 21, 1991.

1. What did Japan do in the years since 1973 to make it less dependent on the oil that it must import?

2. What did the Tokyo worker mean when she said, "The gulf crisis is like looking at a fire on the other side of the river"?

The Ten Most Heavily Populated Japanese Cities		
CITY	ISLAND	POPULATION (1990)
1. Tokyo	Honshu	8,200,000
2. Yokohama	Honshu	3,200,000
3. Osaka	Honshu	2,600,000
4. Nagoya	Honshu	2,200,000
5. Sapporo	Hokkaido	1,700,000
6. Kyoto	Honshu	1,500,000
7. Kobe	Honshu	1,500,000
8. Fukuoka	Kyushu	1,200,000
9. Kawasaki	Honshu	1,100,000
10. Hiroshima	Honshu	1,050,000

Sources: *Facts and Figures of Japan,* 1991 Edition; *Nippon: A Charted Survey of Japan, 1990/1991*

largest city, is home to over 2.5 million Japanese. There are eight other cities, from Sapporo in the north to Fukuoka (foo-koo-OH-kuh) and Kitakyushu (kee-tah-kyoo-shoo) in the south, with populations of more than 1 million people. Many of Japan's farming and fishing villages are declining and much of their traditional way of life is disappearing.

As you have read, most of Japan's major cities are located on the coastal plains, which make up only a small part of Japan's land area. Over half the population, about 115 million people, lives on just 2 percent of Japan's land area. This land area is roughly equal in size to the state of Connecticut. The concentration of such a large number of people in so small an area gives Japan a **population density** that rivals China and Bangladesh, the world's most densely populated countries. Japan, about equal in size to California, has a population over four times that of California.

Tokyo, Osaka, Kobe, and Japan's other large cities are crowded, bustling centers of business and industry. Tall office buildings, banks, and apartment houses compete for scarce available space. Virtually every square inch and kilometer of city land is fully used. Narrow city

11

Tokyo, Japan's capital and largest city, teems with people.
To house its growing population, tall apartment buildings
have replaced most of the city's older wooden houses.

streets are clogged with traffic not only during rush hours but through-out the day. Exhaust fumes from cars, buses, and trucks combine with the pollution of factories and warehouses, often located within or right next to these cities, to create unhealthful urban landscapes. Of the major cities, only Kyoto, the ancient capital, with old Buddhist temples, Shinto shrines, and lovely gardens, retains its link with Japan's past. The city is still the home of small factories and workshops that produce fine textiles, enamel ware, and ceramics.

Housing in Cities.   City housing consists mainly of apartment dwellings, since only the very wealthy can afford the cost of a private home. Land is so scarce and expensive in Tokyo, for example, that even a modest house for a family of five on a small plot of land might cost several million dollars. Obviously, few Japanese can afford such homes. As a result, in Tokyo and other large cities, most families live in modern apartment buildings of four to ten stories. The average city apartment consists of two or three very small rooms.

Since the large cities are so expensive, many Japanese who work there live in distant towns and cities where housing and living costs in general are lower. Those who live in distant towns and cities commute to work on trains that require a two- or three-hour daily trip each way, as

12

you read in the introduction to this chapter. Fortunately, Japan has an excellent system of mass transportation. High-speed "bullet trains" traveling at speeds of over 100 miles (160 kilometers) an hour connect the main cities. Tokyo and other cities also have efficient subways that, while tightly packed with passengers, speed workers to their jobs.

The Agricultural Setting. Even though Japan has become an **urban,** or city-centered, nation, farming is still a vital segment of the nation's economy. Today, only 14 percent of Japan's land is used for agriculture. Every bit of soil that can be cultivated in the coastal plains and valley lowlands, as well as terraced farm land on mountain slopes, is put to use to grow food.

As in other industrial countries of the world, Japan's impressively large output of food is produced by a relatively small number of farmers. Today, just over 4 million families, less than 18 million people, are engaged in farming. Farmers make up less than 7 percent of the population. Most of them work only part time in agriculture. Holding down jobs in large cities or nearby towns, over 70 percent of Japan's farmers earn more than half their income from sources other than farming.

Rice is still the most valuable crop grown in Japan. Nearly half of all **arable** land, or land on which crops can be raised, is devoted to growing rice, and it accounts for nearly 31 percent of the value of all farm production. Japan produces more than 90 percent of the rice its people consume. It also grows large crops of soybeans, wheat, barley, and vegetables. In total, Japanese farmers raise nearly 70 percent of the nation's food. Additional supplies of these crops and other food are imported from abroad. Among the imports are meat, which has increased in popularity in recent years, and wheat, which is used to bake the European-style bread that many Japanese families now prefer to rice.

Despite the need to import food, the productivity of Japan's agriculture is remarkable. Much of Japan's farmland has poor soil and requires fertilization, constant irrigation, and improved seeds. Most farms are so small, averaging 2 to 4 acres (.8 to 1.6 hectares), that special farm machinery must be used. The Japanese have developed motorized rice planters not much larger than lawn mowers that are pushed along by hand. They also use small threshing machines and tractors that can be maneuvered over the fields.

The Bounty of the Sea. Unlike the land, in many ways the sea has been Japan's most dependable and abundant natural resource. From earliest times, fish have been the main source of protein, an essential element in the human diet, for the Japanese people. This remains true even today, when Japan's vast modern fishing fleet harvests and processes this staple of the nation's dinner table. The Sea of Japan and the Pacific Ocean supply an endless bounty of tuna, mackerel, sardine, halibut, bonito, shrimp, and herring. Octopus and squid are also widely consumed. In most Japanese homes today, fish and other food from the sea are usually served as part of the meal.

To harvest this rich resource for its people, Japan developed a fishing industry that is now the largest in the world. It has over 400,000 fishing vessels. They reap their catch both from nearby waters and from fishing grounds in many other parts of the world. To supplement the catch from the seas, the Japanese have established fish farms where fish are raised. Another part of the Japanese diet from the seas consists of seaweed that is cultivated in farms along the coasts. Seaweed is a rich source of vitamins and minerals.

THE PEOPLE OF JAPAN

The earliest inhabitants of Japan may have been the people now called the Ainu. They may have started living there about 100,000 years ago. Scientists believe that the ancestors of the present-day Japanese migrated there during the last Ice Age, which lasted until about 11,000 years ago. These people came from what is now China and Korea.

The Early Japanese.   The early Japanese people gradually spread throughout the four main islands of the archipelago. At first, they were hunters and fishers who lived together in small groups. Then, with the introduction of rice cultivation, the Japanese began to lead a more settled life in small farming villages. (You will learn about the early history of Japan in Chapter 2.)

Over a period of time, the Japanese forced the Ainu from their lands, pushing them back to the northernmost island, Hokkaido. Today, only about 16,000 Ainu remain in Japan.

Characteristics of the Japanese People.   The people of Japan early began to form their identity as a people and to develop traditions and ways of life that set them apart from neighboring peoples in Asia. Over many centuries, the people developed a culture that was uniquely Japanese.

As the Japanese settled and developed their island nation, they became a **homogenous** people. That is, they became a people with a

School children pose in front of a giant statue of Buddha. Buddhism is one of the many features of Chinese culture that the Japanese borrowed from their East Asian neighbor.

common culture and ways of life. During their long history, the Japanese have shared a common language, common religious and ethical beliefs, and the same values and traditions.

This quality of the Japanese people was reinforced by the geographic isolation of Japan. More than any other major country, Japan's separation from its neighbors permitted it to develop as a nation without needing to fight against invaders. (Another island nation, Great Britain, was invaded many times.) At the same time, Japan was close enough to the Asian mainland to have contact with the people there. As a result, Japan borrowed many features of the cultures of China and Korea. From China came its writing system, forms of its early government, and Confucianism, one of Japan's religious systems. Another set of religious beliefs, Buddhism, came from China and Korea. Many other nations have borrowed from their neighbors, in a process called **cultural adaptation.** Yet, unlike most of such nations, quite remarkably, Japan absorbed what it borrowed into its culture in such a way that the culture retained its special Japanese character. This process of borrowing without changing the essential nature of the Japanese culture has been a feature of Japanese history through the ages. Even today, after Japan borrowed its industrial technology from the nations of the West, it remains very much a "Japanese" country.

Japan's geography also played an important role in establishing the Japanese identity. As you have read, the mountainous landscape required its people to settle close together in small valleys and in limited areas along the few coastal plains. This also strengthened the people's feelings of **group identity**, or sense of belonging to the same group. As you will read in Chapter 4, identification with the group is an important part of many aspects of Japanese life.

As a farming and fishing nation, Japan's people learned early in their history that they must work together in order to survive. The lack of good, fertile farmland posed special difficulties. However, families found that by working together in groups to terrace hilly land, build irrigation systems, and cultivate rice by hand they could create a dependable food supply. This difficult feat reinforced the important role of the group in their lives.

Throughout their history, the Japanese have been proud of their achievements as a people. They have taken unusual pride in their ability to work together to achieve common goals, even in the face of great obstacles. They tend to think of themselves as a special people who

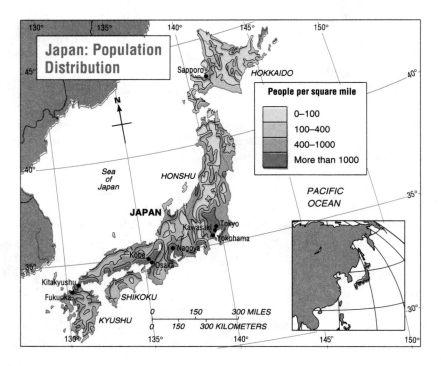

The tea ceremony is an ages-old tradition that is still observed by Japanese women. It is a link to the country's long history, of which the people are very proud.

have talents and abilities that are different from and perhaps superior to those of other peoples, whom they think of as foreigners. This quality has often helped the Japanese overcome adversity and hardships. However, it has also had other, less fortunate consequences, and it has sometimes caused the Japanese to treat other people unfairly.

Early in Japan's history, as you will read, Koreans arrived in Japan and made important contributions to Japanese culture. Some Koreans remained in Japan, and in the early and mid-1900s other Koreans were brought forcibly to Japan as laborers. Today, there are about 700,000 Koreans living in Japan. Yet Japan refuses to allow them to become citizens and discriminates against them in many other ways. The 60,000 Chinese in Japan, too, are not treated as equals. Even the 16,000 Ainu in Hokkaido are regarded as being different from other Japanese.

This attitude also influences the way they treat a group of their own people, the *burakumin* (boo-RAH-koo-meen). The more than 1 million *burakumin* are descendants of people who were butchers and leather tanners in early Japan. Since the Buddhist religion, practiced by many Japanese today, does not believe in killing animals, the *burakumin* still suffer from prejudice. Most Japanese families avoid contact with them and refuse to allow their sons and daughters to marry anyone in this group. Many *burakumin* are forced to live in separate urban slums.

Today, the Japanese view of themselves as a special people has complicated Japan's new role as a great trading nation and economic superpower. The leaders of Japan's government attribute their nation's remarkable economic success to the enterprise of their managers, the hard work of their labor force, and their skillful cooperation in working in groups. It is these qualities, they claim, that have enabled the Japanese to capture world markets in automobiles, VCRs, camcorders, microwaves, cameras, TVs, and CD players. They suggest that Americans and other peoples are unable or unwilling to work together in this way to become as productive as the Japanese.

THE JAPANESE LANGUAGE

The Japanese language is distantly related to the language of Korea. Both of them belong to a family of languages believed to have originated in central Asia. Until the mid-1800s there were many **dialects**, or varieties, of Japanese spoken in Japan. Many were so different from one another that people in one part of the country often could not understand people in another part. The written form of the language, however, was the same in all parts of the country. Now the dialect of the city of Tokyo is the standard speech of Japan, although people in various parts of the country speak it with a variety of local accents.

Written Japanese. The written form of the Japanese language is one of the most difficult writing systems to learn. It uses a combination of phonetic symbols to represent sounds, as well as Chinese characters to represent words. As you will read in Chapter 2, the Japanese adopted Chinese characters for their written language in the third and fourth centuries A.D. These characters are called *kanji* (KAHN-jee) by the Japanese. Since the *kanji* characters were not well suited to the sounds of Japanese, they were simplified and used to represent Japanese syllables rather than complete words. In this system, called *kana* (kah-nah), every Japanese syllable is represented by a Chinese character that has been adapted in form.

There are two kinds of *kana*. In one form, the original Chinese character is written but in a flowing, or cursive, style. In the second form of *kana*, an abbreviated form of the Chinese character is used. An example of all three kinds of symbols is shown below.

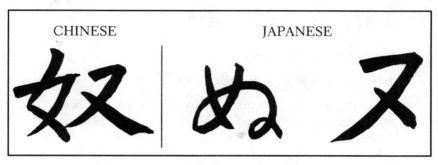

CHINESE   JAPANESE

The Chinese character, on the left, means "slave." The first Japanese character is an adaptation, representing the syllable nu. *The character to the right is an abbreviated form that uses part of the original Chinese character.*

Since the writing system consists of thousands of individual symbols, the Japanese government attempted to simplify the written language after World War II. The spellings of Japanse words were changed to conform to the pronunciation then in use. The number of *kanji* characters was reduced, and the way of writing them was simplified.

The Use of English and the Latin Alphabet. English is the language of international trade, which is a mainstay of the Japanese economy. Hence, many Japanese have learned to speak it, and English is widely taught in Japanese schools. However, the huge differences between the grammatical structure and sounds of the two languages make it difficult for speakers of Japanese to master English (just as speakers of English have difficulty learning Japanese). Often there are no accurate literal translations of words or phrases from one language into the other.

Many Japanese language experts believe that the present system of writing Japanese is outdated and hinders communication with people in other parts of the world. Therefore, an attempt has been made to introduce the Latin alphabet that is used in most Western languages. However, not many Japanese are in favor of such a radical change. They believe that the present system, while it might be further simplified, is a vital part of the treasured Japanese tradition and for this reason should not be abandoned.

REVIEWING THE CHAPTER

I. Building Your Vocabulary

Match the definitions with their terms.

archipelago   megalopolis   homogeneous
maritime   urban   *burakumin*
typhoon   monsoon   *kana*
Pacific Ring of Fire

1. wind that changes direction with the seasons

2. pertaining to people of a single ethnic group

3. an area of nearly continuous cities

4. pertaining to the sea

5. a chain of islands

6. a violent tropical wind

7. part of the Japanese writing system

8. Japanese people who are discriminated against

9. a region of volcanoes and earthquakes

10. pertaining to cities

II. Understanding the Facts

Write the letter of the correct answer to each question next to its number.

1. The most populous island of Japan is:
   a. Honshu.   b. Shikoku.
   c. Hokkaido.   d. Kyushu.

2. In what areas of Japan do nearly 90 percent of the people live?
   a. in the mountains   b. along the Korea Strait
   c. on the coastal plains   d. along the rivers

3. The part of the United States that Japan's climate is most similar to is:
   a. the east coast.   b. California.
   c. the South.   d. the Middle West.

4. Japan has long been subjected to all of the following *except:*
   a. earthquakes.   b. volcanoes.
   c. avalanches.   d. typhoons.

5. Which one of the following best describes Japan's cities?
   a. densely populated   b. mostly seaports
   c. sparsely populated   d. far from the sea

III. Thinking It Through

Write the letter of the correct answer next to its number.

1. Present-day Japan's greatest challenge is:
   a. rapid population growth.
   b. limited natural resources.
   c. a harsh climate.
   d. lack of trained people.

2. Japan's location off the coast of East Asia helped shape its history and culture because:
   a. it protected Japan from invasion and conquest.
   b. it isolated Japan from contacts with China and Korea.
   c. it helped Japan become an industrial nation.
   d. it forced Japan to become a farming nation.

3. Japan's agriculture was limited by:
   a. the lack of farm machinery.
   b. shortage of people who wanted to work the land.
   c. shortage of land that could be cultivated.
   d. its system of land ownership.

4. Which statement below best describes Japan's natural resources?
   a. Japan has always lacked enough iron ore, coal, and other resources.
   b. Japan has most of the resources it needs except oil.
   c. Japan must import oil and many other resources it requires.
   d. Japan's resources have limited its growth as an industrial nation.

5. Which of the following is an outcome of Japan's location as an island nation?

   a. Its people became expert swimmers.

   b. It always had a strong navy.

   c. It used the seas as a source of food.

   d. It did not have to depend on internal transportation facilities.

DEVELOPING CRITICAL THINKING SKILLS

1. Describe how Japan's location as an island nation influenced its history.

2. Explain how the geography of Japan has determined where people in that nation live.

3. Describe some of the factors that led to the Japanese becoming a homogeneous people.

4. Describe the attitude of the Japanese people to minorities in Japan and foreigners.

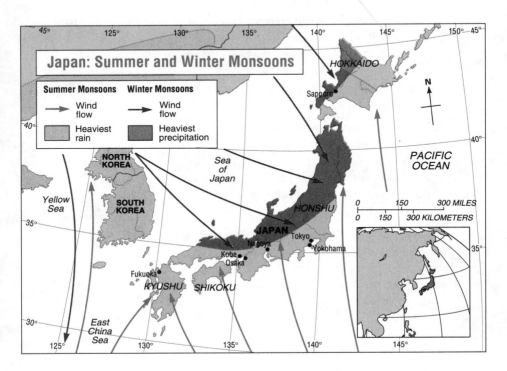

22

INTERPRETING A MAP

Study the map on page 22. Then answer these questions.

1. Over what bodies of water do the monsoons pass?

2. Which of the main Japanese islands are not affected by the winter monsoons?

3. What impact do the monsoons have on Japan's climate?

ENRICHMENT AND EXPLORATION

1. Consult a reference work to learn more about the Ainu, the people who lived in Japan before the Japanese. Make a checklist of the major differences between them and the early Japanese.

2. Japan and Great Britain are both island nations. Do research to find out in what ways their geography is similar and different and how these factors have affected each nation's history.

3. If you could arrange a summer vacation trip to Japan for you and your family, list the places you would want to visit and why. Collect brochures from a travel agent and consult travel magazines to help you decide.

THE LEGACY OF EARLY JAPAN

c. 8000 B.C.–A.D. 1853

c. 8000 B.C.–250 B.C.	The Jomon Period
2500–1500 B.C.	*Indus Valley civilization*
1200 B.C.	*Olmec civilization*
600 B.C.	Traditional date of Jimmu, Japan's first emperor
750 B.C.	*Kush conquers Egypt.*
461–429 B.C.	*Golden Age of Greece*
c. 250 B.C.–A.D. 250	The Yayoi Period
250–710	The Yamato Period
300–900	*Mayan civilization*
645	The Taika Reforms adapt Chinese culture.
710–1184	The Nara and Heian Periods
800–1000	*African kingdom of Ghana*
858	Fujiwara Yoshifusa becomes regent.
1020	*The Tale of the Genji* by Lady Murasaki
c. 1040	*Chinese invent movable type.*
1185–1333	The Kamakura Shogunate
1185	Minamoto Yorimoto establishes the first shogunate.
1200–1450	*African empire of Mali*
1338–1573	The Ashikaga Shogunate
c. 1450	*The Inca establish an empire in the Andes.*
1450–1600	*African empire of Songhai*
1502–1521	*Montezuma rules Aztecs.*
1543	Portuguese traders bring guns to Japan.
1585–1867	The Tokugawa Shogunate
1603	Ieyasu Tokugawa becomes shogun.
1641	Japan isolates itself.
1853	Commodore Perry arrives in Japan.

2 The Legacy of Early Japan (c. 8000 B.C.– A.D. 1853)

In A.D. 747 the Emperor Shomu (SHOH-mooh) gave the order to begin work on a huge statue of the Buddha and a temple to hold it. In doing so, the emperor hoped to express his deep devotion to the symbol of Japan's new religion. He believed that the great temple and giant statue would make his nation's new imperial capital at Nara (nah-rah) the center of Buddhism in Japan. For the next five years, 50,000 men worked on the construction of the enormous Todaiji (toh-DEYE-jee) Temple. Thousands of skilled metal workers cast the huge bronze figure of the Buddha, over 53 feet (16.54 meters) high. They used over 3 million tons (27 million kilograms) of copper, tin, and lead, and 15,000 pounds (6,800 kilograms) of gold.

Finally, the great task was completed. In 752 Emperor Shomu's magnificent Buddhist shrine was dedicated with elaborate rituals befitting the occasion. This dedication was the greatest ceremony to take place thus far in Japan's history. More than 10,000 Buddhist priests presided at this ceremony. Monks and other visitors from China, Korea, and from lands as far away as India were present.

The Japanese emperor had now become the leader in establishing Buddhism as an official national religion. Within a few years, more than 42 Buddhist temples sponsored by the emperor were built at Nara. As you will read, Buddhism was to become a traditional religion and a vital influence in Japanese culture.

EARLY JAPANESE HISTORY (c. 8000 B.C.–A.D. 710)

Our knowledge of the early history of the Japanese people, like that of the beginnings of most peoples, is still incomplete. However, the find-

25

ings of archaeologists and evidence from Chinese documents have helped historians reconstruct the beginnings of Japan's history. Also helpful in reconstructing the story of Japan's early years have been official histories of Japan that Japan's rulers ordered written. By the A.D. 700s, these rulers regarded keeping a detailed record of their people's history as one of their major duties. The records combined myths with well-documented facts. Later historians have been able to separate out the myths and legends that were included to build a reasonably accurate story of what actually happened in the early years of Japan's history.

The Jomon and Yayoi Periods (c. 8000 B.C.–c. A.D. 300). Little is known about the earliest people of Japan, but archaeologists have been slowly filling in the details of how they lived. The early Japanese were fishers and hunters and food gatherers. They lived in dwellings dug into the earth with thatched roofs, and they made pottery that they decorated with ropelike designs. The designs were made by pressing a rope, called *jomon* (joh-mohn), into wet clay. The period from about 8000 to 250 B.C. has been called the Jomon Period after this design.

The introduction of wet-field, or irrigated, rice growing from China in about 250 B.C. brought important changes to these early people's lives. With a dependable food supply, agriculture and settlement now became important features of Japanese life. This so-called Yayoi (yah-YOY) Period, which takes its name from a district in Tokyo where a kind of pottery typical of the time was found. It lasted 500 years, to A.D.

Even in Japan's Jomon period, the earliest in its history, craftworkers had the skill to fashion this elaborately decorated female figurine.

250. At this time, bronze and iron tools came into use. These metals were introduced from China and Korea, possibly through trade with these countries. By A.D. 200, people from Korea may have invaded and settled in Japan. China's rulers had sent representatives to visit Japan as early as A.D. 57. The Japanese may also have established some trade with these Asian lands during this period.

Beginning in the Yayoi Period, the people lived in family units called *uji* (OO-jee). The *uji* were groups of families that were thought to be descended from a common ancestor. The early *uji* were headed by chieftains, both men and women, who were religious and political leaders. The *uji* chieftains were Japan's earliest rulers.

By A.D.300 powerful *uji* were living in central and western Japan along the Inland Sea. Much of our information about this period comes from the huge tombs in which *uji* chieftains were buried. The largest tomb, in central Japan, is 2,700 feet (823 meters) in length. The pottery and clay figures found in these tombs reveal the great wealth and power of the chieftains. They were served by small groups of aristocratic warriors on horseback who fought with iron weapons. Iron was also beginning to be used for farm tools.

The Yamato Period (c. A.D. 300–710). Rivalries among the *uji* led to conflicts. The most powerful *uji* conquered their weaker rivals and gradually consolidated their territory into larger holdings. By 400, one of strongest groups of *uji*, the Yamato (yah-MAH-toh), had become the dominant power in central Japan. Based on the Yamato, or Nara, Plain, they became leaders of a **coalition,** or union, of other *uji* and united much of Japan. At the same time, they invaded Korea and occupied land there. In this way, the Yamato further increased their power and prestige. The ruler of the Tenno *uji*, one of the most powerful of the Yamato group, became the first emperor of Japan and established the dynasty that has ruled Japan ever since.

By about this time, the Shinto religion was widely practiced in Japan. **Shinto** means the way of the gods. Believers in Shinto worshiped many gods, called *kami* (kam-ee), which were found in nature, such as mountains, lakes, rivers, rocks, and trees. In ancient times, anything that was outside the ordinary, that possessed superior virtues, or that inspired awe, was called *kami*.

Contacts with China. The growing power of the Yamato was due in part to the skill with which its leaders applied ideas they imported from the mainland. From the 4th century through the mid-6th century, the

Yamato were in close touch with southern Korea. Then, by the 7th century, China, which was enjoying one of the greatest periods in its history, became the focus of the Yamato's interest. From the 5th century on, Japan was deeply influenced by the culture of China. As you have read, Japan had had contacts with China and Korea for many centuries. However, as Japan itself became more unified, Chinese civilization played an increasingly vital role in shaping Japanese culture.

The introduction of **Buddhism** by monks and scholars from China about 552 not only helped shape Japan's religious tradition but also helped introduce Chinese learning and philosophy as well as Chinese styles in art, literature, sculpture, and architecture. At first, some of the leading Yamato families opposed Buddhism, fearing it would destroy their people's Shinto beliefs and even weaken their own roles as Shinto priests. Shinto rituals continued to be observed, and Shinto ceremonies were carried out alongside Buddhist rites.

One of the most important Yamato rulers was Prince Shotoku (SHOH-toh-koo). He is remembered for two achievements. First, he set the country on the road to a **centralized** state. Using the principles of Buddhism, he established a constitution that set forth the duties and rights of the emperor, his ministers, and the people.

Prince Shotoku's other great achievement was to begin the imperial policy of **cultural borrowing** from China, which continued for nearly 300 years. In 607 Shotoku sent the first of many official Japanese missions to China to study Chinese culture and institutions. Included in the missions were Buddhist monks, scholars, painters, musicians, and writers, all eager to learn the Chinese ways and to bring them home to Japan. Chinese culture was especially admired by the nobility.

The Taika Reforms. The influence of Chinese ways on Japan was intensified when the powerful Fujiwara (foo-jee-WAH-rah) family gained control of the imperial court in 645. It then issued the **Taika** (TEYE-kah) **Reforms,** or "Great Changes," which adopted the main features of the Chinese system of taxation, land ownership, and the organization of government. During the next hundred years Japan successfully carried out many parts of this plan. The government modified elements that were unsuited to Japanese society and rejected others that did not fit with Japanese traditions. To ensure the success of these reforms, the Fujiwara and their supporters overcame those *uji* that were opposed to these changes. They also forced the *uji* to recognize the Yamato ruler as emperor of all Japan.

Perhaps the most important of the Taika Reforms was to set up a stronger central government under the emperor with power over the *uji*. Modeled on China's imperial government, Japan's government was organized into ministries with high officials responsible to the emperor. Equally important, a large **bureaucracy**, or group of government officials, was appointed to help administer government laws and decrees. Unlike China, where the bureaucracy consisted of scholars, in Japan members of the noble court families were asked to administer the government. Japan's aristocratic tradition and the strict hierarchy based on each person's inherited position in society made this adaptation seem natural.

At the same time, Japan was divided into 66 provinces, with counties and villages in each. These provinces, the lands that were the home of the *uji*, were to be ruled by officials sent by the central government. Moreover, all land in Japan was declared the property of the imperial government, and it was to be divided equally among the people. However, these reforms, which were also modeled on the example of China's imperial government, were never fully carried out. In Japan, the government did not exercise much control over the provinces or the lands there. Despite these weaknesses, the Taika Reforms were a major step in helping transform Japan from a land ruled by clans into a country with an organized central government.

The Role of the Emperor.   Nevertheless, strong *uji* continued to challenge the power of the central government. Certain noble court families often challenged the authority of the emperor. Thus, the Taika Reforms did not succeed in making Japan's emperor an all-powerful ruler. As a result, the emperor was to become the symbolic leader of his people during much of the country's history.

Regarded as the descendant of the sun goddess, the emperor remained as Japan's spiritual leader and the symbol of government no matter which group exercised the real power at various periods in Japan's history. The Japanese did not accept the Chinese view that the emperor could be overthrown by the people if he failed to protect them or to carry out all his other responsibilities to them. Thus, the imperial dynasty that began with the Tenno *uji* continues in power today, and is the oldest ruling house in the world. In this way, the emperor helped unify the Japanese people and anchored their sense of identity as a special people.

Continued Chinese Influence.   From the 6th to the 9th centuries, Chinese influences continued to mold Japanese society and its culture.

Chinese written characters became the basis of Japan's first writing system. Interestingly, the Chinese writing system was not well adapted to representing the sounds of Japanese. Consequently, the Japanese invented the writing system called *kana* (see Chapter 1) to be used alongside the Chinese characters, making possible the creation of a great body of Japanese literature. Japanese scholars now began to record their nation's history, as you have read, basing it in part on early legends and stories. (See the Case Study, page 33.) Chinese literature, music, dance, and painting were studied as models by Japanese scholars, musicians, artists, and writers, who soon began to compose their own works at the imperial court. The Chinese calendar was introduced, and its system for dating periods of history was now followed in Japan. Buddhism, in its various forms, soon spread throughout Japan, and its beliefs were adopted by the nobility and the common people alike. The Japanese adapted these cultural borrowings so that in time they became truly Japanese in character. In the end, the Japanese used what they learned to develop a rich, unique culture of their own.

The Yamato Legacy. By the end of the Yamato period in 710, several features of Japanese life had already developed that were to leave a lasting imprint on the island nation.
- The role of the family as the basic unit in the *uji* confirmed the importance families were to have in Japanese society.
- A society had developed in which people's rank and position were fixed at birth.
- The appearance of a warrior class emphasized the role that military power was to play in Japanese society and government.
- The twofold role of *uji* chieftains as priest-rulers was to be carried out by Japan's later rulers, who had both religious and political functions.
- The fact that *uji* and noble families continued to be strong foreshadowed the difficulty that future rulers of Japan would face when they attempted to centralize power.
- Finally, the cultural borrowing and adaptation of the Yamato rulers showed Japan's remarkable ability to adopt ideas and to make them part of the country's own culture.

CLASSICAL JAPAN (710–1185)

With the groundwork of Japanese culture laid by the time the Yamato Period ended, the Japanese people moved into a new historical period.

*The building of the magnificent Todaiji Temple in the
ancient city of Nara in 752 marked the adoption of
Buddhism by the emperor as the state religion of Japan.*

During the next 400 years, although they continued to borrow from
China, they established a truly unique civilization. This period of cultural advance came to be known as the period of Classical Japan.

The Nara and Heian Periods (710–1184). With a centralized political
system in place, the Japanese felt the need to establish a new capital
from which the country could be administered. In 710, therefore, they
built their first capital city at Nara (nah-rah), just east of the present city
of Osaka. Modeled on China's capital, Nara became the center of
Japan's new, developing culture. At Nara, the influence of Buddhism
grew at the imperial court. It was here, in 752, that the emperor Shomu
built the huge Todaiji Temple and giant bronze statue of the Buddha
that you read about at the beginning of this chapter.

About 10,000 Buddhists were connected with the Todaiji Temple
and other Buddhist temples that were built in Nara. They became so
influential in the political life at Nara that they threatened the power of
the Taika reformers. Partly to escape this growing Buddhist influence,
in 794 Emperor Kammu built a new capital, called Heia (HAY-ah) west
of Nara. Later known as Kyoto, Heia remained the capital of imperial
Japan for more than a thousand years, until 1868.

Culture at the Heian Court. At Heia, the Japanese emperors ruled
over a brilliant court, where a new Japanese culture was created. This
classical era in Japanese history, the Heian Period, lasted until 1185.

Many scenes from Lady Murasaki's The Tale of Genji, *a classic of Japanese literature, were the subject of paintings by Japanese artists. This panel shows ladies of the court.*

One of the great achievements of the Heian Period was the development of the new system of writing mentioned earlier. The literature and poetry created at this time were among the finest in the world. During the late 900s and early 1000s, the members of the nobility at the imperial court devoted much of their time to literary pursuits. Nobles continued to use the Chinese system of writing, which they considered superior, and spent long hours perfecting their **calligraphy,** or the art of producing beautiful Chinese characters with a brush. However, women at the imperial court adopted *kana* for their writings. These women of noble families often kept diaries in which they recorded the customs and the events at the court. Their diaries and poetry provide important evidence of the impressive cultural achievements of the Heian Period.

Two of the greatest works of Heian literature were written by noblewomen. *The Pillow Book* of Sei Shonagon (SAY SHOH-nah-gohn), a lady-in-waiting to the Japanese empress, was filled with interesting descriptions of daily life at court. Here is one example:

> Through a partition one hears a lady's hushed voice, followed by the youthful voice of someone answering her and a rustling of clothing as she approaches. It must be time for the lady's meal; for then comes the sound of chopsticks and spoons, and then the clatter made by the handle of a jug as it falls on its side. . . .

The other great work of Heian literature written by a noblewoman was *The Tale of Genji* (GEN-jee), one of the world's first novels. Its author was Lady Murasaki (moo-rah-SAH-kee), another member of the

CASE STUDY:
The Tale of Genji

In the following excerpt from *The Tale of Genji*, Lady Murasaki tells how 12-year-old Prince Genji, a son of the emperor, met his intended bride and how he felt about his engagement to her.

Genji . . . was constantly at the Emperor's side. He was soon quite at his ease with the common run of Ladies in Waiting and Ladies of the Wardrobe. . . .But. . . . only one [Princess Fujitsubo] was pretty and quite young as well, and though she tried to hide from him, it was inevitable that they should often meet. . . .

He was now twelve years old and the time for his Initiation was come. . . . .Genji arrived at [3 p.m.]. He looked very handsome with his long childish locks. . . .

Duly crowned, Genji went to his chamber and after changing into man's dress went down into the courtyard and performed the Dance of Homage [respect], which he did with such grace that tears stood in every eye. . . .

His sponsor, the Minister of the Left, . . . began to think he would offer [his daughter] to Genji. . . .That night. . . . his betrothal [engagement] was celebrated with great splendor. It was thought the little Prince looked somewhat childish and delicate, but his beauty astonished everyone. Only the bride, who was four years older, regarded him as a mere baby and was rather ashamed of him. . . .

Everyone seemed to make a great deal of fuss about Princess Aoi, his betrothed [fiancée], but he could see nothing nice about her. The girl at the Palace now filled all his childish thoughts and his obsession became a misery to him. . . . After an absence of five or six days he would occasionally spend two or three at his betrothed's house. . . . The Shigeisa, one of the rooms which had belonged to his mother, was allotted to him. . . . "If only I were going to live here with someone I liked," thought Genji sadly."

From Lady Murasaki, *The Tale of Genji*, translated by Arthur Waley. New York: Modern Library, 1960.

1. How did Prince Genji feel about the bride selected for him?

2. What do you learn from this selection about marriages of male members of the imperial family?

empress's court. A thousand pages long, this novel portrayed the luxurious life of members of the imperial court. It centered on the fictitious character of a young prince, Genji. Lady Murasaki's work, which appeared about 1020, is still considered one of Japan's greatest and most influential novels.

Other significant developments in Japan's culture were seen in the lovely scroll paintings produced by Heian court artists. These paintings often provided visual histories of battles, court ceremonies, and other significant events of the Heian Period. Japan's skillful adaptation of Chinese architecture in the construction of imperial palaces and Buddhist temples also attested to the development of a unique Japanese culture at the Heian court.

However, the emphasis on art, literature, music, and ceremonial display at the Heian court had little relationship to the events that were beginning to reshape the political landscape throughout Japan. The centralized government, adapted from the Chinese, began to give way to domination of the country's rule by a single aristocratic family. The power of the nobility at the imperial court, and even of the emperor himself, was challenged by the powerful Fujiwara family.

Fujiwara Rule (858–1159).   The Fujiwara were the largest owners of private estates in the country. In the 300 years of their rule, the emperor became the ruler of Japan in name only, while real power rested with the Fujiwara and other aristocratic families. In 858, Fujiwara Yoshifusa* (yoh-shee-FOO-sah), made his grandson emperor and named himself **regent**, or person who rules in place of the emperor. With that act, he established a system by which the Fujiwara virtually took over Japan's imperial government. The Fujiwara took power by providing wives for the emperors from their own family ranks and then arranging to have themselves named as regents, who held the real power in the country. This was one step in the gradual process of depriving the emperor of power that was to go on for centuries.

Only a few emperors, such as Go-Sanjo (goh sahn-joh) in 1068, seriously attempted to regain the power of the imperial throne. However, it was not the emperor who soon threated the Fujiwara dominance of Japan. Rather, this threat lay in the rise of warrior families, a military aristocracy in the provinces that was increasingly beyond the control of the imperial court.

---

* Japanese names used the family name first, then the person's given name.

Rise of the Warrior Aristocracy. In the provinces, aristocratic families, often junior members of the noble court families, gradually established their independence from the provincial officials appointed by the court. Since they had often spent large sums and great effort to build terraced rice fields on their lands, they no longer regarded these lands as imperial holdings. Rather, they looked upon them as their own private property. Many no longer paid taxes to the imperial government, which did little to preserve order or to protect them from bandits.

The members of these powerful families were called **samurai** (SAM-uh-reye). Most samurai were descendants of *uji* families of old. They were skilled warriors on horseback, who used force to protect their large estates. Sometimes, several related samurai families even joined together to form a larger, more powerful warrior group. Many accumulated great wealth and dominated the local peasants, who, willingly or not, served them in the rice fields as well as in battle.

The challenge of these military aristocrats set in motion a long era of change that would make Japan quite different from China, the country from which the Japanese had borrowed so heavily. Most dramatic would be the departure of the Chinese model of government. Beyond changes in government were those in society, religion, and the arts.

MEDIEVAL JAPAN (1185–1867)

Beginning in 1185 the authority of the emperor collapsed, along with that of the central government. This was a 500-year period of strife and turmoil. Warfare and a political and social system known as **feudalism** dominated Japan as warrior families fought for control.

The Kamakura Shogunate (1185–1333). When the emperor died in 1156, the court nobility quarreled over who was to come to the throne. Unable to agree, two powerful groups, the Taira (TEYE-rah) and the Minamoto (mee-nah-MOH-toh), fought a series of battles. In 1185, the Minamoto, under the leadership of Minamoto Yorimoto (yoh-ree-MOH-toh), finally defeated the Taira. Yorimoto's victory was a turning point in Japanese history, for it began a 700-year period in which the military warrior class ruled Japan.

Yorimoto moved quickly to consolidate his power. In 1192, he forced the emperor to appoint him **shogun** (SHOH-gun), the most powerful samurai and the commanding general of the imperial armies. Yorimoto also was given the right to pass this office of shogun on to his descendants.

This furious battle between the Taira and Minamoto families was but one of the armed conflicts that raged in the 1100s and finally led to the triumph of the Minamoto.

Yorimoto remained apart from the politics and intrigues of the Heian court by establishing his headquarters at Kamakura (kah-mah-KOO-rah), near the city of Edo (present-day Tokyo) on the Kanto Plain. The Fujiwara and other court nobles still held high-sounding titles at court, but they, too, no longer had real power. The era of rule under the **shogunate,** or government by the shoguns, which was in many ways a military dictatorship, had begun in Japan. The Kamakura shogunate was the first of three that were to rule the country until 1868.

Feudal Japan. The feudal system under which Japan lived for hundreds of years was very similar to European feudalism that prevailed at a somewhat earlier time. The essential bond of both systems was loyalty— loyalty of each group in society to the next highest group. In Japan, the emperor occupied the highest social position, but he had little or no political power. The actual ruler of the country was the shogun.

The shogun gave some of his lands to lesser samurai in return for their military service and personal loyalty to him. Guiding the lives of the samurai was a strict code of conduct known as *bushido* (BOO-shee-doh), or the way of the warrior. A samurai was expected to live a life of bravery, honor, discipline, and self-control. Unquestioning loyalty to his lord was a guiding principle of a samurai's life, even more important than loyalty to his family, friends, or the emperor. Any violation of *bushido* was regarded as a loss of honor, which a samurai was expected to acknowledge by committing *seppuku* (SEP-poo-koo), or ritual suicide.

Under Japanese feudalism, women led restricted lives, with fewer rights than in earlier times. Nevertheless, the wives of samurai warriors could inherit land, and, since husbands spent much time fighting, their wives were often required to manage their estates.

The Mongol Invasion.   One dramatic event engraved itself on Japanese history in the Kamakura Period. Powerful armies, led by the Mongol emperor Kublai Khan, twice attempted to invade Japan in the late 1200s. After conquering a mighty empire stretching from the Middle East across central Asia to China and Korea, Kublai Khan demanded that Japan recognize him as its ruler. The Japanese refused and amassed armies of samurai warriors in northern Kyushu. In 1274, the Mongols sent an army across the Korea Strait but soon withdrew their forces in the face of a severe storm.

In 1281, the Mongols returned to the attack, launching the largest seaborne invasion in medieval history. They landed an army of nearly 140,000 in Japan. Vastly outnumbered, the samurai armies, who had never fought large-scale battles, managed to maintain their defenses.

Fierce samurai warriors, armed with swords and lance, protected by armor, terrorized their opponents as they fought the shoguns' battles for hundreds of years.

For several weeks the fighting raged. Then suddenly, a fierce typhoon struck the area and the Mongol fleet was destroyed. The Japanese defenders rejoiced at their miraculous victory, which they believed was the work of benevolent *kami* (see page 27). They called the typhoon *kamikazi* (kah-mih-KAH-zee), or the divine wind, that had been sent to protect Japan. This, again, was proof to the Japanese that their island nation was the land of the gods, who would protect them from invasion.

The End of the Kamakura Shogunate.   The Mongol invasion did, however, weaken the power of the shogun. Many samurai warriors had spent vast sums preparing their armies to beat back the Mongol attack. They expected the shogun to reward their efforts with grants of additional land. Yet the Kamakura shogun failed to provide them such land grants. The samurais' bitterness grew when they learned that Buddhist monks had been rewarded by the shogun for their prayers against the Mongols. Thus the loyalty to the shogun of strong groups of samurai began to weaken.

In 1331, a new emperor, Go-Daigo (GOH DEYE-goh), attempted to regain the power of the imperial throne from the Kamakura shogun. The forces sent by the shogun to defeat Go-Daigo deserted and threw their support to the emperor. Their leader, Ashikaga Takauji (ah-shee-KAH-gah TAH-kah-oo-jee), then decided to seize power himself. He led his forces into Kyoto, the imperial capital, in 1336 and proclaimed himself shogun in 1338.

The Ashikaga Shogunate (1338–1573).   During the rule of the Ashikaga shoguns, Japan entered a period of turmoil and civil war that lasted for more than two centuries. The Ashikaga shoguns only exercised effective control over the Ashikaga's own domains centered about their capital at Kyoto. The samurai warriors now ruled their own estates in the provinces with little concern about the shogun. Though the Ashikaga tried to strengthen the shogun's power, this effort had little success. By the end of the 1300s, rival warrior groups were engaged in constant warfare throughout Japan.

During the 1400s, conditions in Japan grew even more chaotic. The power of the Ashikaga shoguns was challenged constantly by warrior groups who controlled the provinces. These groups now were organized as small armies, with footsoldiers using iron pikes as weapons. They were commanded by skilled military leaders on horseback.

In 1467, a civil war broke out in Kyoto among the Ashikaga leaders over the selection of a new shogun. This bloody struggle, known as the

Onin War, soon spread throughout Japan. When it ended ten years later, the Ashikaga shogunate was as powerless as the emperor, who ruled the nation in name only. Powerful warrior groups in the provinces, each led by its military leader, known as a **daimyo** (DEYE-myoh), were now Japan's real rulers.

The daimyo, meaning "great names," commanded armies of samurai, who wore metal armor and rode on horseback, carrying steel swords. These armies also included peasants, who served as footsoldiers and were armed with light weapons. As the shogun's control over the provinces disappeared, the daimyo were free to expand the territory they ruled. The daimyo turned their homes into castles protected by walled fortresses. The daimyo's armies moved into these fortresses after battle. Peasants and craftworkers in each area also began to seek protection and shelter within the castle walls. Once there, they provided necessary services for the daimyo. Important towns and cities began in this way. Osaka, Tokyo, Nagoya, and Nagasaki all began as castle towns during the Ashikaga Period. These and other important developments in Japanese society occurred even amidst the warfare and conflict that beset Japan in the 1500s.

A revolution in warfare in Japan also contributed to the growing power of the various daimyo. In the 1500s, Portuguese traders introduced guns and cannon to Japan. The use of this modern military technology enabled the strongest of the daimyo to conquer their rivals and to increase their power. By the late 1500s, several daimyo had unified large areas of Japan and begun a struggle for control of the nation. For a time, the daimyo allowed the Ashikaga shoguns to remain in power in Kyoto. But in 1573 the Ashikaga shogunate ended as one powerful daimyo made Japan a unified nation for the first time in its history under a new shogunate. Before we study this new shogunate, however, we must examine some of the changes that were taking place under the Kamakura and Ashikaga shogunates.

The Spread of Buddhism in Japan. Under the Kamakura and the Ashikaga shogunates, Buddhism gained great popularity among the Japanese. As you recall, Buddhism had come to Japan in 552, but for many centuries its religious beliefs had been adopted mainly by the nobility at the court. Gradually, simpler forms of Buddhism were spread that taught that salvation and entrance into paradise were possible by an individual's strong faith in the Buddha and in his grace and mercy. These newer forms of Buddhism were better suited to Japanese society than the older ones. Priests were allowed to marry and temples were built in towns and villages as well as at traditional religious centers. During the troubled years of feudal warfare between 1338 and 1573, Buddhism's importance in the lives of the people continued to grow.

Zen Buddhism, one of the newer forms of Buddhism, was adopted by the samurai and warrior groups during the Kamakura shogunate. Zen Buddhism emphasized the need for deep meditation and communion with nature in order to achieve self-understanding, or enlightenment. Japan's samurai warriors embraced Zen Buddhism as a means of self-discipline and self-control, attitudes equally required for success in battle.

Zen Buddhism also had a lasting impact on many aspects of Japanese culture. It introduced the tea ceremony, with its simple group rituals. Zen's emphasis on simplicity gave rise to rock gardens with their great beauty defined by a special tree or stream or small grouping of stones, and the careful arrangement of a few flowers or blossoms. These Zen Buddhist contributions are still found throughout Japan today.

The Growth of Japan's Economy. Despite the civil war and instability of the Ashikaga shogunate, Japan continued to trade with China. Japanese merchants brought Chinese porcelain, raw silk, medicines, pottery, and books. But they also exported raw materials like copper as well as Japanese-made products such as silk cloth, swords, lacquer ware, and hand-painted screens and fans. As this trade flourished, it led to the growth of towns along Japan's coast at easy stopping points near natural harbors. As merchants carried these goods inland, marketplaces also grew up where goods were sold to the warrior groups and peasants of the provinces. This growing trade allowed small centers of industry to develop in Japan devoted to papermaking, weaving, and metalworking. These centers themselves became important sources of Japan's own growing internal trade in raw materials and manufactured goods.

The increased use of money, chiefly copper coins from China, was another significant step in the development of Japan's economy. Such economic growth meant that land no longer was the sole source of wealth. Merchants, traders, and manufacturers were beginning to lay the foundations of their future prosperity.

Japan's trade with China also indirectly increased the wealth of the daimyo. Many of them hired samurai to attack trading vessels and capture their valuable cargoes. These samurai pirates thus supplied the daimyo with the goods and money they needed to complete their conquests. Sometimes, the pirates even attacked coastal towns in China and Korea, bringing back valuable loot for the daimyo.

Japan's agricultural economy made important gains in these same years. Wet-rice cultivation spread as the estates of the warrior groups grew in size. Improved irrigation by better control of streams helped expand Japan's terraced cropland. New farm tools and the increased use of animals in farming also improved agricultural productivity on the great estates. In addition, important new crops like soybeans and tea were now being cultivated.

These improvements in agriculture and trade were sufficient to support a relatively large population, one that continued its growth even in the difficult centuries of feudal warfare. Despite a terrible smallpox epidemic in the 730s that killed a third of the people, it is estimated that Japan's population had grown to about 10 million in the 1200s. By the late 1600s, the population had nearly doubled, reaching 18 million.

THE AGE OF CENTRALIZED FEUDALISM (1573–1867)

Late in the 1500s Japan's civil wars ended with the establishment of a new regime, the Tokugawa shogunate. Able military leaders brought powerful daimyo under their authority and established a new centralized government. The Tokugawa shogunate held Japan in tight control for almost 300 years.

The Tokugawa Shogunate (1585–1867). In 1568, Oda Nobunaga (oh-dah noh-boo-NAH-gah), one of Japan's most powerful daimyo, led his forces into Kyoto, the imperial capital. To establish his dominance, Nobunaga brutally destroyed a stronghold of Buddhist warrior-priests and forced the Ashikaga shogun from power. Then, in 1582, just as Nobunaga completed his conquest of central Japan, he was assassinated.

One of Nobunaga's best generals, Hideyoshi Toyotomi (hee-day-YOH-shee toh-yoh-TOH-mee), then took control to prevent civil war. Hideyoshi was a remarkable man. The first Japanese leader from a poor family, Hideyoshi defeated all rival daimyo and forced them to become his **vassals,** or subjects.

Hideyoshi did not rule as shogun, because his ancestors had been peasants. Instead, he had the emperor appoint him as chancellor. However, he completely controlled the government and used its wealth to finance his warfare. He also forced the peasants to turn in their weapons, thus making the samurai the only warriors. In this way, the samurai now became a professional military class, no longer masters of their own estates but vassals who served their feudal lords.

41

The actions of Hideyoshi Toyotomi belied his mild appearance. He attempted to conquer Korea as a first step on the way to the conquest of China.

Hideyoshi next undertook an extraordinary adventure of conquest against Korea. In 1592, he sailed with an army of 200,000 across the Korea Strait and invaded Korea, advancing north until Chinese troops forced the Japanese to withdraw. The following year, Hideyoshi again attacked Korea, but was unable to complete his conquest before he was killed in 1598.

On Hideyoshi's death, five of his most powerful daimyo served as regents for his young son. However, they soon quarreled in a struggle for power, which was settled by the victory of Tokugawa Ieyasu (toh-koo-GAH-wah ee-ay-yah-soo) at the battle of Sekigahara (seh-kee-GAH-hah-rah) in 1600. Ieyasu, who had been granted control of Edo and surrounding lands by Hideyoshi, kept his headquarters there when he became shogun in 1603. By 1615, Ieyasu had firmly established the power of the Tokugawa shogunate, which united and ruled Japan for the next three centuries.

The Tokugawa Feudal System. Ieyasu continued Hideyoshi's policy of using the samurai as a professional soldier class that served the daimyo, the great feudal lords. Ieyasu also took strong steps to establish control over the daimyo themselves. Ieyasu and his successors carefully divided all the great estates in Japan. The Tokugawa kept all the land around Edo, which also included nearly all the important towns, seaports, and iron and copper mines. The rest of Japan was divided among the 245 to 295 daimyo, whose lands and armies were still very powerful.

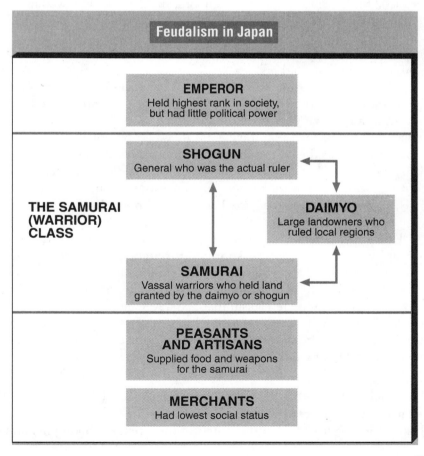

Feudalism in Japan

EMPEROR
Held highest rank in society, but had little political power

SHOGUN
General who was the actual ruler

THE SAMURAI (WARRIOR) CLASS

DAIMYO
Large landowners who ruled local regions

SAMURAI
Vassal warriors who held land granted by the daimyo or shogun

PEASANTS AND ARTISANS
Supplied food and weapons for the samurai

MERCHANTS
Had lowest social status

To gain control over the daimyo, Ieyasu set up three ranks of daimyo. The "related" daimyo were junior members of the Tokugawa family whose large estates were in the lands closest to Ieyasu's Edo domains. In the second rank were "hereditary" daimyo, the **fudai** (foo-DEYE), who had owned their estates before 1600 and were Ieyasu's vassals. Most of the *fudai* lands were in central Japan. Together, the "related" and the "hereditary" daimyo held more than half the rice-growing agricultural land. The **tozama** (toh-ZAH-mah), or "outer" warlords, were those daimyo whose bonds of loyalty to Ieyasu were weakest. Their estates were largely in the northern and western region, far from Edo.

Ieyasu and his successors were determined to prevent any of the daimyo, especially the "outer" warlords, from trying to overthrow the Tokugawa. To ensure this, by the mid-1600s they had placed many restrictions on the daimyo. For example, the Tokugawa shogun had to grant permission before any daimyo could enter another daimyo's lands. As vassal to the shogun, his sovereign lord, the daimyo also owed many feudal duties. When the shogun commanded it, the daimyo had to provide armies to meet his military needs. The daimyo also were required to build castles and forts for the Tokugawa as well as to pay for building roads and improving harbors.

However, the Tokugawa's most significant measure to control the daimyo was to require that they build a residence in Edo, where their families had to live year-round, and where they themselves had to remain for part of each year. Living in Edo was very expensive, and this expense as well as the cost of their other duties consumed nearly all the daimyo's income. In this way, the shogun increased the authority of the central government as he limited the power of the daimyo. (Interestingly, at about the same time, the French king Louis XIV used a similar system to control the nobles of France.)

Under this system of centralized feudalism, the shogun was the feudal lord whose authority was supreme throughout the land. All the daimyo were his vassals, who swore loyalty to him and owed him many feudal duties. This form of Japanese feudalism under the Tokugawa was very different from the feudalism that had developed earlier in Europe. There, the monarchs' vassals remained so strong a force that they kept most European kingdoms divided and prevented their weakened monarchs from uniting their lands.

The Social Structure. The class structure of Japanese society grew even more rigid between the mid-1600s and the mid-1800s. The Tokugawa shoguns adopted the beliefs of the Chinese philosopher and

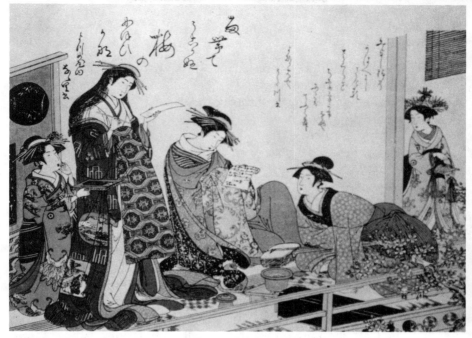

Elaborately dressed, ladies of the court during the Tokugawa shogunate remained secluded and were not expected to be concerned with the serious issues that occupied the men.

teacher Confucius about the four ranks in society. These mirrored Japan's class structure. At the top were the samurai, who made up about 7 percent of the population. The samurai warriors now were divided into many different grades. Some were high government officials, vassals of powerful daimyo at Edo and other towns. Others were foot soldiers. But all samurai still ranked above the rest of the populace. They were forbidden to marry below their class. They also were entitled to wear certain dress and to carry two swords as symbols of their rank.

Below the samurai in the class system came the peasants, more than 80 percent of the population, who, as farmers, were considered to be the source of Japan's most valuable wealth. Ranked below the peasants were the craftworkers, who made pottery, wove cloth, made clothing, produced metalware, and provided the other goods local people needed. At the bottom of society were the merchants, who were considered by the shoguns as contributing little to society, since they produced nothing and only bought and sold products made by others.

Completing Japan's centralized feudal society, but in some ways almost unrelated to it, was the imperial dynasty. The emperor and his court remained at Kyoto throughout the Tokugawa shogunate. The emperor continued to be an important living symbol, but he was virtually powerless, as he had been for hundreds of years.

The Arrival of Europeans in Japan. In the years when the Tokugawa shoguns were coming to power, Portuguese traders reached Japan. (See page 39.) By 1600, Dutch and English merchants were also beginning to trade there. In 1549, Francis Xavier, a founder of the Roman Catholic Jesuit order, also arrived. He and his missionaries soon converted nearly 150,000 Japanese to Christianity, and their numbers had nearly doubled by the early 1600s. Some daimyo encouraged their people to become Christians, hoping to gain wealth from trade with Europeans that would follow their conversion. Other daimyo were especially interested in the guns and cannon the Europeans had brought.

At first, Hideyoshi and Ieyasu welcomed the Catholic missionaries, since they might become a threat to the powerful Buddhist temples that opposed these leaders. Soon, however, they worried more about the threat of European conquest because of events in the Philippines. There the Spanish had taken over the islands after Catholicism had arrived there. The Tokugawa shoguns also worried that Japanese who became Catholics might owe their loyalty to the pope rather than to them. They also believed Catholics would support future enemies who might attempt to overthrow the shogunate. With these fears in mind, the Tokugawa shoguns launched a campaign against Christians. They first banned Catholic missionaries from Japan, then persecuted all Christians until they had systematically wiped them out by 1638.

This fear of foreign influence also led Japan to limit and soon virtually end all foreign trade. The Tokugawa viewed European trade as a source of wealth for Europeans, not for the Japanese. Now that the Japanese had learned how to make the new guns and weapons the Europeans had introduced, they believed that Japan itself could supply all its other needs. All Japanese merchants were now forbidden to trade or travel overseas. After 1641, no European ships were allowed to land anywhere in Japan except at a small Dutch trading post at Nagasaki. In this way, Japan's new leaders isolated their nation just as it was becoming unified.

Peace and Stability in Japan. From the 1640 to 1853, Japan turned the energies of its people to building a strong government and a peaceful and prosperous society. Though the Japanese had only limited contacts with other countries, they enjoyed lasting peace and stability throughout these years. This was in sharp contrast to the preceding centuries of warfare and bloodshed.

One indication of Japan's new era of peace was the changing role of the samurai. This warrior class now had to adapt to a society that had little need of fighters. Some samurai, of course, remained as officers serving the shogun and the daimyo. Others took jobs as teachers of military arts and science. Many educated samurai, however, devoted themselves to scholarship and learning, a Confucian value highly honored in Japan. By the 1700s and 1800s, they had become leaders of Japan's intellectual class, gaining fame as writers, artists, painters, and poets. The Japanese so highly valued education that they achieved one of the highest rates of literacy in the world. Moreover, despite this change in the role of the samurai, many aspects of the strict, demanding samurai code of honor continued as an important guide to behavior among the Japanese. Loyalty as the key to all relationships, to the lord, to subordinates, to family, and to friends was to be honored by Japanese of all classes.

In this period of peace, the arts flourished. In the cities, people flocked to see a lively new kind of drama, called **kabuki** (kuh-BOO-kee), with elaborate, colorful stage settings. Also popular were **bunraku** (boon-RAH-koo), or puppet plays, and **sumo** (SOO-moh) wrestling. At about this time, a new kind of poetry called **haiku** (HEYE-koo) was admired. A haiku is a short poem of 17 syllables in three lines that conveys a mood or paints a nature scene. Here are two examples of haiku:

> Having viewed the moon
> I say farewell to this world
> With heartful blessing.

> Stubborn woodpecker
> Still hammering at twilight
> At that single spot.

While the Confucian hierarchy of the four-class society remained the model (see page 45), it corresponded less and less to developments in Japan's expanding economy. Merchants now played an increasingly important role as their businesses increased. The rice that provided the daimyo with much of their income increasingly was being shipped to merchants in Osaka and Kyoto. Merchants paid an annual fee to the daimyo for this privilege. The merchants then often sold the rice at much higher prices than they had paid for it. Merchants used this wealth to establish shops, small factories, and other enterprises. Some merchants also became money lenders and wine makers.

Japanese agriculture, the basis of the economy, also made important advances in the 1700s and 1800s. The daimyo increased the amount of land under cultivation by draining swamps, terracing hillsides, and altering other land to produce more crops. In addition, the great expense

The bookshop in the background attracts strollers in Edo, later named Tokyo, in the 1830s. With an increase in the literacy rate, books became more popular.

required of the daimyo living in Edo, the shogun's capital, encouraged them to grow surplus crops or even produce manufactured goods on their estates to produce more income. This, in turn, stimulated the nation's economic growth and made the great estates an integral part of the economy instead of the separate, uncoordinated production facilities they had been in the past.

Another sign of Japan's increasing prosperity during these peaceful years was the rapid growth of the nation's cities and ports in the 1700s and 1800s. Under the Tokugawa shogunate, Japan was becoming a nation of city dwellers. The population of Edo had grown to over 1 million by the 1700s. Osaka and Kyoto each had about 300,000 people, and there were nearly 250 other towns with populations of from 3,000 to 20,000. In these cities and towns **barter**, or trade by the exchange of goods, now was replaced by the use of paper money and coins. Thus a commercial, trading economy was developing in the cities, just as a prosperous agriculture was flourishing in the countryside.

Clearly, Japan's feudal society was becoming transformed by major changes in its economy. Yet most of the institutions and customs of its feudal past remained in place. During the Tokugawa shogunate, Japan had again demonstrated its ability to adapt to changing conditions while preserving traditional institutions and values. Nevertheless, an event was to take place in the mid-1800s that set Japan on a dramatic new course in its history—the arrival of ships of the U.S. navy, led by Commodore Matthew C. Perry.

48

REVIEWING THE CHAPTER

I. Building Your Vocabulary

Match the definitions and the terms.

calligraphy	*kami*	*kamikazi*
uji	samurai	daimyo
bureaucracy	shogun	*seppuku*
bushido	vassal	feudalism

1. the gods of the Shinto religion
2. the body of lower government officials
3. small groups of families with their own priest-rulers
4. skilled warriors on horseback
5. brush paintings of Chinese characters
6. powerful samurai who controlled provinces under the Ashikaga shogunate
7. typhoon that stopped the Mongol invasion
8. the samurai code of conduct
9. feudal chief *daimyo*
10. ritual suicide
11. a system of society based on loyalty
12. one who is the subject of a person next highest on the social scale

II. Understanding the Facts

Write the letter of the correct answer to each question next to its number.

1. Which country served as a model of Japan's system of government as well as of its forms of land ownership and taxation?
   a. Portugal   b. Korea   c. China

2. Which of the following was the most important event in Japan's history during the late 1200s?
   a. arrival of Portuguese traders   b. the Mongol invasion
   c. arrival of Catholic missionaries

3. How did the Tokugawa shoguns gain control over the daimyo?
   a. The daimyo were forced to give up their estates.
   b. The families of the daimyo were required to live in Edo, the shogun's capital city.
   c. The daimyo became Christians.

4. Which group was at the bottom of Japanese society?
   a. the peasants   b. the artisans   c. the merchants

5. Which of the following best describes Japan under the Tokugawa shogunate?
   a. a peaceful and prosperous nation
   b. a land facing civil war
   c. an isolated nation dominated by China

III. **Thinking It Through**

Write the letter of your correct conclusion to each sentence next to its number.

1. China helped shape Japan's history because:
   a. Chinese invasions forced Japan to become a military nation.
   b. Japan borrowed and adopted many features of China's culture.
   c. China's emperors were related to Japan's imperial family.
   d. Japan's Shinto traditions were borrowed from China.

2. During the classical era of Japan, Japanese at the imperial court at Heia:
   a. rejected Chinese culture but borrowed many ideas from Korea.
   b. adopted the traditions and customs of Zen Buddhism.
   c. followed Shinto traditions as well as Christianity.
   d. blended Chinese and Japanese ideas to create a new Japanese culture.

3. During the Yamato Period, the rise of a warrior class was important because it showed:
   a. the role that military power was to have in Japan in future centuries.
   b. that people's rank and position were fixed at birth.
   c. that the *uji* were the basic units in society.
   d. that the emperor had more power than the shogun.

4. During the civil wars and fighting in the 1400s and 1500s, Japan's economy:
   a. depended completely on goods imported from China.
   b. grew as trade expanded and farmers produced larger crops.
   c. was based on the products captured by samurai pirates.
   d. remained undeveloped and depended on goods imported from Korea.

5. From the mid-1600s to the mid-1800s, Japanese society under the Tokugawa shogunate was based on:
   a. system of centralized feudalism.
   b. new cultural traditions brought by European traders.
   c. the rule of the all-powerful emperor.
   d. a strict class hierarchy in which the merchants were the most highly regarded class.

DEVELOPING CRITICAL THINKING SKILLS

1. Explain why the tombs of the Yamato clan chieftains help us to understand Japan's early history.

2. Describe the changes in the lives of the samurai from the 1100s to the 1600s.

3. Explain why the emperors continued to rule in Japan after the shoguns gained control of the real power of government.

4. Explain how *The Tale of Genji* helps historians understand what life was like at the imperial court in the 1000s.

5. Describe the results of the rapid growth of Edo, Osaka, and other towns in the 1700s and 1800s.

MAKING A TIME LINE

Make a time line of the main events of Japan's early history. Then answer the following questions.

1. What was the earliest period of Japanese history called?
2. During which dynasty was the first shogunate established?
3. Which shogunate dynasty ruled Japan the longest?
4. How long did the Nara and Heian periods last?
5. In which years did the Mongols attempt to invade Japan?

ENRICHMENT AND EXPLORATION

1. Use an encyclopedia and other library references to learn more about the Mongol invasions of Japan. Imagine that you were a samurai warrior who helped defend Japan against the large Mongol army in 1281. Write a short account of the battle you took part in and describe your feelings before and after the terrible typhoon struck.

2. To help you review the important contributions made by three of Japan's greatest leaders, prepare a chart titled "Founders of the Tokugawa Shogunate." Use a separate heading for each of the great rulers: Nobunaga, Hideyoshi, and Ieyasu. Then for each man show the years he was in power, list the methods he used to govern, and give his main accomplishments.

3 The Emergence of Modern Japan (1853–1952)

Shortly before noon on September 1, 1923, a huge earthquake jolted Tokyo and Yokohama. The great shock was followed almost immediately by an even more destructive fire. The jolt had rocked the capital just as Japanese families were preparing their lunch. The red-hot coals from tens of thousands of hibachis, the small charcoal-burning grills the Japanese used for cooking, ignited the city's tens of thousands of wooden houses, with their paper windows and straw-mat floors. On that terrible day, more than 130,000 people died in the fires that swept through Tokyo, and another 10,000 lost their lives as the quake caused large buildings to collapse. Yokohama, too, suffered great damage.

Yet, four years later, Tokyo had been rebuilt into a modern city. The city's huge new railroad station was now surrounded by tall office buildings, banks, and many other impressive steel and reinforced-concrete structures. The bustling capital, like Japan itself, had shown its age-old weakness. It had also displayed its remarkable ability to adjust to change. In many ways, Tokyo seemed a fitting symbol of the new urban society that was emerging in Japan. The new factories and industries that had replaced those destroyed in 1923 were equipped with the most modern machinery and the latest technological advances. Yet it was only 70 years earlier that Japan had begun the great changes that transformed it from a feudal society into a modern nation.

THE DOWNFALL OF THE TOKUGAWA SHOGUNATE

In the more than 200 years of the Tokugawa shogunate, Japan had developed into a strong centralized feudal society. During this period, Japan had enjoyed years of relative peace and stability as well as prosper-

THE EMERGENCE OF MODERN JAPAN

1853–1952

1853	Commodore Matthew C. Perry's "Black Ships" arrive in Tokyo harbor.
1854	Kanagawa Treaty is signed.
1858	"Unequal treaty" with the United States is signed.
1868	Tokugawa reign is ended.
1868–1912	Meiji era
1871	Feudal system is abolished.
1884–1914	*Almost all of Africa comes under European rule.*
1889	New Japanese constitution is enacted.
1895	Japan wins war with China.
1905	Japan wins Russo-Japanese War.
1910	Japan occupies Korea.
1910–1917	*Mexican Revolution*
1914–1918	*World War I*
1917	*Communist Revolution in Russia*
1919	Treaty of Versailles
1929	Great Depression begins.
1931	Japan seizes Manchuria.
1933	*Hitler becomes ruler of Germany.*
1937	Japan starts war with China.
1939–1945	World War II
1941	Japan attacks U.S. naval base at Pearl Harbor.
1945	United States drops atomic bombs on Hiroshima and Nagasaki. Japan surrenders. Allied occuption of Japan begins.
1947	New Japanese constitution goes into effect.
1948	*State of Israel is established.*
1949	*Communists take over in China.*
1952	Allied occupation of Japan ends.

ous economic growth. Deliberately isolated from other nations, Japan's people strengthened their own culture and traditions. In doing so, they renewed their unity and identity as a people. Then, in the mid-1850s, powerful forces within Japan, spurred by the actions of foreign powers, suddenly ended its isolation. Japan then entered a period in which it was transformed within a few decades into a modern nation.

Perry's "Black Ships."   Early in July 1853, an impressive American naval force sailed into the harbor of Edo, present-day Tokyo, and dropped anchor. Uneasy Japanese on the shore eyed the four steam-powered warships with black hulls. Under the command of Commodore Matthew C. Perry, these ships had been sent to open diplomatic and trade relations with the Japanese. Perry carried a letter from U.S. President Millard Fillmore to the Japanese emperor. The letter made a number of demands on Japan: that it open its ports for trade with U.S. ships, protect U.S. sailors who are shipwrecked in Japanese waters, and allow U.S. ships to stop at Japanese ports for fuel and supplies.

Perry had been instructed to present his demands and then depart. He was to give Japan's government time to consider these requests. It was clear, however, from the guns and cannon on the "black ships," as the Japanese called them, that Perry might be prepared to use force when he returned.

The Tokugawa shogun, who was the actual ruler of Japan, was alarmed by Perry's demands. He realized that they were backed by modern naval power that Japan could not match. Moreover, the Japanese, though they were cut off from trade and cultural contacts with other nations, were well aware of what was happening in Asia and the Pacific. They knew that European nations as well as the United States were now taking a new interest in Asia and the Pacific. They knew that China already had been forced to open its ports to the British after losing the Opium War in 1842 and that the United States and other European nations also had forced China to grant them trading rights. The Netherlands, France, and Britain also were establishing colonies in Southeast Asia. The shogun now understood that Japan, too, might soon come under the domination of foreign nations. Clearly, how he responded to the demands of the United States was a matter of grave importance to Japan.

The Tokugawa shogun took the unusual step of consulting not only with his own advisers but with the most powerful daimyo. Also, for the first time in several centuries, the shogun asked the emperor at Kyoto for advice. The shogun's advisers and the daimyo were split, with the

北亜墨利加
洪和政治洲
欽差全権國王使年
海軍水師提督せリリ
上官眞像之寫

武州本牧横濱
上陸應對之御容

嘉永神奈

In Japanese eyes, the newly arrived, unwelcome Westerners like Commodore Perry were ugly, with long noses.

majority in favor of rejecting Perry's demands. Some even urged military action to drive the Americans away. Yet some of the shogun's key advisers took a more carefully thought-out view. They maintained that Japan would serve its own long-range interests best and preserve its own sovereignty by agreeing to negotiate with the United States. The shogun finally accepted this view. When Commodore Perry returned in early 1854, this time with eight warships, the shogun signed an agreement known as the Kanagawa Treaty.

The "Unequal Treaties."   In the Kanagawa Treaty, Japan agreed to allow U.S. ships to refuel and resupply in Japanese ports, to aid shipwrecked sailors, and to trade with the United States—but only in two small ports. Not long after, Great Britain, the Netherlands, and Russia signed similar agreements with Japan. Japan's centuries-long isolation from the world was at an end.

In 1858, the United States persuaded the shogun to sign a new trade treaty. In this treaty, Japan was required to open Yokohama and other major ports to U.S. ships. Japan's **tariffs**, or taxes on imported goods, were fixed at low levels, which would open the nation to a flood of foreign goods. In addition, Americans living in Japan were to be subject to the laws of the United States rather than those of Japan. This right, called **extraterritoriality,** was humiliating to many Japanese because it symbolized the superiority and power of the United States in its dealings with Japan. Immediately, the European powers demanded these same privileges in Japan. The shogun was reluctantly forced to grant them. In Japan, the agreements, which became known as "the unequal treaties," injured the nation's pride and became a source of bitterness. They spurred the Japanese to undertake major changes in their government and in society itself.

By 1860, it seemed as if Japan might soon suffer the same fate as China and other Asian nations that were becoming carved into **"spheres of influence"** or annexed as outright colonies of foreign imperialist powers. However, Japan was learning a different lesson from this same frightful experience. Many Japanese quickly concluded that by skillfully adapting to these changes, rather than resisting them, their nation might emerge from these troubled years stronger than ever.

One of the shogun's advisers reflected this view when he argued that Japan should agree to Perry's demands:

> He will capture our junks [ships] and blockade our ports. . . . In time the country would be put to an immense expense, and the people plunged into misery. Rather than allow this, as we are not the equals of foreigners in the mechanical arts [technology], let us have relations with foreign countries, learn their drills and tactics . . . and it will not be too late then to declare war.

However, this policy was not put into effect until after a group of skilled new leaders gained control of Japan in 1868.

The Overthrow of the Shogun.   The "unequal treaties" exposed the weakness of the Tokugawa shogunate. Even before this, several powerful daimyo groups in southern Kyushu, Shikoku, and western Honshu had opposed the shogun's rule. Now, however, these daimyo believed the shogun had betrayed Japan's honor by yielding to foreign powers. They took the lead in opposing the U.S. and British trade agreements. They began to acquire the superior weapons of the Europeans to build up their own forces. They also engaged the shogun's army in several battles, using mixed armies consisting of samurai and peasants from their domains.

Finally, these daimyo, aided by some nobles at the imperial court, seized control of the government in 1868. To rally support, they adopted as their motto "Revere the emperor and expel the barbarians." Acting in the name of the 15-year-old emperor, they forced the shogun to give up power and declared that Japan's emperor was restored to his ancient power. Having ended the 700-year rule of the shogunate, they also moved the capital from Kyoto to Edo (renamed Tokyo). The shogun's castle at Edo was converted into the imperial palace. The events that brought about these dramatic changes in Japan's government and its subsequent achievements are known as the **Meiji Restoration.**

THE MEIJI RESTORATION

The term Meiji (may-jee) means "peace and enlightenment," and in many ways it is a meaningful description of the historic changes in Japanese society from 1868 to 1912.

The Meiji Reformers. The leaders of the new imperial government were a remarkably talented group of energetic young men. Numbering about 100, most of these former samurai and court nobles were in their early thirties. This small group was to provide highly skilled leadership for their nation during the next four decades—among the years of greatest change in Japan's history. As they grew older, these leaders were referred to by the Japanese as **genro** (gen-roh), or elder statesmen. Holding complete power, the reformers nonetheless ruled in the name of Emperor Mutsuhito (moo-tsoo-HEE-toh), whose reign from 1868 to 1912 is known as the Meiji era. Once in power, the reformers continued to "honor the emperor" by ruling the government in his name. They knew that by doing so they were assuring the solid support of the people, who still regarded the imperial dynasty as the descendants of the gods and goddesses, the symbols of the nation.

However, the Meiji reformers had no intention of trying to expel the Western "barbarians." On the contrary, the reformers used Westerners to help them make the necessary changes in their nation. In doing so, they used the age-old Japanese practice of borrowing from other countries while keeping the essential Japanese character of the nation. They were convinced that by taking from the West what it considered essential, Japan could build itself into a truly modern nation. This new Japan would be equal in military, economic, and political power to the West without sacrificing its ancient traditions and cherished values. Once Japan had achieved this equality, it would then be able to end the "unequal treaties" and again take control of its own

Emperor Meiji posed for his portrait in a full-dress Western-style military uniform.

future. Thus, in 1868, the government declared, "Knowledge shall be sought throughout the world so as to invigorate [stimulate] the foundations of imperial rule."

Accordingly, the Meiji reformers made it the center of their planning to borrow the Western inventions, technology, and institutions that would enable Japan to take its place among the world's great powers. The reformers were to succeed brilliantly in their goal. In this achievement, they followed in the path of their ancestors more than a thousand years before when they adopted China's great culture and modified it to fit their needs.

Domestic Reforms. The Meiji reformers realized that in order to modernize Japan, they had to end feudalism. Their goal was summarized in the slogan, "a rich nation, a strong army." Thus, in 1871, they had the emperor declare that the feudal system was abolished. The domains, the lands held by the daimyo that made up nearly three fourths of Japan,

To encourage the Japanese people to imitate Westerners, the women of the Meiji court as well as the emperor and his son quickly adopted Western-style clothing.

were now divided into **prefectures** ruled by governors. In return, the daimyo were paid for their lands with government bonds. The daimyo, with their financial future tied to the success of the reformers, now had good reason to support the reforms.

The Meiji government then moved to abolish the feudal class system itself. The Meiji reformers clearly saw that basic changes in the social structure were needed in order to establish a modern military system. Hence they ended the samurai's official status as the warrior class in 1873 by requiring peasants to serve in the military on an equal basis with the samurai. The salaries that were paid to the samurai were sharply decreased. In addition, in 1876, the ancient samurai privilege of wearing two swords, which was symbolic of the power of the samurai, was revoked.

These social changes caused great hardship among the samurai, and it was not surprising that they resisted the new order. Although some of the samurai gained posts as officials in the Meiji government and some entered business, most samurai lacked such opportunities. Many of them determined to fight to retain their power. In 1877, Saigo Takamori (sah-EE-goh tah-kah-MOH-ree), a Meiji reformer who had split with the other leaders, led an army of 40,000 samurai to overthrow the Meiji government. However, after nine months of bloody fighting, the rebellion was finally crushed and Saigo committed *seppuku*, or ritual suicide in the ancient samurai tradition. This ended the samurai threat. Most Japanese understood and respected the actions of these rebels, even as they supported the government's action to end the revolt.

Financial and Communications Reforms. Ten years after taking power, the Meiji reformers were firmly in control of Japan. By then they had already set about reorganizing the government and its finances. They were determined to finance the building of a new industrialized economy using only the resources and talents of their own people. They refused to take the easier route of financing the transformation of the economy by borrowing from foreign nations. They knew this would involve huge debts that would make Japan dependent on outside powers. Worse still, those nations might intervene in Japan's affairs and attempt to gain control of its destiny.

To establish a firm base of revenue, the Meiji leaders first reformed the tax system. In 1873, they ended the traditional taxes peasants had paid. These had taken the form of giving a part of each year's rice crop to the government. Instead, taxes were now based on the value of the land, and they were paid in money. In this way, for the first time, the peasants were recognized as the owners of the land they farmed if they paid these taxes. In the early years of the Meiji restoration, the new land tax provided most of the funds it needed to carry out its ambitious programs of economic and political reforms. In 1870, the land tax comprised 72 percent of total government revenue. By 1912 it accounted for less than 20 percent—dramatic evidence of the success of the nation's new industrial base and economic diversity.

To raise additional money, the government sold bonds and borrowed money from wealthy daimyo and local banking families. A new monetary system, based on a unit of currency called the **yen**, together with a new, modern banking system, also greatly helped to strengthen the nation's economy.

The Meiji reformers also introduced modern communications systems. During the 1870s, Japan's first postal system was launched. Railroad lines soon connected Tokyo and Yokohama as well as other key cities and ports. At the same time, a telegraph network was built to link Japan's major cities. By the early 1890s, Japan had 2,000 miles (3,200 kilometers) of modern railroads and 4,000 miles (6,400 kilometers) of telegraph lines. The government also improved the harbors at Tokyo and Osaka to help Japanese shipping and trade.

Establishing Light Industries. Under the "unequal treaties," tariffs on imported products were fixed at 5 percent, a rate so low that it threatened to flood Japan with foreign goods. If permitted, it would discourage the growth of Japanese industries. To prevent this, the Meiji government took the lead in establishing factories and mills to industrialize the nation. The government leaders brought in business experts and engineers from Western nations to advise them in building factories, shipyards, and mines. They also set up technical schools to train young Japanese in business methods, engineering, and factory production and management skills.

Model factories were set up by the Meiji government to encourage industrial development in many different fields. Pilot plants helped mechanize the silk industry and develop cotton textile mills. These were soon to become Japan's leading industries. Similar factories were built by the government to produce cement, glass, chemicals, and woolen cloth. These light industries formed the basis of industrialization in the first decades of Meiji rule. Other government efforts also helped develop new copper, iron, and coal mining industries. The Meiji also opened weapons factories and naval shipyards in an effort to build up Japan's military power. At the same time, the government helped mechanize and improve agriculture, which remained Japan's largest economic activity and the source of funds for much of the new industrialization. Wet-rice farming was improved, and tea became a more important crop. In all of these activities, the government took an active role. It did so not only in planning the changes, but in **subsidizing**, or supplying the money, to carry out the plans. This practice became typical of the government's relation to the economy and is still carried on today in one form or another.

The Rise of the Zaibatsu. By the 1880s, the government had gone heavily into debt through its subsidizing of the nation's economic development. The government's financial picture was worsened by the expense involved in ending the samurai revolt of 1877. In addition, serious **inflation,** or rapid increase in prices, caused the government's debt to rise still faster and forced it to introduce unpopular new taxes on tobacco and wine.

In the early 1880s, finance minister Matsukata Masayoshi (mah-tsoo-KAH-tah mah-sah-YOH-shee), one of the talented Meiji reformers, moved to reduce government spending. One of his major efforts to get the economy back on an even keel was to sell many of the government's pilot factories and mills to private Japanese business families. In the past, several Japanese families, known as **zaibatsu** (zeye-baht-SOO), had grown wealthy in domestic businesses and banking. These families became interested in the new factories and industries developing in Japan. Some of the zaibatsu had established close links with the government under the Tokugawa shoguns. Now the Mitsui (mih-TSOO-ee), Mitsubishi (mih-tsoo-BEE-shee), Sumitomo (soo-mee-TOH-moh), and other wealthy business houses bought many of the factories, shipyards, mines, and other government enterprises. Members of these powerful family business groups also had many personal ties with members of the Meiji government. The zaibatsu gained increasing influence and control over Japan's economy in subsequent decades, and these same families continue to be a dominant force in Japan today.

Western Influences.   From the beginning, the Meiji reformers turned to Western nations for examples of the new ways of doing business and technologies Japan needed to become a modern nation. In 1871, a group of more than 100 Meiji reformers traveled to the United States and several European nations. The main purpose of their trip was to negotiate a revision of the "unequal treaties" with these nations. Yet, though they did not achieve their goal, they learned at first hand the great progress underway in those nations.

Their trip thus became a learning experience. They visited major cities and centers of industry and talked to government officials in various fields. They also met with businesspeople and industrialists, experts in banking and finance, and military leaders and planners in these nations. This was the first of many similar Japanese missions abroad, and it also accelerated the use of foreign teachers and experts in Japan itself.

A New System of Education.   A new national system of education was established in 1872, requiring both boys and girls to attend school. The Meiji reformers looked on education as essential to train the Japanese to learn the skills they needed as members of a modernizing society. The education law declared:

> In order for each person to make his way in life, husband [manage] his wealth wisely, enjoy prosperity in his business, and attain the goal of his life, he must . . . broaden his knowledge, and cultivate his talents. . . . For this reason, schools are established. . . . Learning is like an investment for success in life.

The Japanese school system was modeled on that of France, but U.S. textbooks and teacher-training methods also had an important influence. Hundreds of Western educators also visited Japan to provide their experience and advice. The new educational system enjoyed great success, and by 1907, all Japanese children were receiving six years of schooling.

The government also set up secondary schools and universities for advanced study. Tokyo University and other institutions became important centers of learning whose graduates were soon to become the leaders of business and government in Japan. Thus, the success of the Meiji goals for education had immense importance for the Japanese. It meant that a person's role in life was no longer fixed at birth, as in the past, but would be based on his or her education and training.

In education, as in other Meiji institutions based on Western models, the Japanese continued their own traditions and adapted them to fit their needs. In the schools, Japanese history was emphasized to instill a love of country. Every school taught **"morals classes,"** or courses that were used to reinforce such traditions as reverence for the emperor, filial piety (the respect and obedience due parents and elders), and the value of cooperation and group loyalty. These values were designed to mold citizens who would follow the fixed patterns of acceptable social behavior, in sharp contrast to the Western emphasis on individualism and self-fulfillment. Indeed, they were deemed all the more important by the Meiji government to make sure that the Japanese would retain their identity as a people even as they adopted Western models.

The Constitution of 1889. The Meiji reformers had discussed the idea of a formal plan of government for Japan for many years. In 1881, the reformers had the emperor issue a decree stating that a new form of government would be established within nine years. During the 1880s, a few important leaders had formed new political parties, which also were beginning to demand a voice in the government.

To head a commission to draft a constitution, the reformers chose Ito Hirobumi (ee-toh hih-roh-BOO-mee). Ito was especially attracted to Germany, where the monarch and a powerful chancellor held nearly all government power. When he returned home, Ito and his aides drafted Japan's new constitution, in secrecy. Then in 1889, the reformers, now increasingly referred to as the *genro*, had the emperor proclaim the constitution as law. They made it clear, however, that the constitution was a gift given to the people by the emperor, not a recognition that the people had the right to govern themselves. Coming from the emperor, who was the symbol of authority and unity in Japan, the new constitution was quickly accepted.

The Constitution of 1889 established a legislature called the **Diet**. The Diet was composed of two houses. The members of the lower house, the House of Representatives, were to be elected by male taxpayers (about 1 percent of the population). The upper house, the House of Peers, consisted of hereditary nobles and appointed members from the new leadership. The emperor retained the supreme power of government, including the right to command the army and navy, direct foreign affairs, and veto all bills passed by the Diet. In reality, however, the full power of government remained in the hands of the reformers. In the early years of the constitutional government, they became the prime ministers and the cabinet members who actually ran the government.

Despite these limitations, Japan for the first time had a parliamentary system of government based on law. In this way, the reformers also hoped to gain greater support among the Japanese people. They also wanted to impress the foreign powers by becoming the first nation in Asia to adopt a Western-style **parliamentary government.** (In a parliamentary government, the executive and legislative powers of the government are based on the parliament, or national legislature.) In this they were successful, for the British and other nations began to put an end to the "unequal treaties" soon after the constitution took effect. Japan, with its growing industrial economy and political power, was now ready to take its place on the world stage.

The Rise of Nationalism. In 1892, Ito Hirobumi, the Meiji *genro* who had been responsibile for drafting the constitution, became prime minister of Japan, 25 years after the Meiji Restoration had begun. During that quarter century, nearly every aspect of Japanese life had been transformed. Japan's population had increased rapidly, from about 30 million in 1868 to nearly 45 million by the late 1890s. Japanese farmers increased rice and barley production, but could scarcely keep up with the food needs of the nation.

However, many farmers, now faced with heavy money taxes, did not share in the growing prosperity. In increasing numbers, they became tenant farmers, working land owned by others. Many also abandoned their lands and moved their families to cities in search of jobs in small shops and factories. This flood of workers to the cities caused a surplus of labor in many industries. At the same time, women became a large part of the workforce, since they were willing to work for lower wages than men. Increasingly, Japan's limited supplies of coal, iron ore, and other resources were in danger of being used up as Japan began to establish the industries it now needed to compete with Western nations.

Despite these problems, however, by the 1890s, the spirit of **nationalism** stirred in Japan, with the emperor as its focus and symbol. Ancient Shinto rites centering on the emperor were revived. Patriotic fervor was especially strong among the new army, made up largely of peasants, who had been drafted and were taught the divinity of the emperor and the superiority of the nation he ruled.

IMPERIAL JAPAN

Growing numbers of Japanese agreed with the Meiji *genro* that their nation must become a military power in order to increase its trade and gain access to raw materials. Japan now turned its attention to nearby East Asian nations that might enable it to achieve this goal.

War with China. In 1876 Japan had forced neighboring Korea to sign a treaty opening that country to Japanese trade and granting Japan the right of extraterritoriality. China long had claimed Korea as part of its empire but without the power to enforce its claim. Growing tensions between Japan and China over Korea led to war in 1895. Japan's armies

By the time of the Sino-Japanese War of 1894-1895, the Japanese army not only was wearing Western-style uniforms but was also using Western military techniques.

quickly overran Korea and moved into Manchuria, a Chinese region rich in iron ore and coal. The Japanese navy destroyed the Chinese fleet as well. Japan's easy victory caused an outburst of national pride among its people, and also stirred grudging admiration and new-found respect for Japan among the Western powers.

In the Treaty of Shimonoseki (shih-moh-noh-SAY-kee) that ended the war with China, Japan forced China to turn over the island of Formosa (present-day Taiwan) off China's coast, the Pescadores (pes-kuh-DAWR-eez) Islands, and the Liaotung (lyoo-DOONG) Peninsula of Manchuria. However, Germany, France, and Russia, not yet ready to accept Japan as a full-fledged imperial power, forced Japan to return the Liaotung Peninsula to China. Then, when Japan withdrew from the area, Russian troops moved in and seized control of the naval base at Port Arthur. Japan then tried unsuccessfully to negotiate a settlement of the issue with the Russians.

The Russo-Japanese War.   However, Japan was quick to learn how great-power diplomacy worked. In 1900, foreigners in the Chinese capital of Peking were threatened by an uprising called the Boxer Rebellion. Japan then joined with the Western powers and sent troops to free the Westerners. Next, in 1902, it arranged to sign a treaty of alliance with Great Britain, which agreed to back the Japanese in order to limit the growth of Russian influence in Asia. With the support of Britain, the world's leading naval power, Japan launched a surprise attack on Port Arthur in 1904, sinking part of the Russian fleet stationed there. Japan achieved final victory at the battle of Tsushima (tsoo-SHEE-mah) in May 1905, where it completed the destruction of the Russian fleet, destroying 38 warships.

U.S. President Theodore Roosevelt arranged the final peace treaty that ended the Russo-Japanese War. Under the terms of the Treaty of Portsmouth, Japan received the southern half of Sakhalin (SAK-uh-leen) Island, just north of Hokkaido, as well as Russia's rights to the Liaotung Peninsula and its railroads in Manchuria. Japan's victories over China and Russia now gave it a free hand to move into Korea. In 1910, the Japanese occupied Korea, where they would remain for the next 35 years. Thus, in a few short years Japan had gained an empire and had become an imperialist power.

Japan's Role in World War I.   Although its interests were not directly involved, Japan joined its ally Britain when World War I broke out in

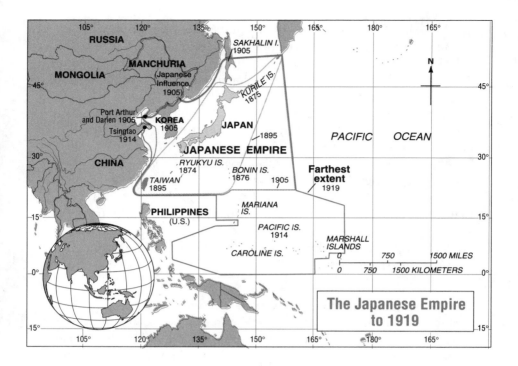

The Japanese Empire to 1919

1914. Since the main conflict was in Europe, Japan had a nearly free hand to expand its growing empire in Asia. At the peace conference in 1919, the victorious Allies drew up the Treaty of Versailles. As one of the "Big Five" powers, Japan was now an equal partner with the leading nations of the world.

In the peace settlement, Japan received Germany's former colonies in the Pacific—the Caroline, Marshall, and Mariana Islands—as **mandates**, or commissions, from the League of Nations. It also was directed to negotiate with China to decide the fate of the German naval base of Kiaochow (kee-OW-joh) Bay in China. Japan gained control of that base in 1922. Japan also joined the new League of Nations, which was established to keep the peace, and was granted a permanent seat on the League's Council. Japan clearly had taken its place as one of the great world powers.

During the war, in 1915, Japan's military leaders had presented China with the so-called Twenty-one Demands. These included Japanese possession of German-held Shantung, extension of Japanese rights in Manchuria, and a half interest in iron and steel mills in central China. In effect, the Twenty-one Demands attempted to bring China under Japanese domination. A weak Chinese government was forced to give in to most of the demands. Japan was now the most powerful nation in East Asia.

JAPAN DURING THE 1920s

Japan's emergence as a major international power coincided with the end of the Meiji Restoration. A new generation of leaders and political parties took over the government. The 1920s were years of great change in the nation's economy, with the growth of heavy industry and an influx of the rural population to the cities. Japan's parliament and new political leaders gained power, and Western culture became popular among the growing urban population.

A New Generation of Leaders.   With the death of Emperor Mutsuhito in 1912, the Meiji era came to an end. The new emperor, Taisho (tah-EE-shoh), weak and in ill health, ruled until 1926, but had little influence on the government. Only a few of the Meiji leaders still were active in politics, and a new generation of Japanese leaders had appeared. In 1918, for the first time, the government was headed by a leader who had not been selected by the Meiji rulers. Hara Kei (hah-rah KAY-ee), the new prime minister, was the first of many prime ministers during the 1920s who were selected because they were leading members of Japan's political parties.

In 1925, the Japanese people seemed to gain a greater voice in their government when all adult males, not only those who paid taxes, gained the right to vote. However, the democratic thrust of this period had important limitations. For example, the same year that adult males gained the vote, efforts of radical groups like the communists and socialists to form political parties were harshly restricted. In 1928, a special police force was established to seek out "dangerous thoughts" among the people. Laws passed by the Diet banned any effort to try to change Japan's political system or to try to abolish private property. The major political parties received much of their financing from the zaibatsu. In accordance with their supporters' views, the parties often stayed in office by exploiting labor unrest and rural protests. Equally important, most of the electorate consisted of rural farmers, who still firmly held conservative traditional values in which democracy had little meaning.

Japan's Economy in the 1920s.   During the 1920s, Japan was rapidly becoming an urbanized nation. Nearly half the population now lived in

69

cities, and the standard of living of these city dwellers was rising. Japanese industries had rapidly expanded during World War I to provide for the needs of the military. Japan also had greatly increased its trade with other Asian nations, whose commerce with European countries was interrupted by the war. Steel, shipbuilding, and other heavy industries continued to expand after the war, to meet Japan's new needs as an imperialist power.

Further, a small number of zaibatsu controlled an ever-larger part of Japan's major factory complexes, shipyards, mines, and banks. At the same time, most Japanese companies were small, employing relatively few workers. Over 50 percent of all Japanese factories had workforces of between five and nine workers. More than half of the workers were women. Workers in the large, zaibatsu-controlled industries were gaining higher wages and improved conditions that would soon result in lifetime job security.

Japanese farmers did not share in the general prosperity of the 1920s. Crop prices declined throughout the decade as food production increased slightly faster than the population grew. As a result, farm incomes shrank. Farmers were soon to suffer even greater hardships in the worldwide Great Depression of the 1930s.

THE ROAD TO WORLD WAR II

In 1929, a worldwide depression struck. This Great Depression caused nations to withdraw behind high tariff barriers in an effort to protect their own economies. Japan, as a new industrial power, suffered greatly from this loss of trade, on which its economy depended. Military leaders and conservative politicians believed that the solution to the country's problem was to secure a greater colonial empire than it already had. This effort led the Japanese into a world war that ended disastrously for them.

The Rise of Military Leadership. During the 1920s, many Japanese were growing unhappy with the new political parties governing Japan. To them, the parties were corrupt and controlled by the zaibatsu, who manipulated government policies in their own self-interests. The Japanese also opposed the growing influence of Western culture in their nation. They were especially critical of young people in Japan's large cities, who eagerly adopted Western-style clothing and hairdos, flocked to foreign movies and jazz clubs, and took up tennis, golf, baseball, and other Western sports. These young people were referred to as "modern boys and girls," who, by rejecting their traditional culture, were regarded as "un-Japanese." Conservative Japanese looked back to the past, in which they believed loyalty and honor alone had motivated their rulers. Events soon followed in which Japan's military leaders seemed to possess the qualities these people sought.

In 1923, Japan and the Western powers had reached an agreement at the Washington Naval Conference, which had been held to limit the size of nations' navies and to prevent the building of new bases and fortifications in the Pacific. Some Japanese military leaders believed this agreement unwisely prevented the nation from building the naval force it needed. Then in 1924, the United States banned Japanese from immigrating to the country, as Australia had done earlier. This action was considered a deliberate insult by many Japanese, who charged that the Western nations were racists. To the Japanese, who took special pride in their nation and its ancient traditions, this discrimination was particularly painful. They believed their rapidly growing population had an equal right to move into other regions of the world. It soon became clear that China offered the nearest and most profitable target.

When the emperor died in 1926, his son, Hirohito (hihr-oh-HEE-toh), ascended the imperial throne and remained in power until 1989. This long reign, called the Showa (shoh-wah) Period, or "Enlightened Peace," ironically was to be the stormy age of Japan's attempted conquest of a Pacific empire and prolonged fighting in World War II.

The Japanese Conquest of Manchuria.   In September 1931, Japanese troops in the part of Manchuria that China had leased to Japan blew up a railroad bridge and then claimed that the explosion had been an attack on its forces in the area. The Japanese army used this as an excuse to quickly conquer Manchuria. The next year the Japanese set up a **puppet state** called Manchukuo (man-CHOO-kwoh), with a former emperor of China on the throne, but power completely in their hands. The Japanese prime minister opposed this action, but the Japanese people strongly supported it. The United States and other Western powers condemned Japan's takeover. They and the members of the League of Nations demanded Japan withdraw its troops from Manchuria. Instead, Japan withdrew as a member of the League.

The Japanese people were joyful over the conquest of Manchuria, which covered a land area larger than Japan itself, and had the coal, iron ore, and other resources badly needed by Japanese industry. Japan soon

The 1931 Japanese invasion of Manchuria gave Japan an enormous area rich in the natural resoures that it lacked, but the action was condemned by the Western powers.

built steel plants, railroads, and power plants there and added millions of acres of Manchurian farmland to Japan's own limited agricultural resources.

The conquest of Manchuria brought new prestige and strength to Japan's military leaders. Many Japanese now believed that their nation had found a way to escape the suffering caused by the Great Depression. They also hailed the conquest as a step in fulfilling their nation's mission to liberate the people of Asia from Western control. Increasingly, they looked to the military for leadership. Though many political leaders feared the nation was being led down the path to war, most of them were powerless to oppose the generals and admirals. In 1936, several political leaders who opposed military aggression in China were assassinated, and a year later a general took office as prime minister of Japan. That same year, fighting again broke out between Japan and China.

Japan's Aggression in China. In July 1937, minor fighting between Chinese and Japanese forces began near Peking (now Beijing). This time, Chinese troops led by General Chiang Kai-shek struck back forcefully. However, Japan's superior forces soon conquered Shanghai and

Nanjing, then continued their invasion until they controlled North China and Inner Mongolia. Nevertheless, Chiang Kai-shek's forces hung on and retreated inland, refusing to surrender.

The United States and other Western powers protested Japan's aggression in China. In 1938, the United States government imposed an **embargo,** or ban, on all military goods for Japan. In 1940, after Japan had invaded Indochina in Southeast Asia to gain oil and rubber needed by its military force, the United States stopped all shipments of scrap iron and steel to Japan. It also joined with Britain and the Netherlands in cutting off shipments of oil. This oil embargo eventually crippled Japan and convinced the nation's military leaders that it must fight, if necessary, to end this threat.

Meanwhile, World War II had begun in Europe after the German leader Adolf Hitler invaded Poland in September 1939. Japan welcomed this dramatic event as an opportunity to join with Germany and Italy in the fight against Britain, France, and the Netherlands. These nations were opposed to Japan's actions on the Asian mainland. Then, in the spring of 1940, Japan signed a **non-aggression treaty** with the Soviet Union, under which each side promised not to attack the other, to protect itself against any possible attack from the north.

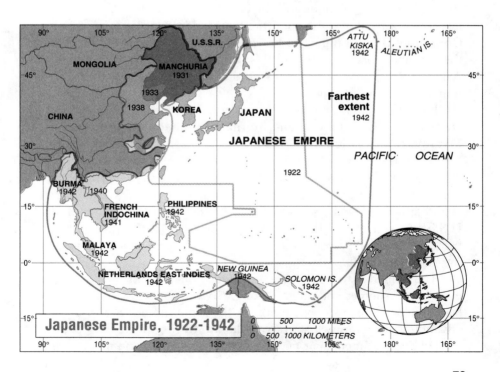

Japan now also determined to have a showdown with the United States to force an end to the oil embargo. In October 1941, after several months of negotiations, Japan agreed to withdraw from Indochina if the United States would end its cutoff of oil and help negotiate peace between China and Japan. However, the United States, doubtful of Japan's real intentions, insisted Japan must first withdraw its forces from China, Manchuria, and Indochina. At the same time, the Japanese government already had decided to go to war if the United States refused to reach a settlement by December 1.

World War II. On the morning of December 7, 1941, a fleet of Japanese aircraft carriers launched their planes on a bombing attack against the Pacific fleet at Pearl Harbor in Hawaii. Caught by surprise, a large part of the U.S. fleet was sunk or badly damaged. Yet, despite the terrible damage inflicted, the Japanese had seriously miscalculated. Japan's military leaders had based their planning on a quick knockout blow that would defeat the United States in a brief war. They had underestimated the United States' will to fight, as well as the enormous resources and labor reserves it would now mobilize against Japan.

Japan's government and its military leaders had based their war strategy on an easy conquest of the countries of Southeast Asia and the Pacific. Nearly all of these countries were colonies of Western nations. Consequently, the Japanese believed, these people would welcome them as liberators. To carry out this plan, Japan set up a **"Greater East Asia Co-Prosperity Sphere"** to coordinate its domination of the new united Pacific-Asian region.

By 1942, in a series of coordinated invasions, Japan had achieved its goal of establishing a vast empire that stretched from Burma (now Myanmar) into much of China and Southeast Asia and across the Pacific to the Aleutian Islands off Alaska. However, the people of these conquered lands and islands strongly resisted Japanese rule. Meanwhile, the United States, which quickly rebuilt its military might, launched counterattacks at Japanese strongholds throughout the Pacific. With the U.S. victory at the battle of Midway in June 1942, the tide of battle turned. The naval power of the United States began to force a Japanese retreat in the Pacific.

The United States had twice the population of Japan and far greater economic resources and military power. By the end of 1944 it had won back much of Japan's new empire. At the same time, U.S. forces were advancing closer and closer toward Japan. In the spring of 1945, the United States launched air raids against key industrial and military centers in Japan, including Tokyo itself. Massive destruction and the death of 100,000 civilians in that city were but a prelude to the horror that was soon to be visited on Japan. In the Pacific, U.S. forces occupied the islands of Okinawa and Iwo Jima, after inflicting terrible casualties on the Japanese forces there, and prepared for an invasion of Japan.

Germany surrendered in May 1945. Japan now stood alone against the power of the United States and its allies. With much of its military power destroyed and its cities in ruins, Japan and its people faced starvation and defeat. Yet, the morale of the Japanese remained high. United around the emperor, Japan appeared willing to continue the war even if U.S. forces invaded their land. Then, in July 1945, the United States and its allies demanded that Japan surrender. The Japanese government refused. After much debate within the U.S. government, it was decided to attack Japan with atomic bombs rather than risk the deaths of hundreds of thousands of U.S. troops in an invasion of Japan. On August 6, the United States dropped an atomic bomb on Hiroshima, followed two days later by an atomic attack on Nagasaki. More than 200,000 people were killed in these bombings. Thousands of others were exposed to fatal radiation. Even then, Japan's military commanders were divided on continuing the war, but on August 14, Emperor Hirohito made the decision to surrender. In a dramatic broadcast, he announced to his people that the war was over.

THE U.S. OCCUPATION OF JAPAN

Japan formally surrendered to U.S. General Douglas MacArthur on September 2, 1945, aboard the U.S. battleship *Missouri* in Tokyo harbor. Japan itself was now a nation in ruins, its economy in collapse, most of its major cities destroyed, and more than 3 million of its people killed. A brief seven years later, in 1952, when the U.S. occupation ended, Japan was rapidly rebuilding and about to enter the most prosperous period in its history.

General MacArthur in Control. General Douglas MacArthur, who had been head of the Allied forces in the Pacific, took control of Japan as the Supreme Commander of the Allied Powers. He quickly set up a new U.S.-controlled government, which he headed, and also commanded the U.S. troops that now occupied Japan. MacArthur proved to be a strong and skillful leader who soon won the respect of the Japanese people. They firmly supported his plans for rebuilding Japan into a peaceful unified nation.

Japanese gather at the memorial that honors the victims of the atomic bombing of Hiroshima. The flame in the foreground marks the spot where the bomb exploded, while the bombed-out building in the background stands as a symbol of the attack.

On Sept. 2, 1945, aboard the U.S.S. Missouri, U.S. General Douglas MacArthur and his fellow officers watch a Japanese officer sign the surrender document that ends World War II.

MacArthur acted decisively to achieve two immediate goals: to disarm Japan and to institute a new democratic government. Japan's army and navy were demobilized, and its warships and weapons were destroyed. The nation's armed forces of more than 6 million were brought home to Japan and returned to civilian life. Japan's wartime leaders and top military commanders were put on trial as war criminals. Seven were executed and 16 were imprisoned for life. The Japanese empire was broken up, and its conquered lands were restored to their prewar status.

Even in defeat many Japanese admired MacArthur's boldness in ridding their nation of the military leaders who they felt had betrayed them in losing the war. The U.S. army of occupation also played a key role in winning the confidence of the Japanese people. It treated its defeated enemy fairly and did everything it could to help restore the people's morale.

77

Japan's New Constitution. MacArthur and his advisers drew up a new democratic constitution for Japan, which the Japanese Diet put into effect in 1947. The emperor remained in power, though he now became a symbolic figurehead without constitutional powers. The Diet, whose members represented the people, was given the supreme power in the government. The prime minister and the cabinet were responsible to the Diet. A national system of courts also was established. In addition, the rights of the Japanese people to freedom of speech, religion, and the press were spelled out. Women were given the right to vote, for the first time in Japanese history. The equality of women and men, the right of workers to join unions, and the right of all citizens to an education were other important features of the Constitution of 1947.

One clause of the constitution was especially applauded by the Japanese. Article Nine provided, "The Japanese people forever renounce war as a sovereign right of the nation and the threat or use of force in settling international disputes." In these few words, Japan was forbidden to have an army, navy, or air force for the purpose of waging war, or to use force in its dealings with other nations. The people of Japan welcomed the lifting of the heavy burden of militarism that they had borne for so many years.

Economic and Other Reforms. General MacArthur and his advisers made major changes in Japan's economy. The zaibatsu, which had exercised such extensive control over the nation's economy, were ended. Most of them were broken up into many smaller companies. Many of these companies then were sold to the public. Eventually, however, the zaibatsu regained much of their power. This occurred when it became clear that their power and organization were needed to hasten the rebuilding of Japan's economy.

A fundamental reform in land ownership was carried out during the U.S. occupation. Large landowners were required to sell most of their land to the government at very low prices. Many of these owners had controlled the land as part of their great estates and domains since feudal times. The Japanese government then gave small farmers the right to buy small parcels of land, averaging 2.5 acres (1.01 hectares), at very low prices. In this way, tenant farmers, who made up nearly 70 percent of the rural population, now became landowners. Japan thus became a nation of small landowners.

Important changes in education also were made during the occupation. The public school system was remodeled after that of the United States. Nine years of education was made compulsory. A new curricu-

CASE STUDY:

The Occupation: a Challenge for Japan

Wataru Hiraizumi, a member of the Diet from the Fukui district of Honshu, recalls what his father had explained to him about the main challenge facing the Japanese when the U.S. occupation ended.

> For my father, the central question was . . . how to succeed in modernizing without losing our traditional culture . . . our sense of who we are . . . our belief in Japan. He saw a world in which modern, Western cultures clashed with and overwhelmed ancient, traditional cultures. To him, that was the greatest danger to Japan. As he saw it, some Asian nations had already succumbed by going Communist. That was the worst possible outcome. They had confronted the West . . . and had been attracted to it, and lost their souls. Suddenly, all their rich cultural traditions and values, thousands of years old, had lost their flavor and color. But they were too proud to just imitate the West and join it or become copies of it. Their answer was to try to leap ahead of the West by adopting Communism, the ideology [beliefs] of the future . . . the next stage. Well, he was afraid that could happen to Japan.
>
> After the war, through the fifties and sixties and into the 1970s, he was very unhappy at the Americanization of Japan. . . . But then . . . he started to reconcile [persuade] himself. He began to believe that perhaps the Japanese were going to keep their character and their soul. . . .
>
> Well, so far, Japan is a rare case. We seem to be modernizing, industrializing, and even learning how to deal with foreigners without losing our traditions. Of course, geography counts. . . . The oceans insulate [separate] us. . . . I think my father helped us to do what we have done . . . to build this prosperous, modern, international Japan that still has its soul.

[From Martin E. Weinstein, *The Human Face of Japan's Leadership*. New York: Praeger, 1989.]

1. What was the speaker's father's fear about what would happen to Japan under the occupation?

2. How did the father feel in later years about what had happened to Japan?

lum included social studies courses intended to encourage critical thinking in place of the rote memorization and indoctrination of the "moral education" courses in the old system. New private colleges were founded, and many junior colleges were set up to encourage higher learning among the new postwar generation.

During the U.S. occupation, the Japanese displayed the same unity and self-discipline that they had in the great era of change under the Meiji Restoration. Moreover, the Americans allowed the Japanese Diet and its leaders to participate in the making of the changes, thus making it possible for them to be modified as required in some cases. This process of implementing postwar changes helped give them legitimacy and made them easier for the Japanese people to accept.

The effectiveness and success of the policies of the U.S. occupation were clear by 1951, when the United States and the Allies signed a treaty of peace with Japan. Under the terms of the treaty, Japan regained its sovereignty and independence. It lost all the territory it had conquered overseas. Japan now consisted again of its ancient land—the four main islands of Honshu, Shikoku, Hokkaido, and Kyushu, and small surrounding islands. After occupation forces withdrew, Japan was allowed to establish a National Police Reserve, a force of 75,000 men for domestic security needs. The United States also signed a security treaty with Japan that allowed it to maintain military bases in Japan. It also pledged the United States to provide for Japan's defense.

The changes introduced during the occupation transformed Japan. Many people wonder whether the changes would have been made by the Japanese themselves in time. There is general agreement that this probably would have been true. Here is how one expert on Japan states the case:

> The occupation reforms succeeded in large part because they were headed in the same direction forces within Japan were pushing. The dynamic leadership of external military authority perhaps channeled these forces more narrowly, and thus made them flow more swiftly than might otherwise have been the case, but basically the occupation facilitated [made easier] rather than determined [decided] the postwar development of Japan.

From Enemy to Ally. After the **Cold War** began between the United States and the Soviet Union, Japan's location in Asia and the economic recovery that began during the U.S. occupation soon changed Americans' view of their former enemy. The U.S. government now was concerned with helping Japan rebuild its economy as quickly as possible to prevent the spread of communism there. Therefore, by 1948 it no longer pressed for the breakup of the zaibatsu holdings. When the Chinese communists won control of their country in 1949, the U.S. fear of communist expansion grew greater still.

Gradually, the U.S. policy toward Japan changed still more as Americans began to view Japan as a possible strategic partner in opposing the spread of communism and Soviet power in Asia. At the same time, the Japanese government itself worried about the growth of the Communist party in Japan and the increasing radicalism of the labor unions. Japan's conservative political parties grew stronger. Yoshida Shigeru (yoh-SHEE-dah shi-geh-ROO), who served as prime minister during most of the period from 1946 until 1954, also skillfully worked with MacArthur to strengthen Japan's parliamentary party system and consolidate conservative power. Japan's two conservative parties merged in 1955 to form the Liberal Democratic party, which was to dominate Japanese politics throughout the postwar period.

The outbreak of the Korean War in 1950 strengthened the growing ties between Japan and the United States. Japan's rebuilt industries turned out many of the supplies needed by U.S. military forces in Korea, and the United States now became one of Japan's main trading partners. The United States also provided financial aid and advanced technology, which helped Japan establish new, more modern plants in such basic industries as steel, chemicals, shipbuilding, and electric power. It also encouraged the Japanese government to undertake centralized planning to guide the rebuilding of the nation's economy and the use of its resources.

But it was the Japanese people themselves who were largely responsible for their nation's recovery. Once again, Japanese traditions of hard work, group loyalty, shared values, and belief in themselves as a people were harnessed to achieve the rebuilding of Japan's economy. You will learn about the results of this "economic miracle" in later chapters as you study Japanese society today.

REVIEWING THE CHAPTER

I. Building Your Vocabulary

Match the terms and the definitions.

extraterritoriality	yen	*genro*
zaibatsu	the Diet	morals classes

1. school courses used to reinforce Japanese traditions

2. basic unit of Japanese currency

3. Japanese lawmaking body

4. the right of foreigners in Japan to be tried in their own courts

5. wealthy Japanese families who owned the chief industries of the country

6. elder statesmen

II. Understanding the Facts

Write the letter of the correct answer to each question next to its number.

1. The main purpose of Commodore Perry's mission was to:
   a. invade Japan.
   b. make peace between Japan and China.
   c. cut off all trade between the United States and Japan.
   d. open Japan to U.S. trade.

2. The "unequal treaties" between Japan and the Western nations:
   a. ended Japan's isolation and spurred the Japanese to make major changes in their country.
   b. provided that China and Japan join under Western rule.
   c. made Japan a colony of Western nations.
   d. ended the power of the Japanese empire.

3. The government leaders who built Japan into a modern nation by cultural borrowing from the West were:
   a. the Edo daimyo.   b. the Meiji reformers.
   c. the samurai.   d. the zaibatsu.

4. Japanese government leaders traveled to the United States and other Western lands in the 1870s and 1880s to:
   a. study the governments, businesses, industries, and military and educational systems of these nations.
   b. spread Japanese culture.
   c. establish better relations with those lands.
   d. protest the "unequal treaties."

5. Japan's conquest of Manchuria marked the beginning of the growing power in Japan of:
   a. the *genro*. b. the military.
   c. the emperor. d. the shogun.

III. Thinking It Through

Write the letter of the best choice next to the number of each question.

1. During the Meiji Restoration, the cultural borrowing by Japan:
   a. helped it become a modern, Westernized nation.
   b. helped it become a modern, Westernized nation that preserved its ancient traditions and values.
   c. led to the overthrow of the shogun.
   d. led to the wars with China and Russia.

2. The Meiji government set up pilot plants to:
   a. develop an industrial economy and build up Japan's military power.
   b. encourage the replacement of its light industries.
   c. prepare for an invasion by the Russians.
   d. take industrial power from the zaibatsu.

3. The main purpose of the new system of education in Japan was to:
   a. teach students to read and write.
   b. instill in students a love of their country.
   c. prepare the people to accept the Constitution of 1889.
   d. teach the skills the Japanese needed as members of a modern society.

4. The military leaders of Japan defended their aggression in Asia before World War II by claiming that:
   a. Germany was preparing to attack Japan.
   b. they were liberating the people of Asia from Western control.

c. they needed to have a source for the oil and scrap iron the United States had stopped shipping to Japan.

d. they needed a place to send Japan's rapidly growing minority population.

5. When the U.S. occupation of Japan ended in 1952, Japan was:

a. a defeated nation whose cities and industries were in ruins.

b. rebuilding its economy and becoming more democratic.

c. sending troops to fight in the Korean War as the ally of the United States.

d. preparing to recapture the empire it had lost during World War II.

DEVELOPING CRITICAL THINKING SKILLS

1. Describe how the Meiji reformers used Western technology and institutions to modernize Japan.

2. Describe the changes that took place in Japan as its feudal society began to end after the 1870s.

3. Describe Japan's system of government established by the Constitution of 1889.

4. Summarize the reasons that led Japan to fight in World War II.

5. Describe some of the reforms introduced during the U.S. occupation of Japan and explain how they affected the lives of the Japanese.

ENRICHMENT AND EXPLORATION

1. Consult reference books in your library on World War II in the Pacific. Then make a time box to summarize the main events that took place there from 1941 to 1945. For each major battle or event, list the date and place it occurred, who the opponents were, and the reason why the engagement was important to the outcome of the war.

2. Imagine that you were the chief adviser to the Tokugawa shogun in 1853 when Commodore Perry's ships arrived in Tokyo. He has asked you to prepare a report to help him decide how to reply to the U.S. demands. List the main things you believe he must consider and briefly explain why they are important to Japan. For each item, describe what you think will happen if he follows your advice and what will happen if he does not.

84

4 Japanese Society Today

Foreign tourists who visit one of Japan's famous Shinto shrines or Buddhist temples often are astonished to see the busloads of students who are visiting these same sites. Yet they probably are even more surprised when they observe these groups of young people more closely. The high school group nearby, for example, seems to be enjoying every minute of its trip, listening intently to every word their teacher utters. There are no troublemakers in the group, no students who are disrupting the field trip by showing off or playing tricks on their classmates. The students seem to need no reminders from their teacher to behave themselves. These young Japanese are obviously learning important aspects of their nation's past, and having fun doing so.

Another thing foreign tourists notice about the people at the shrine is that there are few individuals who seem to be there alone. It is clear that the groups of students as well as groups of older people make up nearly all the visitors to the shrine. During their stopover here, the tourists have done more than visit an important religious center. They also have begun to learn about the importance of groups and people's behavior in groups in Japanese society.

THE IMPORTANCE OF GROUPS IN JAPANESE SOCIETY

Unlike the foreign visitors in Japan, most Japanese would expect groups of students to act like those you have just read about. In fact, the Japanese stress on the importance of the group is perhaps the most distinguishing feature of Japanese society.

The People of Japan and Other Countries

COUNTRY	POPULATION	RURAL/ URBAN RATIO	LIFE EXPEC- TANCY	INFANT MORTALITY (per 1,000 live births)	LITERACY RATE
Japan	123,778,000	23 / 77	76 M 82 F	5.0	99%
Brazil	153,771,000	24 / 76	64 M 69 F	67.0	76
Canada	26,620,500	24 / 76	73 M 80 F	7.3	99
China	1,130,025,000	54 / 46	68 M 70 F	33.0	70
France	56,184,000	23 / 77	72 M 80 F	8.2	99
Germany	79,070,000	14 / 86	73 M 81 F	6.0	99
India	844,000,000	72 / 28	57 M 58 F	91.0	36
Russia and the Commonwealth*	285,000,000	34 / 66	64 M 74 F	25.2	99
United Kingdom	57,121,000	7 / 93	72 M 78 F	13.3	99
United States	248,879,000	24 / 76	72 M 79 F	9.1	99

*Includes Georgia
M = Male
F = Female

Source: *World Almanac, 1992*

The Advantages of Groups.   In Japan, membership in various groups throughout a person's life allows him or her to participate fully in society and make contributions that strengthen society. At the same time, groups provide each person with a sense of identity and worth as a responsible member of society. Groups teach the Japanese many important things about living in Japanese society. These include knowing how to get along with other people and what conduct and behavior is expected of group members. They also provide the satisfaction of being accepted as a loyal and productive member of society.

From infancy through old age, the family group, the school group, the work group, and many other formal and informal groups require the

Japanese to cooperate and become members of a team. The Japanese become acutely aware of their responsibilities to the various groups to which they belong. Effective group behavior is taught and reinforced at every stage of a person's life. Of course, many of the same groups that the Japanese belong to also exist in the United States and most other countries. But perhaps nowhere else are these groups so decisive in shaping people's lives.

The Group in Japanese History.   There are many reasons why group membership has become such a dominant feature of Japanese life. Japan's history as an island nation provides one important clue. From very early times, the Japanese developed a homogeneous society. This provided a solid base for group cooperation among people who shared the same historical and cultural background. Moreover, the Japanese had to depend on one another to build terraces for growing rice and to irrigate their small plots of land. In a land constantly threatened by earthquakes, typhoons, and other disasters, nature also encouraged people to depend on one another in order to survive such experiences. Religion, too, played a part in strengthening the group nature of Japanese society. Buddhism taught the oneness of the universe as well as the goal of freeing the individual to merge with the cosmos. The Confucian teachings adopted from China also emphasized strict respect for rank and status in each person's relations with others. This code of conduct was useful in functioning in group settings.

The Japanese also have made group activity a central feature in their society for many other, practical reasons. Groups enable a large population living close together in a small area to enjoy social harmony. Groups provide firm guidelines and standards of conduct required of their members. By promoting cooperation and reducing concern about the often-conflicting needs of individuals, groups help promote a peaceful, stable society.

This group emphasis helped Japan to become a modern nation. The Japanese developed a deep sense of loyalty and pride in themselves as a people. The Japanese, in this fashion, came to regard themselves as a tight-knit nation to which all Japanese owed their loyalty. As Japan emerged from its feudal era during the Meiji Restoration, the Japanese sense of themselves as a special people was well developed. This sense of "we Japanese" and their confidence that they could do difficult things that others could not do enabled Japan to modernize in traditional ways without becoming Westernized.

In their small modern apartment, the members of this Japanese family still observe the practice of sitting on the floor while at the table having their dinner.

THE JAPANESE FAMILY

The family is the basic group to which nearly all Japanese owe their loyalty. The typical Japanese family today is a **nuclear family**—that is, one that consists of parents and their children. Most families live in Japan's overcrowded cities, in two- or three-room apartments less than half the size of a U.S. apartment and crowded with modern appliances.

Until recent decades, the normal family was an **extended family**, consisting of a married couple and their children plus grandparents and other older relatives. In rural areas and even in some cities, homes were large enough to accommodate all these family members. The Japan tradition called for an adult, expecially a son, to take care of an older parent. Today, however, with most of the large urban population living in small apartments, there is barely enough room for the married couple and their children.

Yet, there are still families where the two grandparents or a widowed grandparent somehow share this tiny space. If the mother works at a full- or part-time job, the grandmother may take over many of the household duties, preparing meals, cleaning the apartment, and doing the shopping for the family.

The Family Structure.   In most Japanese homes, the mother is the dominant member. She assumes nearly all of the responsibilities for raising the children, even when she has a job outside the home.

In most middle-class Japanese families, the father is away at work until late in the evening, often six days a week. After he finishes work, he usually spends his evenings socializing with groups of his co-workers. Since he seldom sees his children during the week, the father is sometimes called their "Sunday friend." It is also not uncommon for many Japanese businessmen to accept a job assignment in another part of Japan or even in another country for a year or more, leaving their families behind.

It is not surprising, then, that the strongest bonds in a Japanese family are between the mother and the children. Often these bonds are even stronger than those between husband and wife. Many marriages in Japan are still "arranged" marriages, or **omiai** (OH-mee-eye). In many such marriages, the partners learn to love each other after they are married. Increasingly, though, young couples marry for love.

The Role of the Mother.   The typical Japanese mother devotes much of her time to teaching the children the behavior that is expected of them in dealing with other people. She teaches them to show respect to other people. Such respect is based on people's age, their job, and their position in society. The mother encourages her children to become team players, to learn to put their own preferences aside, and to accept the standards of the various groups to which they will belong. She also teaches them to be considerate of their fellow students, to exercise self-discipline, and to contribute to their class's success in school.

Mothers usually take charge of their children's education, actively encouraging them to study hard in order to become successful. They take a very active part in helping their children with their daily lessons and in preparing for tests.

Although women handle most of the tasks of raising the children, they seldom punish them. In fact, mothers often seem to spoil their children. Most mothers regard childhood as a time of freedom, as years of preparation for the difficult roles their children will face as adults. Thus, young children and teenagers, especially if they are boys, usually have few duties in the household.

89

THE STATUS OF WOMEN

Japanese women have achieved full equality with men under the law. They were granted the rights to vote and to sue for divorce under the 1947 Constitution. Yet the equality of Japanese women is in many respects more theoretical than real. Present-day Japan is still very much a man's world. Women play a subordinate role to men in most aspects of life. Yet, this is changing as women become more independent of men and some women achieve equality with men in the workplace.

Family or Career? Most Japanese women continue to believe that their role as mothers who are responsible for raising the children and carrying out the major functions of the family is their most important duty. To them, few jobs or careers could be more rewarding or confer greater status. Understandably, therefore, Japan has not experienced a vigorous woman's movement like that in the United States. Nevertheless, since the end of the U.S. occupation in 1952, Japanese women have achieved gains in their legal rights and educational achievements.

As in other industrial countries, women's role as housewives have been transformed by a flood of household appliances like dishwashers, vacuum cleaners, refrigerators, and microwave ovens. Many families now have cars, which wives use during the day for shopping and driving their children to school and after-school "cram-schools" and club groups. All this has meant far greater freedom for most women from routine tasks and opportunities to do things that interest them.

Women in the Workforce. The birthrate in Japan has been steadily falling. As a result, women have become an increasingly important source of labor outside the home. Therefore, working women have been able to secure benefits that were unheard of in the recent past.

Despite the fact that Japanese women continue to prize their traditional roles as homemakers, a substantial number have entered the workforce in recent years. Today, almost half the women have jobs outside the home, and six out of ten working women are married. A woman professor of social psychology at Keio University, Iwao Sumiko (ee-WAH-oh soo-mee-koh), reports:

> Working women now fall into two main groups: a small, very talented elite [select group], whose ambitions may run even higher than men's, and a great mass majority, whose members do not want to work so hard that it will interfere with their family responsibilities and enjoyment of nonwork activities.

Women in Japan's Work Force, 1960-1990			
YEAR	NUMBER EMPLOYED (in thousands)	PERCENT OF FEMALE POPULATION EMPLOYED	PERCENT OF WORKING WOMEN IN TOTAL WORKING POPULATION
1960	17,440	51.8	40.8
1965	18,080	48.1	39.1
1970	19,550	48.2	39.0
1975	19,120	44.0	37.1
1980	20,960	45.7	38.4
1985	22,530	46.3	39.3
1990	24,860	48.0	40.3

Source: U.S. Department of Labor, Bureau of Labor Statistics

Working women in general fall into two age groups. One group consists of women between the ages of 20 and 24. The other group consists of women between the ages of 40 and 49. The women in the younger group enter the workplace after graduating from high school or junior college. Then they work for a few years until they marry. The vast majority of these women work at routine jobs in electronics or textile factories or become salespersons, clerks, elevator attendants, or waitresses. When they marry, most of them leave their jobs and spend their time establishing their households and raising children.

Women in the older group are usually married and return to work after their children are grown. Many do so because their families need their additional income to help meet home mortgage payments, to pay for their children's after-school "cram schools" (see below), and to keep up with the constantly rising cost of living. A second reason is that, as Iwao Sumiko has noted, increasingly women are seeking to have careers of their own outside the home, in the business or professional world.

Many older women work at the same kinds of jobs they had before they "retired" to look after their children. They are considered as *pato* (PAH-toh), or part-time employees, and earn the same low wages as before even though they may work full time. Nor are they eligible to have the lifetime jobs with their firms or receive the bonuses and other benefits that male employees receive.

Women graduates of junior colleges or even universities often work as secretaries or as "office ladies" in business and factory offices. "Office ladies" keep the office clean and serve tea to the men. In their spare time they also may do typing and filing jobs.

Gains of Educated Women.   As Iwao Sumiko has pointed out, however, the prospects for some women in the workplace has been changing drastically. Nearly 30 percent of Japanese women now receive higher education. As the number of women who attend junior colleges and universities has increased, large Japanese companies have begun to provide on-the-job training for new women workers. This move was encouraged by the Equal Employment Opportunity Law passed in 1985. This law forbade discrimination in hiring based on a person's sex. More and more companies are paying women executives and managers at the same rate as men.

Many women with higher educations have been finding career opportunities in Japan's small businesses. In such businesses, of which there are thousands in the country, more and more women are able to enter a career track and achieve leadership positions in a firm. Educated women also are achieving greater success in certain professions. This is especially true of education, where women make up more

Women now make up a substantial part of the Japanese workforce. Here women join men in the painstaking work of assembling high-quality cameras.

than half the teachers in Japan's schools. More women are also becoming doctors, engineers, computer programmers, and journalists.

In general, though, not many women have been able to achieve the success in business, government, and the professions that is often enjoyed by men. The average woman worker in Japan earns only 53 percent of the salary received by a man. Women have made slow progress in government and politics. While many women's groups play an active part in local government, few women serve in the national government. Fewer than 30 women were elected to seats in the Japanese Diet in each of the national elections during the 1980s. In 1992, there were only 10 women in the House of Representatives of the Diet, which has a total membership of 512.

SCHOOL GROUPS AND EDUCATION

Education is highly valued in Japan for two reasons. Education is critical in determining a person's future career and position in Japanese society. It is also an important means for training children to adapt to the society in which they live.

Japanese Schools. The structure of the Japanese school system is similar to that of the United States. Six years of elementary schooling is followed by three years of junior high and three years of senior high school. In Japan, however, children attend school $5\frac{1}{2}$ days a week, 240 days a year, compared with 5 days a week and 180 days a year in the United States.

The long school year reinforces the teaching of the self-control and social skills needed to achieve success in class. School teaches the rewards of group loyalty. Students study and recite together in small groups led by the teacher. The teacher encourages each person to study hard and regard each assigned task as something that must be done well, to the best of one's ability.

From elementary school through high school, most students take their education seriously and study very hard. Starting in the first grade, students have daily homework assignments. Social studies, science, math, music, art, and physical education are taught. Most students also study English. Learning to read and write Japanese requires considerable classroom time because the written language is difficult. Students are expected to learn and memorize enormous amounts of information from their textbooks and their teacher's instruction. To help them do

These boys are attending a science class at a juku, *or "cram school."* Juku *prepare students for the stiff entrance examinations of the best schools and colleges.*

this, many pupils attend *juku* (joo-koo), or "cram schools" that give private classes after school. The *juku* also help prepare students to pass the tough exams necessary to enter the best high schools.

In the first two grades, children have the same teacher and study, play, and eat lunch together. This develops students' focus on the group and their responsibilities as members of their class. In elementary school classrooms, small groups within each class take turns helping clean and straighten up the room. In elementary and junior high school, members of each class often work together on an assignment or project.

Schools arrange frequent class field trips to historical and cultural sites. These often last two or three days and students usually remember them fondly for a lifetime. Students in junior and senior high school also join a great variety of extracurricular activity groups. They participate in clubs devoted to many of the sports and hobbies that are popular in Japan. Tennis, baseball, and *kendo,* a form of fencing, attract many students. Clubs in dramatics, calligraphy, and art offer instruction in these subjects. These activities are another means of teaching an individual to participate according to the standards of the group.

Universities and Careers. There are over 460 universities as well as more than 600 junior colleges and technical schools in Japan. Yet getting admitted to one of several top-level schools like Tokyo, Osaka, or Kyoto University is the highest goal of virtually every Japanese student. Competition for admission to these and a few important private universities is fierce. Only the students who score highest on an entrance exam are admitted. As a result, many Japanese students spend several hours after school during their high school years at *juku* preparing for their university exam. Students rightly refer to this tense, strenuous period in their lives as "examination hell." Most often, students' mothers also help their sons and daughters study for these crucial tests, earning them the nickname *kyoiku mama* (KYOH-ee-koo mah-mah), or "examination mothers."

Nearly 95 percent of Japanese students graduate from high school, and nearly 40 percent go on to universities or junior colleges. Being accepted by Tokyo, Osaka, or Kyoto University (but especially Tokyo University) virtually assures a person's future success. Japanese businesses and government ministries hire nearly all their employees from these top universities. Thus, their graduates are likely to become the future business and government leaders of the country. In this way, modern Japanese democracy is firmly based on highly educated citizens who gain their positions in government and industry through their own merit rather than through family status or wealth, as in the past.

A high school student observes her chemistry teacher. The emphasis of Japan's schools on science and mathematics has paid off in the high quality of its industrial products.

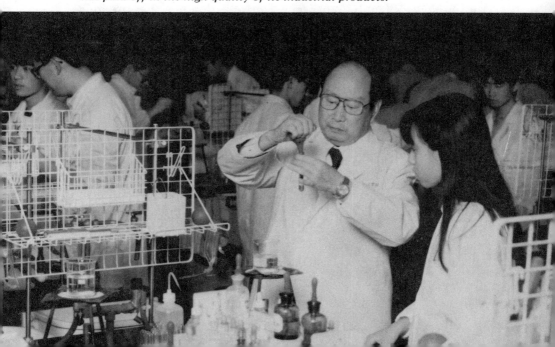

THE JAPANESE WORKFORCE

With the world's second-largest economy, surpassed only by that of the United States, Japan has one of the highest living standards in the world today. This great accomplishment has been due in large part to the dedication, traditions, skill, and hard work of its people.

Composition of the Workforce.   More than 25 percent of all Japanese workers have jobs in manufacturing. Japan's factories turn out a great variety of products, ranging from textiles to automobiles to microchips for computers. Among the leading industries are automobile manufacturing, shipbuilding, electronics, chemicals, and iron and steel manufacturing. Another 10 percent of the workforce is engaged in mining and construction.

The largest number of Japanese, about 59 percent of the total workforce, are employed in service industries. This includes all those who work in banking, insurance, financial services, real estate, and retail stores. Another large group of service workers hold jobs in government, hospitals, and schools, and in other businesses that provide services for communities, companies, and the public.

Groups in the Workplace.   Working for a large business firm today usually assures employees a lifetime job. About 22 percent of Japanese workers enjoy this benefit, which also includes many social benefits for the employee's family. When new workers are hired, they are judged not only by their job skills and experience but also how well they will fit into the work group. In some ways, the business has taken the place of the traditional extended family that is rapidly disappearing in Japan. (See page 88).

Workers tend to regard the people they work with and the executives who run the firm almost as members of their family group. The management of the company, in turn, treats its workers in a **paternalistic**, or fatherly, way. Workers are highly motivated to work hard for the benefit of the firm. Most new employees receive training in programs designed to develop strong, lasting loyalty to their company.

Workers show pride in their jobs by performing well and learning from others how to improve their skills. They often put in long hours of overtime without extra pay and sometimes even do not take their paid vacations. They seem quite willing to put the success of the company ahead of their own personal needs.

As in many Japanese companies, these workers exercise before starting work. Such activity strengthens workers' sense of the group and solidarity with their company.

Japanese workers identify themselves as employees of a particular company rather than in terms of their occupations as engineers, accountants, parts assemblers, or other kinds of workers. The more highly regarded and respected the company is, the higher is the **status**, or standing, of those who work for it. The Japanese judge businesses and the individuals who work for those businesses the same way they rank high schools and universities. Thus, persons who work for Mitsui or Mitsubishi or other key Japanese businesses become respected members of society.

A worker's social life also revolves around his or her associates in large companies. Male workers especially spend many hours socializing after work. They also join clubs to pursue hobbies with their co-workers and play on company sports teams. Most important, fellow workers and their families form the workers' closest circle of friends. Except for school friends, most workers have few close friends outside their company groups. In this way, the work group's solidarity is greatly strengthened, and the worker and his family increasingly regard their social life and their work life as one and the same. A man's co-worker or some-

CASE STUDY:

Lasting Friendships

Kazuo Aichi graduated from Tokyo University and then pursued a successful career in politics. He served as a member of the House of Representatives of the Japanese Diet from a farming district in northern Honshu. Here he tells about the lasting friendships he made in a singing club he joined at the university while he was a student there.

My main activity at college was an all-male, all-university choral group called the *Dansei Shibugasho* [literally, the male quartet] . . . . Does [it] seem strange to you that I could learn more from a choral group than from my law courses? Well, I think I did. In my sophomore year, one of the officer positions on the chorus became vacant, and I was selected to fill it. Well, I was very enthusiastic, and I worked hard at it, and in my next year, . . . I became the leader of the *Dansei Shibugasho*. I was responsible for organizing the group activities and leading them.

That was the most valuable experience I had at Todai. It is something I will never forget. I still continue the friendships I made in that chorus. Even now, twenty-five years after graduating, every two or three months at least ten of us get together for an evening of . . . singing. They are my closest friends—all working at different professions, and some in important positions now. . . .

How can I explain it? . . . Well, in order to sing together . . . in good harmony . . . the hearts have to blend together. There must be good feelings among all the members of the chorus. Human relations— *nigen kankei*—is the most important thing. Often those strong-minded, big men on campus were ready to quarrel with each other or even to split up the group. As the leader, I had to find a way to settle their differences. They knew I was not against them. They helped me to settle their differences, and so we all stuck together. . . . That was the most important lesson I learned at Todai.

From Martin E. Weinstein, *The Human Face of Japan's Leadership*. New York, Praeger, 1989.

1. What was the most important lesson the author learned at Tokyo University?

2. How does the author's experience illustrate the role of groups in Japanese society?

times even his boss may act as **nakodo** (nah-KOH-doh), or go-between, in introducing him to young women as possible marriage partners.

Building Group Harmony in the Workplace.   Managers and other business executives know that the success of their business depends on the loyalty, cooperation, and hard work of their employees. Therefore, they consider that building group harmony and consensus is far more important than giving orders and setting arbitrary work schedules.

Japanese workers have grown accustomed to suggesting ways by which they can improve their own productivity and that of their work group. Managers value workers' ideas and respect their views. Often, before executives carry out important decisions on new production methods or changes in job responsibilities, they consult with the workers who will be affected by these decisions. After meeting with the workers and listening to their ideas, the manager or executive groups may change their plan or even abandon it. Sometimes, however, they may decide to go ahead with the plan despite the workers' views or objections. In either case, the workers are satisfied at having taken an active part in this group decision-making process.

In Japan this method of reaching decisions by consulting with members of the group is known as **nemawashi** (NEH-mah-wah-shee). *Nemawashi* assures that once a decision has been reached or a plan agreed upon in this way, workers will put aside any disagreement they may have had, and work hard to carry it out. With *nemawashi*, company officials build trust among their workers. This is one reason why Japanese workers, even those who belong to unions, seldom go out on strike and have higher productivity rates than workers in most other countries.

Hierarchy in the Workplace.   In all of Japanese society, the question of how highly a person or a group is regarded by others is of extreme importance. Unlike the United States, where equality of people and groups is thought of as an ideal, the Japanese are accustomed to thinking in terms of certain people and groups being higher or lower in status than others. This idea of **hierarchy** (HEYE-uhr-ahr-kee), or different levels of status, is just as important in a factory, office, or other workplace as it is in other parts of Japanese society. Although most workers in Japan are employed in companies that have fewer than 100 employees, they observe the same patterns of status and hierarchy as workers in the biggest companies. As one expert on Japan has remarked, "Behavior that recognizes hierarchy is as natural [to the Japanese] as breathing."

99

Hierarchy in the workplace is based on several factors. Clearly, the officials and the managers of a company have the highest status and prestige. The status of other members of the firm is determined by education, age, and length of service.

Education is usually the most important factor in a person's status in the workplace hierarchy. As mentioned earlier, the prestige of a college or university from which one graduated determines the prestige—and status—enjoyed by its graduates. Similarly, those individuals whose education ended with high school are ranked according to the status of their school.

The workers' age and the length of time they have been with the company also help determine their status in the workplace hierarchy. In places where everyone is performing the same tasks, older workers and those who have held their jobs in the firm the longest enjoy higher status than younger workers or more recently hired employees. Even the skill with which a worker performs his or her job is reflected in the status he or she is awarded. Workers' salaries, in turn, are largely determined by these same factors.

At lunch, these shipyard workers are discussing how to solve a problem that faces them on the job. Such group cooperation is a regular part of the work routine in Japanese industry.

INDIVIDUALISM IN A GROUP SOCIETY

Foreign observers and even some Japanese often wonder if Japan's group-based society has not crushed the spirit of individuals who resent having to conform to uniform standards of behavior. They admire the Japanese work ethic and the great economic and cultural achievements of present-day Japan. Yet they find it difficult to understand how the Japanese can so constantly follow the strict codes of conduct that prevail in modern Japan and still maintain their individuality. Most Japanese, however, do not feel any conflict between their roles in groups and their own individuality.

The Individual and the Group.   Individuals in Japan are no less ambitious than people in other nations. They wish to excel and have their own strong self-identities. The Japanese, however, establish and maintain their individuality in ways that are socially acceptable in Japan. In fact, emphasizing themselves as individuals above their membership in groups is regarded as selfishness. The Japanese term for individualism, **kojin-shugi** (koh-jeen SHOO-gee), is seldom used for that reason. In Japan, socially acceptable individualism stems from the individual's own cluster of hobbies or other activities that set him or her apart from people with different interests. Achievement in any one or more of the acitvities provides distinction without threatening the group.

Expressions of Individualism.   Many Japanese express their individualism by turning to nature for their inspiration. The Japanese age-old love of nature stemming from the Shinto worship of *kami* spirits (see page 27) is still a strong force in Japanese society. Modern Japanese express their individualism through many decorative arts associated with nature. Cultivating **bonsai** (bohn-seye), or miniature trees, requires painstaking efforts over a period of many years by those with the will and discipline to undertake it. Another expression of individualism, which requires enormous discipline and will power, is the planting and arranging of tiny gardens. In such gardens, there are only a few carefully chosen shrubs and rocks surrounded by borders of small pebbles that are raked each day to form a perfect landscape. The traditional art of arranging flowers, known as *ikebana* (ee-kay-bah-nah), is very popular. *Ikebana* requires an understanding of the rules for arranging flowers that developed over the centuries. A person's achievement in *ikebana* stems from demonstrating a command of the rules. Many Japanese people write poetry, using traditional haiku and tanka styles. Here, too, individual achievement comes from expressing ideas within the rigid form of these types of poetry. Millions of other Japanese read novels that focus on characters' feelings about maintaining their self-identity in modern Japan. Music, dancing, painting, and photography also are outlets for self-expression as well as enjoyment by many Japanese.

Even activities considered more as sports or hobbies in other countries are used in Japan to help define the lives of their followers. Young people often spend long hours on ski trips or hiking. Japanese businessmen, like those in Western countries, often regard their golf scores as noteworthy badges of individual achievement.

Most Japanese also find the many informal groups they belong to important in building their self-identity. At universities, groups of students get together to study, but they also go together to coffee shops and take part in various sports. Japanese women, too, usually belong to several informal groups of friends. Membership in these groups enables people to gain new experiences and fulfill their role in the group.

Individualism and *Danchi* Families. With private housing in the cities scarce and expensive, more and more Japanese families have moved into modern apartment house complexes called **danchi** (DAHN-chee). Built with government money, *danchi* make it possible for people with limited incomes to live in or near cities at reasonable rents.

A *danchi* apartment complex usually consists of 50 to 100 buildings with 4 to 10 stories each. Each story of the building has from 16 to 30 identical apartments. These apartments are of several different sizes—all of them small. One feature that is especially attractive to many families is that each apartment has a flush toilet, since most Japanese apartments and houses still lack such toilets. In addition, each apartment has a small balcony for drying laundry. There are sliding paper doors that can be used to separate rooms for greater privacy. Mats called **tatami** (TAH-tuh-mee) cover the floors.

Most of the families who live in any given *danchi* tend to have the same educational background and earn comparable salaries. In some, most of the fathers work for government agencies. In others, most of the men work at similar kinds of factory jobs. In addition, most of the families are of similar ages and status.

However, many *danchi* have features that the government and those who live there did not foresee. The arrival of large numbers of families in new *danchi* usually throws a heavy burden on the community where they are built. In keeping with the Japanese practice of making decisions in groups, these problems might be expected to be handled by the families who have made the *danchi* their new home. Yet these families do not know one another. There are no groups in existence that can provide guidance in solving the many serious practical problems they face. These problems often include the need for new schools, adequate transportation, and funds to pay for these and other needed facilities. As a result, strong-willed individuals often step forward to provide leadership that normally would be based on group consultation.

Since most Japanese families base their socializing on the husband's work group, *danchi* families face difficulties in establishing relationships with their neighbors. Because families have such similar backgrounds, it is difficult to determine who has higher or lower status. This makes it very awkward for members of each family to know how to deal with other families.

In many cases, there seems to be no way to establish group standards of acceptable conduct. A U.S. expert on *danchi* living makes this observation:

> The lack of formal structure and status hierarchy in the *danchi* community results in a great deal of latitude [freedom] for individual self-expression in interpersonal relations [relations among people]. There are few effective means for enforcing community norms [standards] since privacy is respected. . . . In fact, there is little knowledge of what norms should be followed, if any, so that people rarely pressure one another to conform to explicit [clear-cut] standards, and the community ideals and goals are less obvious than personal ones.

These are only a few examples of the challenges that the *danchi* present to the group society in Japan. Some observers believe that in the future, Japan's society itself may become more and more like that now found among residents of the *danchi*.

CHALLENGES TO GROUP SOCIETY

In recent years, increasing numbers of Japanese have questioned many aspects of their society. Changes in Japanese society itself also seem to pose serious challenges to present patterns of life.

Complaints of Japanese Workers.   Although work in Japan is rewarding in many ways, as described earlier, there is a darker side to employment. Some businesspeople and white-collar workers, who are commonly referred to as **sarariiman** (a term that comes from the English "salary man") feel burned out by their work and separated from their families. They resent having to do whatever their companies wish. This is especially common among those employees who have been sent by their firms to the United States and other Western nations for a year or two. There, they observe that most workers have a more balanced career, one that allows them time with their families as well as considerable leisure of their own.

While the group continues to play a decisive role in workers' attitudes to their companies, younger employees are beginning to exercise more independence. For example, after-work gatherings have long been a regular part of company life and important in furthering group harmony. Today, many young workers resent the time such meetings take from their personal lives. As a result, companies increasingly schedule such meetings during regular work hours.

Another change has affected the extent to which workers are willing to accept any job assignment offered them. When workers are given an assignment they like, they will, as in the past, work very hard to carry it out. However, if an assignment is not to their liking, many, both men and women, do not hesitate to quit their jobs. The labor shortage has made it easier for such workers to find new jobs.

Reactions of Young People.   Some high school students are protesting the difficult years they must spend studying and cramming during "exam hell." Others consider it unfair that so few young people are able to gain admission to the top universities and thus must almost give up hope of ever achieving high-ranking positions in government, business, or the professions. To escape from the rigid educational system, some young Japanese men organize motorcycle gangs, while young women form dance groups that perform in public places to the beat of electronic music.

Another form of young people's rebellion against the strict Japanese code of conduct is their fascination with Western pop culture. Western rock groups draw large audiences of young Japanese when they appear in Tokyo and other big cities. Some young people dress in the most extreme Western clothing styles. By contrast, however, the use of drugs by young men and women in Japan is rare. Street crime, auto theft, and vandalism also are uncommon among young Japanese.

An Aging Society.   Today, the Japanese people live longer than the people of any other major industrial nation in the world. The average life expectancy for men is 76 years, and for women 82 years. However, this presents the nation with many problems.

Most Japanese workers now retire between ages 55 and 60. Most then must depend on company and government pensions that are seldom adequate to keep up with the cost of living. Though many people have carefully accumulated savings over many years, they try to reserve these for their future needs. Often, when they can, they will take jobs cleaning city streets or doing other low-paying work. Since most will live several more decades, they do not wish to become a burden on their families. Some older people, as you have read, live with their grown children and their families in their crowded city apartments. Even though government health insurance pays for 90 percent of their medical bills, many elderly Japanese face the prospect of living in nursing homes when they are too sick to be cared for by their children.

Japan's aging population poses another challenge to the nation. Now 12 percent of the population, by 2020 persons 65 and older will make up nearly 22 percent of the people, almost doubling in number. Japanese government and university experts wonder whether their nation will be able to afford the enormous costs required to support such a large group of aged citizens.

Overcrowded Cities.   Today, Japanese cities continue to grow, though at a slower rate than in the past. Despite a low birth rate, the urban population is growing largely because of the decline in farm population. Rural people move to the city in the hopes of obtaining a fuller share in Japan's economic prosperity. In cities like Tokyo and Yokohama, scarce land is so expensive that huge newly built apartment complexes and commercial offices continue to spill over into the surrounding countryside. Most of this rapid postwar growth of Japan's cities was poorly planned, and the nation now suffers from this urban sprawl. Since open space is so limited, there are few public parks and playgrounds for people to enjoy. Narrow city streets are packed with traffic that barely seems to move, forcing most people to use crowded subways or trains for most travel.

The Challenges in Perspective.   Many of the challenges described here seem to be reducing the Japanese dependence on groups. They also seem to be moving Japanese society in the direction of accepting behavior similar to that in the West. However, Japan in the 1990s is still a country that only outwardly seems Western. Japanese society still reflects centuries-old traditions adapted to 20th-century ways.

Chapter 4:
CHECKUP

REVIEWING THE CHAPTER

I. Building Your Vocabulary

Write the correct term that matches the definition.

omiai	*nemawashi*	paternalistic
juku	hierarchy	*danchi*
kyoiku mama	status	*pato*
nakodo	*sarariiman*	

1. person who acts as "go between" in introducing young couples

2. part-time employee

3. mother who helps her children study, especially to pass exams to enter a university

4. "cram schools" that help prepare students to pass tough exams

5. the different levels of a group

6. reaching decisions by consulting with members of the group

7. an "arranged marriage"

8. standing or position in a group

9. large group of modern apartment buildings

10. businesspeople and white-collar workers in Japanese companies

11. in a fatherly way

II. Understanding the Facts

Write the letter of the correct answer to each statement.

1. The most distinguishing feature of modern Japanese society is:
   a. its stress on the importance of the individual.
   b. its stress on the importance of the group.
   c. the excellence of its schools.

2. In most Japanese families the person who has the most responsibilities for raising the children is the:
   a. mother. b. father. c. grandmother.

3. In the work group, each person's standing is based on his or her:
   a. occupation.   b. age.   c. position in the group.

4. The statement that is most true of women in the workforce is:
   a. They are usually paid the same as men for the same work.
   b. They face discrimination in most jobs no matter how well educated or talented they are.
   c. They usually do not go back to work after they marry.

5. Individualism in Japan is often expressed by:
   a. cultivating hobbies.
   b. moving to other countries.
   c. meeting fellow workers after the work day is over.

III. Thinking It Through

Write the letter of your correct choice to complete each sentence next to its number.

1. The difficulties of many people who live in large new apartment complexes are often due to:
   a. overcrowding.
   b. the fact that they do not belong to the same group.
   c. their long commute to work.
   d. there are few schools and other facilities.

2. The greater importance of groups in Japan than in the United States is shown by the fact that:
   a. individual Japanese do not do anything by themselves.
   b. they determine people's status and shape people's relationships with one another.
   c. most people make their neighborhood communities the center of their social lives.
   d. people's position in society is determined by where they were born.

3. Most Japanese who work in large business firms enjoy higher status and prestige because:
   a. they are the hardest-working members of the labor force.
   b. these firms hire the best-educated workers and provide them lifetime jobs.
   c. they have the strongest unions, even though most government workers earn higher salaries.
   d. men and women with good educations and job skills have equal opportunities in these large firms.

4. Japanese schools teach students various subjects, but they also encourage them to learn to derive satisfaction from working with their classmates because:
   a. these skills help them learn math and science.
   b. these skills help them succeed in Japanese society.
   c. Japan wants its citizens to learn job skills.
   d. they can learn English and other subjects at cram schools.

5. In company work groups, managers and workers meet to discuss plans and schedules, because:
   a. the government requires them to do so.
   b. managers are not allowed to make decisions without the workers' approval.
   c. this method improves cooperation and productivity.
   d. this is the most common method of individual expression.

DEVELOPING CRITICAL THINKING SKILLS

1. Explain how Japanese turn to nature, sports, and hobbies to express their individualism.

2. Describe the advances that Japanese women have made in recent years.

3. Discuss why Japan's early history and its geography helped groups become the dominant feature of its society.

4. Describe the daily life of a Japanese family living in Tokyo.

5. Explain why the Japanese consider education so important.

INTERPRETING TABLES AND GRAPHS

A. Study the table on page 91. Then answer these questions.

1. How many more women were employed in 1990 than in 1960?

2. What does the table tell you about the change in the percentage of women who worked between 1960 and 1990?

3. Compare the percent of the total working population that was made up of women in 1960 and 1990.

B. Study the graph on page 109. Then answer these questions.

1. a. Which country experienced the greatest population growth from 1900 to 1990?   b. The least growth?

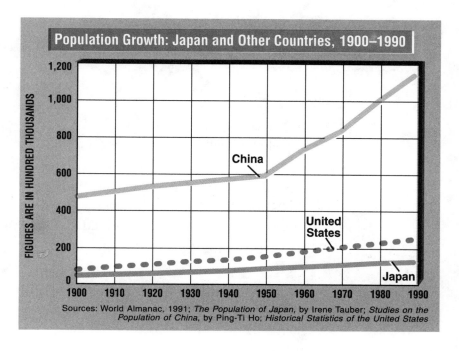

Population Growth: Japan and Other Countries, 1900–1990

FIGURES ARE IN HUNDRED THOUSANDS

China

United States

Japan

1,200
1,000
800
600
400
200
0

1900 1910 1920 1930 1940 1950 1960 1970 1980 1990

Sources: World Almanac, 1991; *The Population of Japan*, by Irene Tauber; *Studies on the Population of China*, by Ping-Ti Ho; *Historical Statistics of the United States*

2. **a.** What is similar about the population growth of the United States and Japan? **b.** What is different about the population growth of these two countries?

ENRICHMENT AND EXPLORATION

1. Choose a small group of your classmates to role play as members of a Japanese company work group. Divide the group into a manager, a supervisor, and several workers. Then have the group hold a meeting to discuss how the company can increase its profits this year. Each group member should talk to other members and act in ways that real Japanese work group members would adopt. Remember that the group's purpose is to listen to all members' ideas and then propose a final plan. Write down the ideas of each member and then describe how the group reached agreement and what it plans to do.

2. Using your textbook and reference books in the library, make a chart comparing education in Japan and education in your state. Use separate headings for the following: the level of government responsible for education, the length of time school lasts, what subjects are studied, how classes are organized, the number of students per class, and extracurricular school activities.

109

GOVERNMENT AND POLITICS IN JAPAN
1952–Present

1952	U.S. occupation ends. U.S.–Japan Security Treaty is signed.
1953	Korean War ends.
1954	Liberal party proposes establishment of national defense force.
1955	Liberal Democratic party is formed.
1960	New treaty with the United States is signed.
1960s	*Many African nations achieve independence.*
1986	First woman heads a major Japanese political party.
1989	*Communism collapses in Eastern Europe.* *Student demonstrations in China are suppressed.*
Late 1980s– early 1990s	Political scandals rock Japan.
1990	*Nicaraguan civil war ends.*
1991	*Persian Gulf War* *Soviet Union becomes Commonwealth of Independent States.*
1992	Japan's economy suffers sharp decline.

5 Government and Politics in Japan (1952–Present)

Angry crowds of students wearing plastic helmets for protection confronted the police. They marched through downtown Tokyo and many other Japanese cities, chanting "Down with the treaty!" The union of railroad workers went out on strike, and dozens of other unions took part in similar work stoppages. Ten million people signed petitions addressed to the government. The Socialist and Communist parties held large rallies and demonstrations. For months during 1960, unrest and turmoil swept Japan as protesters struggled to prevent the government from signing a new treaty with the United States. The treaty allowed the United States to continue to maintain military bases in Japan, as they had since the occupation ended in 1952.

In May 1960, the Japanese government decided to force the Diet, the national legislature, to approve the treaty despite the public outcry against it. However, when the debate on the treaty began, a riot broke out among Diet members favoring the proposal and those opposing it. The police were summoned to remove angry members, who were shouting their disapproval in order to disrupt the session. When the police used force to restore order, the Socialist party members walked out in protest.

Even after the government defied its foes by approving the treaty, opposition to it continued. In June 1960, the planned visit to Japan by U.S. President Dwight D. Eisenhower to attend the official signing of the agreement had to be cancelled after an angry mob in Tokyo attacked the car in which the U.S. ambassador was riding. When the protests, strikes, and violence finally ended, nearly 800 demonstrators and police had been injured and hospitalized.

Despite this turmoil in 1960, the main feature of Japan's democratic government in the years since then has been the political stability and social harmony it has encouraged among the people. As in so much of Japanese life, the system of government and the way it operates is a product of the union of Japanese tradition and Western influences. Having read about the importance of the group in Japanese society in Chapter 4, you will not be surprised to find that the group also plays a strong role in Japanese government and politics.

A PARLIAMENTARY DEMOCRACY

In the decades since the end of the U.S. occupation in 1952, one of Japan's greatest achievements has been the development of a strong democratic government. This government is an outcome of several forces. The Meiji Constitution of 1889 (see Chapter 3) set Japan on the road to representative government, which by the 1920s had many elements of a democracy. The Constitution of 1947, which emerged from the U.S. occupation of Japan, provided the final building block of the political democracy by which Japan is ruled today.

The Structure of the Government.   The form of government in Japan is that of a parliamentary democracy. In a parliamentary democracy, unlike that of the United States, power is centered in a parliament, or legislature. Parliamentary government combines the executive and legislative powers in one branch of government. The legislature names a prime minister and a cabinet to operate the government. The prime minister is the head of the government. As you know, Japan has a hereditary emperor, but he has no power and is merely a symbol of national unity. In its form the government of Japan is very much like that of Great Britain, which has a monarch with little real power and a government that is based in the Parliament.

As in the United States, a Supreme Court and lower courts make up an independent branch of the government. The Supreme Court has the power to declare laws unconstitutional, although it has done so rarely since it was established. The Supreme Court, in fact, has not played a significant part in the government because the Japanese people traditionally have been distrustful of courts and their procedures.

Government in Japan is highly centralized, with the national government having most of the power. Unlike the government of the United States, where the 50 states have considerable power, the local governments of Japan, called **prefectures,** have little authority. Their actions are subject to the direction of the national government.

112

The Organization of the Japanese Government

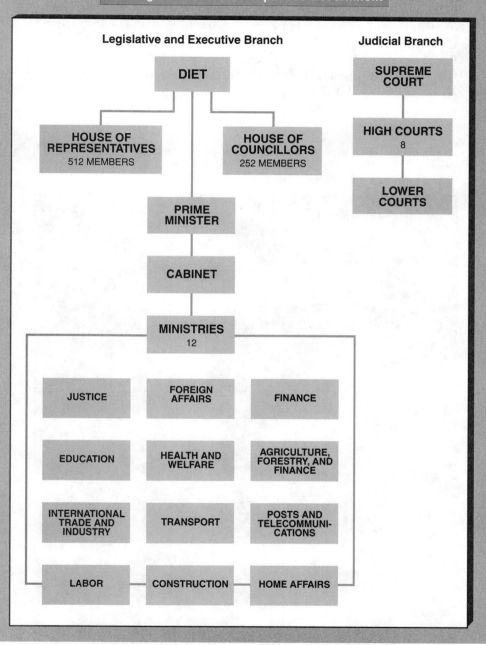

Legislative and Executive Branch

Judicial Branch

DIET

SUPREME COURT

HOUSE OF REPRESENTATIVES
512 MEMBERS

HOUSE OF COUNCILLORS
252 MEMBERS

HIGH COURTS
8

PRIME MINISTER

LOWER COURTS

CABINET

MINISTRIES
12

JUSTICE

FOREIGN AFFAIRS

FINANCE

EDUCATION

HEALTH AND WELFARE

AGRICULTURE, FORESTRY, AND FINANCE

INTERNATIONAL TRADE AND INDUSTRY

TRANSPORT

POSTS AND TELECOMMUNI-CATIONS

LABOR

CONSTRUCTION

HOME AFFAIRS

113

The Diet.   The legislature in Japan is the Diet, which was first established under the Meiji constitution. The Diet is a **bicameral,** or two-house, legislature. The Diet consists of a lower house called the **House of Representatives** and an upper house called the **House of Councillors.** Most of the power of the Diet is vested in the House of Representatives. Its members choose the prime minister.

The Constitution of 1947 made the Diet the center of power in the government. The Diet is elected by **universal suffrage,** that is by the votes of all adult men and women citizens.

Japanese women were given the vote by the 1947 constitution. About three fourths of the electorate votes in national elections, a much higher rate than in the United States.

The two houses of the Japanese Diet meet in separate wings of this building, which dates from 1936. Only Japanese materials were used in its construction.

The prime minister, as the head of the government, is responsible to the Diet for carrying out its laws. The prime minister chooses the members of the cabinet and other appointed officials.

The House of Representatives.   The House of Representatives, although it is known as the lower house of the Diet, has more power than the House of Councillors. It elects the prime minister and the cabinet, controls the budget, and approves treaties with foreign nations.

The House of Representatives has 512 members, who are elected for four-year terms by the voters. However, members of the House usually must stand for election more often than this. The reason is that the prime minister often dissolves the Diet and holds new elections in order to try to increase the size of his majority or for some other political advantage. The House of Representatives also has the right to force the prime minister to resign if he fails to win a majority vote on a major matter. If this happens, he must call for a new election to the House.

The House of Councillors. The House of Councillors, the upper house of the Diet, has far less power than the House of Representatives. Its 252 members are elected to six-year terms. The voters choose 100 of these members from slates of candidates put forward by each party. The other 152 members are elected from the prefectures, Japan's local government units. The House of Councillors has few powers, but governmental matters are considered there more calmly and deliberately than in the often frenzied atmosphere of the House of Representatives. The House of Representatives may override opposition to any of its decisions by the House of Councillors by a two-thirds vote.

The Prime Minister and the Cabinet. As noted earlier, the prime minister in Japan is the head of the government. The prime minister must be a member of the Diet. Most often prime ministers have been members of the House of Representatives. To assist in administering the government, the prime minister chooses a cabinet. Half of the members of the cabinet must be members of the Diet. In practice, almost all cabinet members have been from the Diet, with the remaining members coming from the bureaucracy, the men and women who run the government on a day-to-day basis (see below).

Members of the cabinet head 12 ministries of the government such as justice, foreign affairs, education, and health and welfare. The cabinet members also advise the prime minister and with him provide the political leadership of the country.

Since individual members of the Diet are not expected to introduce legislation, that responsibility falls to the cabinet members. Actually, as you will read, most legislation originates with the bureaucracy.

A successful candidate for prime minister, Toshiki Kaifu, acknowledges the applause of his fellow Diet members.

Although individual cabinet members deal with specific ministries and legislation, the cabinet as a whole takes responsibility for its actions. In keeping with the Japanese tradition of group action, decisions of the cabinet are arrived at by consensus, or general agreement. If a cabinet member disagrees with a decision, he or she is expected to resign or face dismissal by the prime minister.

Elections.   Members of the House of Representatives are chosen by voters in 130 districts throughout Japan. Each of these districts elects three to five members to the House from among the 10 or 12 candidates who generally run for office. However, each voter in these districts can vote for only one member of the House. As a result, the vote in most districts is widely split among the candidates, and most members win election by receiving only 20 to 30 percent of the vote.

In Japan, four or five major political parties put up candidates for election to the Diet. By contrast, in the United States two major political parties compete for power. The Liberal Democratic party (LDP) is the largest party in Japan and has been in power since 1955. There are several other major parties (see below) that are also represented in the Diet.

Two or more members of the same party often run against one another in the district elections for the House of Representatives. Thus, individual party candidates must build strong organizations in their district and gain support from local groups in order to win against their party rivals. These local support groups, called **koenkai** (koh-en-keye), rally to a candidate because of his or her stand on local issues and matters of concern in the district. They often are drawn to the candidate because of his or her personality as well as by party membership. As a result, most members who win election to the House reflect the interests and ideas of the people in the district they represent. At the same time, all candidates usually must win the endorsement of their party if they hope to win. This strengthens the party system but also allows its members to reflect the different factions and viewpoints in the party.

THE BUREAUCRACY

Most of the legislation that the Diet considers when it enacts laws and other measures originates in the 12 ministries and the many agencies that make up the national **bureaucracy.** The bureaucracy is made up of the civil servants who actually run the ministries and agencies of the

CASE STUDY:

A Legislator Is Elected

In 1976, Wataru Hiraizumi was elected to the Diet from the Fukui district in Honshu. In an interview he describes his election campaign for the Diet.

> The essence of parliamentary politics . . . is that people's opinions, even their whims . . . must be courted. This is how one gets on in politics. A good politician knows this by instinct. . . .
>
> Naturally, since my family has always been in Fukui, I went there to my home district, to start building a constituency for the House of Representatives. . . . In 1976, when the next general election was looming, I was asked to see the secretary-general of the party. . . . He told me that I must wait for some time, until there was an opening for me. He said, "If you do not wait, if you force this thing, you will ruin your political future. So be patient and wait. Otherwise, if you run against our wishes, your name will be eradicated [removed] from the list of party members."
>
> . . . We have a four-member district. In the election of 1976, two of the incumbents [members currently in office], both senior, long-standing Dietmen, were defeated and lost their seats. [Despite the secretary-general, I ran and] I defeated a senior LDP Dietman. It was a hard battle. Before the election, our district was represented by three LDP and one Socialist. After the election, three LDP and one Socialist. So you see, nothing was changed. . . .
>
> [During the election campaign] I visited almost every single house in my hometown of Katsuyama, a town of thirty thousand people, door to door. . . . Those last two years before the election were especially intensive. I talked with thousands and thousands of my constituents, again and again, with their groups and clubs. I kept shuttling back and forth from Tokyo. Hard work. A busy schedule. . . . If I tell you any more . . . you will try to steal my seat from me.

From Martin E. Weinstein, *The Human Face of Japan's Leadership*. New York: Praeger, 1989.

1. What part did the LDP play in this Diet member's decision to run for election to the House of Representatives in 1976?

2. Why do you think his campaign in his district was successful?

government. There are about 750,000 civil servants in the entire bureaucracy, most of whom perform lower-level adminstrative and clerical work. Of the approximately 25 percent of these workers who are women, most do work on these lower levels.

The Ministry of Finance, the Ministry of International Trade and Industry (MITI), and the Foreign Ministry are the leading ministries in the bureaucracy. Though members of the prime minister's cabinet are in charge of each ministry, the real power of the ministries is in the hands of the *jimu-jikan* (jee-moo JEE-kahn), or vice-ministers. The *jimu-jikan* head the ministries and carry out their work with the assistance of several hundred bureaucrats in their department.

Status of the Bureaucrats.   The vice-ministers and other high-level bureaucrats often serve in the same government ministry for several decades. By contrast, the officials who serve as cabinet ministers usually hold office for only a few years and are replaced when a new prime minister takes power. Thus the bureaucrats gain great expertise and experience in the affairs of their ministry and in the field of government that it oversees.

The leading members of the bureaucracy enjoy high status and prestige in Japan. Senior bureaucrats are carefully chosen, largely from among the top graduates of the law school of Tokyo University as well as from a few other leading universities. Educational status plays a key role in determining a person's career in government, just as it does in business and the professions (see Chapter 4). Since members of the bureaucracy have attended the same universities as many of the political and business leaders they deal with, they often have close ties to those officials. Later, when top bureaucrats end their careers in the ministry, many take important jobs in business or are elected as members of the Diet. Thus these bonds of trust, which are constantly being reinforced, also help members of the Diet to accept the legislative proposals and the budget planning of the bureaucrats.

The Role of the Bureaucrats.   An officer of a Japanese newspaper was riding a bullet train with a powerful bureaucrat of the Finance Ministry. As the train sped through the countryside, the bureaucrat pointed out the window. "See that bridge over there? I built it." Shortly after, he pointed out again, "See that road? The wide one. That's my work too." After a while, he said, "See that windbreak forest over there? That was one of my most difficult jobs." The newspaperman noted the expression of extreme satisfaction on the bureaucrat's face.

This incident highlights both the extent of the bureaucrats' responsibilities in the Japanese government and the pride they take in their work. They have such power for many reasons. For one, they have large staffs, far larger than those of Diet members. These staffs obtain important information. The bureaucracy also has far greater resources than the committees of the Diet. However, the party in power closely examines the laws and budget planning proposed by the bureaucracy in the various ministries. It evaluates each proposal submitted by the bureaucracy in hearings that any member can attend. Proposals that are approved are sent to the cabinet, which then considers each measure. Usually those measures that are agreed to are returned, in their final form, to the bureaucracy for its review and approval.

When this process is completed, the proposals that the prime minister and the cabinet wish to have enacted are formally introduced in the Diet. These measures are then debated by the committees where they are sometimes first considered, or on the floor of the Diet. In either case, members of the opposition parties have an opportunity to make their views known. If opposition members very strongly oppose a given measure, the party in power may decide to allow it to quietly die without a final vote. In sum, the law-making process in Japan, like so much else, is the result of carefully considered actions taken to build group consensus and support.

THE POLITICAL PARTY SYSTEM

Japan has five major political parties. Most of these parties have existed since before World War II. However, in Japan's multi-party system, one political party, the Liberal Democratic party, has been in power since shortly after the end of the U.S. occupation.

Japan's Political Parties. The Liberal Democratic party (LDP) is the largest party and has been in power continuously since it was formed in 1955. It was created to offset the strength of the Social-Democratic (formerly the Socialist) party and the Communist party. The LDP has consistently won the support of the majority of Japanese voters. In fact, it usually receives nearly as many votes as all the other parties combined. For this reason, people sometimes joke that their nation has "a one-and-a-half party system."

Today, nearly half of the voters do not belong to any party. This means that they do not automatically support the LDP or any other party. Nevertheless, despite its many years in power, the LDP remains a consensus party whose positions reflect the view of most voters. In governing Japan, it also usually considers the views of the opposition parties. As you will read, the party's organization and practical form of politics allow a wide spectrum of opinion to be represented in shaping the government's policies.

Most political parties in Japan are more interested in winning elections than they are in promoting an **ideology,** or set of ideas. For this reason, they support moderate programs favored by the majority of the people rather than legislation that represents a certain point of view and that may divide the nation. As you will learn, this is especially true of the LDP and helps explain why it has been in power so long. Increasingly, this also has become true for several other major parties that, from the 1950s through the 1970s, strongly favored many basic changes in Japan's society.

The Liberal Democratic Party. Since 1955, the Liberal Democratic party has ruled in the Diet, and all of Japan's prime ministers have been members of the LDP. The LDP owes its remarkable success to broad support from all parts of Japanese society. These include large voting blocs of farmers and rural residents, big business groups, small shopkeepers, bureaucrats, and many white-collar workers. Yet, the LDP is not the all-powerful party that these facts might suggest. In fact, the LDP itself is made up of many **factions,** or groups, that support rival leaders within the party and work to help them gain enough strength in the Diet to be chosen prime minister. Usually there are four or five of these factions, called *habatsu* (hah-BAHT-soo), in the Diet whose members support various powerful party leaders.

The heads of the *habatsu* usually are experienced LDP leaders who themselves often have been prime ministers or held other important positions in the government. These leaders aid members of the Diet from their factions by helping them conduct their election campaigns and raise funds to pay for their staffs and office needs. Faction leaders also help members develop contacts with important members of the bureaucracy and business who can provide jobs and services for the voters in the members' home districts. The *habatsu* leaders also may aid more experienced members to gain important posts in the Diet as well as in the party organization. As a result, members find that belonging to the *habatsu* is essential to advancing their careers. Belonging to a faction also provides the kind of small group setting most Japanese are accustomed to.

Despite the *habatsu*, the LDP does exercise broad control over its members in the Diet. Members nearly always support the party's legislation and program proposals in the Diet. They know that their own success and that of the LDP depend on members working together to achieve unity. For this same reason, the prime minister consults with all the main LDP factions on important matters before they are officially proposed in the Diet. He also seeks advice from other factions as well as his own when he appoints cabinet members and other officials. As a result, the factions often are rewarded with key posts in the government. The prime minister himself is also the leader of the LDP, since the party's president always is chosen as prime minister by the members of the Diet. In this way, the LDP usually achieves harmony and unity of purpose among its factions in much the same way that business executives depend on *nemawashi*, or "root-binding," to gain support and greater productivity among their workers (see Chapter 4).

However, the organization and leadership of the LDP alone do not account for its monopoly on government power in Japan. The triumph of the LDP has been mainly due to its success in achieving economic prosperity for Japan and in providing the stability and national unity the Japanese people desire. Its political program and policies have been almost exclusively and effectively geared toward those ends. The LDP, unlike several of the opposition parties, has stressed a long-range program to build modern Japan on the foundations laid by the Meiji reformers in the late 1800s. It has not advocated ideologies borrowed from other nations like those endorsed by the Social-Democratic and Communist parties. The Japanese people have consistently endorsed the LDP's approach. Moreover, the continuing success of the LDP has also meant a lack of success by the other parties. Their inability to elect many members to the Diet and to work together against the LDP has also contributed to the LDP's monopoly on power.

Other Parties.   The Social-Democratic party is Japan's second largest party. In recent years, it has won about 15 to 20 percent of the vote in elections for the Diet. Its chief support comes from members of white-collar and government labor unions. In 1986, it broke tradition by electing a woman, Doi Takako (doh-ee TAH-kah-koh), as its party leader. The Democratic Socialist party, formed by more conservative socialists, usually wins from 7 to 10 percent of the total vote and has its main power base among blue-collar factory workers.

The Communist party of Japan is much more moderate than communist parties in most other countries. Its main support has come from

The only woman to head a Japanese political party, Doi Takako, addresses a rally in Tokyo. Her party, now known as the Social Democratic party, is the largest opposition party.

intellectuals and more radical unions. Though it did not identify itself with the Soviet Union, that nation's collapse may weaken Japan's Communist party even more. The Komeito (Clean Government) party is a relatively new political group, formed in the mid-1960s by members of a religious sect. It has received about 10 percent of the vote in most elections, mainly from poor families in urban areas.

SPECIAL–INTEREST GROUPS

Other groups outside the Diet also often take an important part in shaping the government's policies. They do so by a variety of means. These range from **lobbying,** or trying to influence government members, to working with the subcommittees of the Diet, to trying to influence the bureaucracy, in some cases even by offering bribes.

Big Business Groups. Perhaps the most influential special-interest group is big business. Several organizations represent the interests of Japan's businesses. The most important is the *Keidanren* (kay-dahn-ren), whose members include 700 of Japan's largest companies and more than 100 manufacturers' groups. The *Keidanren* and several other national business organizations help fund the campaigns of Diet candi-

123

dates and give financial support to political parties. During the decades from the 1950s through the 1970s, these business organizations were the leading supporters of the LDP, since that party had the economic recovery and prosperity of Japan as its main goal. Today, big business still strongly supports the LDP, though it also provides funds for some candidates of other parties as well. In turn, the LDP has long had close ties to the nation's top business leaders and has sought their advice on government policies in all fields, but especially measures affecting the economy. As you will see later in this chapter, business's financial relations with the LDP have been criticized.

Farmers' Organizations. Farmers' organizations also have long supported the LDP because that party has helped protect the interests of Japan's declining farm population. The Nokyo, the principal agriculture special-interest group, has been quite successful in its efforts to protect small rice farmers. By persuading the Diet to pass high tariffs on imported rice, Japan's dwindling farm families have been able to survive.

Japanese farmers demonstrating against dropping the high tariff on imported rice. The sign in English refers to the impact of lowering duties on beef and citrus fruits.

Japan's rural districts also still have more representation in the Diet than some urban areas with far larger populations. With proportionately more votes, farmers have been valuable allies of the LDP. In addition, the Nokyo's members have long favored conservative policies and feared the possibility that the Socialist or Communist opposition parties might win power.

Labor Groups.   Several federations, or collections, of labor union workers are active as special-interest groups. They represent the leading unions in business and industry as well as among government workers, teachers, and other white-collar workers. Most of these union organizations have supported the Social-Democratic, the Democratic Socialist, or Communist parties. These unions have worked hard in the election campaigns for the Diet and have contributed most of the funds of these parties. However, the record of labor unions has not been impressive. Although they have often helped elect party members to the Diet, none of these parties has ever been able to elect a prime minister.

Citizens' Groups.   Citizens' groups first began to enter the political arena in the late 1960s and 1970s. Their aim was to protest against and work to correct what the Japanese term *kogai* (koh-gaye), or "public injury." Most of the citizens' groups attacked damage to the environment and pollution. The serious chemical pollution in 1959 of Minamata Bay, off the west coast of Kyushu, marked the beginning of a growing outcry against harming the environment, even in the name of rebuilding Japan's economy. Citizens' groups went to court to claim damages for victims of environmental pollution. Other citizens' groups were formed to force businesses to install antipollution devices and to require companies to pay for damage to the environment. The citizens' groups were largely responsible for court rulings that forced all polluters to pay for the damages they caused. The groups' efforts also led to strict laws protecting the environment.

The citizens' groups were different from other special-interest groups. Their members came from all social groups and had various levels of education and different status. Nevertheless, they were united, not in the concerns of their own individual groups, but in a larger public cause. Some observers believed these groups were more democratic than most traditional Japanese groups, especially since they had little of the hierarchy normally present in small groups. Nevertheless, citizens' groups had to overcome many obstacles. The Social-Democratic and Communist parties attempted to use them at first for their political pur-

125

poses. However, their efforts failed. The LDP, too, tried to attract their support as part of the party's local *komenai* in return for favoring their antipollution work.

Consumer Groups. Beginning in the 1970s, consumer groups became interested in promoting efforts to ensure product safety and reduce risks to consumers' health from contaminated food. These groups, often formed by existing women's groups, have used boycotts and public awareness campaigns to try to remove unsafe products from the market. They also have shared some of the features of the citizens' special-interest groups.

JAPANESE POLITICS THROUGH THE YEARS

After the U.S. occupation ended in 1952, Japanese politics focused on the nation's efforts to restore its economy and to regain its position as a major world power. During these years, the conservative parties, which did not want major changes in the government, attained dominance over the nation's government as the socialist and communist opposition parties remained divided. The Liberal Democratic party won the consistent support of large numbers of the Japanese through policies that aimed at increasing Japan's power at home and its prestige abroad.

The Launching of Democracy. When the U.S. forces left in 1952, Japan launched its postwar democracy. The emperor had formally given up whatever power he had. Since 1947, the Diet had demonstrated its ability to be "the supreme organ of power" in the government. The Japanese people had been guaranteed their freedoms by the new constitution and were, for the first time, citizens living in a democracy.

During the years of occupation, the U.S. military government itself had modified some of its policies as conditions in Japan improved and changed. As the Cold War between the United States and the Soviet Union grew in intensity, the U.S. military government reduced its opposition to the development of a small Japanese military defense force. Increasingly, the United States regarded Japan more as a future ally than as a recently defeated foe, and it no longer worked to prevent Japan from again becoming a major power. The United States also turned away from its efforts to break up the huge zaibatsu combines.

The U.S. growing fear of communism also caused it to support the growth of Japan's conservative parties. By 1952, the conservative Liberal party was in firm control of the Diet. It easily won the approval of the peace treaty signed a few months earlier with the United States despite strong opposition from the Socialist and Communist parties. With this treaty, Japan regained its full independence as a sovereign nation. However, it continued to maintain close economic and political ties with the United States. As you read in Chapter 3, Japan also signed a security treaty with the United States in 1952 by which the United States promised to defend Japan and, in return, was allowed military bases in Japan and the right to station troops there. During the Korean War, from 1950 to 1953, U.S. troops spent periods of rest and recreation in Japan, and military equipment and supplies passed through Japan to the fighting zone in Korea.

"Reversing Course."   During the early 1950s, the government headed by the Liberal party acted to modify some of the policies instituted during the years of the occupation. This plan to **"reverse course,"** as its opponents called it, was intended to return to the central government power that it had lost to local governments during the occupation. Left-wing, or radical, parties fought strong but unsuccessful campaigns against this measure, claiming the government would use a centralized police force to crack down on the opposition. The Diet also limited some of the freedoms of citizens to oppose the government. Fearing a growing threat from Japanese communists, the Diet , controlled by the Liberal party, passed laws to reduce Communist party influence in teachers' unions and in the way subjects were taught in the schools.

In 1954, the government proposed to establish a national defense force. This plan deeply worried many Japanese. The opposition parties were quick to point out that Article 9 of the 1947 Constitution stated that Japan "renounces forever war as the sovereign right of the nation" and that "land, sea, and air forces as well as other war potential will never be maintained" by their nation. They argued that this clause forbade Japan from having a military force of any kind. However, by 1952 Japan already had established a so-called National Police Reserve of 75,000 men, which the government now proposed to enlarge to 250,000 men, under the name of the Self-Defense Forces.

The opposition left-wing parties charged that this was an attempt to remilitarize Japan and drag the nation into the Cold War between the United States and the Soviet Union. In order to obtain approval for the Self-Defense Forces, the prime minister had to agree to limit the amount of money that Japan could spend on the military force and to abandon the plan to establish a new ministry to oversee its operations.

Japan's Self-Defense Forces are shown here on parade. After much discussion as to whether these troops may be used abroad in peacekeeping efforts of the United Nations, the Diet approved this in 1992.

Continuing Conservative Control. To assure continued conservative control of the Diet and the government, the Liberal and Democratic parties merged to form the Liberal Democratic party in 1955. The LDP then began its long monopoly on power. During the rest of the 1950s and 1960s, the LDP's main efforts went into guiding the development of Japan's economy. The resulting "economic miracle" brought its people greater wealth than they had ever known. By the 1970s, under the leadership of the LDP, Japan had become the world's third-greatest economic power. During the following two decades it ranked second only to the United States. (You will read about this "economic miracle" in Chapter 6.)

As you read at the beginning of this chapter, the issue of extending the security treaty with the United States led to a sharp confrontation between the LDP and the other parties in 1960. In that year, the Diet began to debate extending the treaty. The LDP proposed certain changes to give Japan an equal role in the treaty that it had signed as a defeated nation. As a result, a clause giving the Japanese government the right to ask U.S. troops to help end riots or disturbances in Japan was dropped from the treaty. The United States agreed to consult Japan before sending its troops from there into combat in other countries. It also promised not to bring nuclear weapons into Japan.

These proposed changes did not satisfy the Socialist and Communist parties. Many people were convinced that the United States was a threat to peace, and they supported the Soviet Union in the Cold War. Nevertheless, the LDP prime minister, Kishi Nobusuke (kee-shee noh-BOO-soo-kay) was determined to pass the treaty. Instead of working with the opposition to find a compromise, as was usually done, in May 1960 Kishi called for a sudden vote in the Diet. The result was chaos. Fighting broke out between members of the opposition and the LDP. When angry members tried to use force to block a vote on the treaty, a riot occurred. Kishi then called the police, who removed some opposition members from the Diet. Then, after the Socialist members walked out in protest, the LDP approved the treaty.

Kishi's highhanded actions touched off a firestorm of protest across the nation. In July 1960 Kishi was forced to resign. Within a few months, the opposition protests against the treaty faded, and the last postwar challenge to the Liberal Democrats' dominance had ended.

A Record of Achievement.   In the decades since 1960, the LDP continued to attract the support of more voters than any other party. Its vote totals in general elections usually equalled or exceeded the combined vote of the opposition parties. The people kept the party in power because of its role in forging Japan's "economic miracle."

The record of the Liberal Democratic party in responding to Japan's changing needs also was impressive. It developed effective programs to combat pollution and other threats to the environment. It enacted a system of health insurance to provide for the needs of Japan's aging population. It built affordable urban housing for Japan's expanding workforce. It provided efficient transportation networks to link Japan's densely crowded urban centers. The LDP's success in governing the nation also reinforced the domestic stability that characterizes contemporary Japanese society. In many ways, the LDP's success itself accurately reflected the Japanese people's confidence in themselves and in their nation.

Dark Days for the LDP.   However, the prestige of the LPD suffered a severe jolt in the late 1980s and early 1990s. A series of scandals brought down several prime ministers and forced the country to question many aspects of its political system.

Prime ministers and other political figures were discovered to have taken bribe money and other favors from companies that did business with the government between the end of World War II and 1991. In one instance, a company had given shares of its stock to politicians. When this became public, the prime minister and the finance minister were forced to resign. In another case, a leader of a faction of the LDP was arrested for, among other crimes, having given a company details of a planned highway so that it could buy up land along the route. For such favors to the company, he and other members of his faction of the party received the equivalent of about $15 million.

While the public was shocked by these disclosures, reformers pointed out that there had always been a close link between politics and money. It was customary, for example, for the LDP to give gifts to voters. It was said that a vote was worth a refrigerator. As a result, it cost about $8 million to win a seat in the Diet. In the 1990 national election, the LDP spent $1.4 billion on the campaign, almost four times as much as the entire 1988 presidential campaign in the United States. Big business contributed heavily to the LDP campaign. Construction companies were believed to contribute almost 3 percent of their revenues to the LDP. In addition, informal groups of LDP Diet members known as *zoku* (zoh-koo) customarily watched out for different interest groups and interceded in Diet matters in their favor when necessary.

A number of proposals for changes were made. One was to limit the amount of money that could be contributed to political campaigns and instead to fund campaigns from public money. A prime minister, Toshiki Kaifu (toh-SHEE-kee keye-foo), made a number of suggestions for reforms in the political system. One was to scrap the costly custom of having several members of the same party run against one another in the same district for election to the House of Representatives. He proposed, instead, having each district elect only one representative, with opposition candidates being given seats in the Diet through a system of proportional representation. Another proposal was to redraw the boundaries of the election districts so that rural voters would no longer have three times the number of representatives as city people. However, LDP leaders rejected Kaifu's proposals, fearing that they would weaken the party's power.

These scandals angered and embarrassed the Japanese people. In 1989 they expressed their resentment at the LDP by depriving it of its long-standing majority in the House of Councillors of the Diet. While this body has only limited power, this act was taken as a sign that the LDP could no longer take its support by the Japanese people for granted.

Chapter 5

CHECKUP

REVIEWING THE CHAPTER

I. Building Your Vocabulary

Write the correct term that matches the definition.

parliamentary system   prefecture
koenkai   bicameral
lobbying   ideology
habatsu   *kogai*
jimu-jikan

1. a fixed set of ideas

2. vice-ministers

3. government in which the executive and legislative powers are combined

4. factions in the Diet

5. a "public injury"

6. Diet members' local support groups

7. influencing members of the government

8. a division of Japanese local government

9. legislature of two houses

II. Understanding the Facts

Write the letter of the correct answer to each question next to its number.

1. The Diet is the center of power in the government and is elected by:
   a. universal suffrage.
   b. adult males.
   c. wealthy landowners.

2. The prime minister is elected by:
   a. the House of Councillors.
   b. the House of Representatives.
   c. the cabinet.

3. The party that has been in power the longest is the:
   a. Social-Democratic party.
   b. Liberal Democratic party.
   c. Communist party.

4. Most of the legislation passed by the Diet originates in the:
   a. cabinet of the prime minister.
   b. House of Representatives.
   c. emperor's office.

5. The crisis the government faced in the late 1980s and early 1990s was caused by:
   a. a change in the way members of the Diet are elected.
   b. the refusal of big business to contribute money to political parties.
   c. the bribes and other favors members of the government accepted.

III. Thinking It Through

Write the letter of the correct answer next to its number.

1. Because voters can vote for only one of the three to five members elected by their district to the Diet:
   a. most candidates must receive a majority of the vote.
   b. most candidates need to win only from 20 to 30 percent of the vote.
   c. voter turnout is usually low in most elections.
   d. The Liberal Democratic party (LDP) is assured of winning a majority of the seats in the Diet.

2. People in Japan sometimes joke that their nation has a "one-and-a-half party system" because:
   a. the bureaucracy has such a large role in the government.
   b. the House of Representatives has more power in the Diet than the House of Councillors.
   c. the Liberal Democratic party (LDP) has controlled the government since 1955.
   d. Japan's government is so similar to that of the United States.

3. The Liberal Democratic party (LDP) has been successful mainly because:
   a. Japan has enjoyed economic prosperity and stability under its rule.
   b. the Socialist and Social Democratic parties always supported the LDP.
   c. it has been able to completely control the bureaucracy.
   d. it has carried out the programs favored by the special-interest groups.

4. The vice-ministers and bureaucrats have important and lasting power in the government because:
   a. they are civil servants appointed by the Diet.
   b. they hold office for long periods and become experts in the fields their ministries supervise.
   c. they are the highest-paid group in Japan.
   d. they represent the views of special-interest groups.

5. Citizens' groups have helped lead a national campaign to:
   a. protect farmers by placing high tariffs on imported rice.
   b. support the interests of big business.
   c. support the rights of workers to form unions.
   d. protect the environment and reduce pollution.

DEVELOPING CRITICAL THINKING SKILLS

1. Explain how members are elected to the Diet from their local districts.

2. Explain the meaning of this statement: "Most political parties in Japan are interested mainly in winning elections rather than promoting an ideology, or set of fixed ideas."

3. Discuss the role of factions in the Liberal Democratic party in the Diet.

4. Describe the ties between the bureaucracy and the members of the Diet.

5. Explain the causes of the 1960 political crisis in Japan and its results.

ENRICHMENT AND EXPLORATION

1. Use library reference books and magazines to prepare a research report on the present government of Japan. Your report should include the name of the prime minister, how long he has been in office, his political party, some of the main accomplishments of the government, and some of the problems it faces.

2. Prepare a chart comparing the Japanese government with the government of the United States. Use the following headings to identify the main features of each system of government: type of government, the document on which the government is based, the houses of the legislature, the chief executive, the judicial branch, the main duties of government.

6 Japan as an Economic Superpower

Den Fujita smiled as he viewed Tokyo from his modern office on the 44th floor of a tall new building. He was happy because he had just completed a very successful business deal, another in his long career. He had signed an agreement with the Japanese government to open Blockbuster Video, an American chain of video stores, in several of Japan's large cities. Business success like this was nothing new to Fujita. In 1971, he had introduced McDonald's to Japan.

Under Fujita's dynamic leadership, McDonald's expanded quickly and became Japan's leading fast-food chain. By 1991, there were 867 McDonald's restaurants in Japan, and the McDonald's in Tokyo's central business district was one of the chain's busiest stores in the world. The menu at Makudonarudo (the Japanese name for McDonald's) is much the same as it is in the United States. But Fujita, knowing the Japanese food preferences, added several rice dishes to the menu. More recently, the energetic businessman also formed a new partnership with the U.S. company, Toys R'Us, and several stores of that chain are now in operation in Japan.

Fujita built his reputation on his capacity for hard work and his knowledge of how foreign businesses need to adapt in order to prosper in Japan. In many ways, as you will read, he operates differently from most executives and big businesses in Japan. Yet, he also represents a slowly growing willingness to accept change in that style of business that has made Japan one of the world's leading industrial nations.

THE GROWTH OF JAPAN'S ECONOMY
AFTER WORLD WAR II

When Japan entered World War II with its attack on the U.S. naval base at Pearl Harbor in 1941, it was a modern, industrialized power. When the war ended four years later, Japan was a defeated nation that lay in ruins. Nearly 3 million people, many of them civilians, had been killed. The losses of homes and property were enormous. More than half the buildings in Tokyo and Osaka had been leveled, and nationwide nearly one fourth of all Japanese homes had disappeared. Massive U.S. air attacks had destroyed nearly one third of Japan's industrial power as well as 80 percent of its shipping.

Japan also was forced to give up the great empire it had built on the Asian mainland and in the Pacific. It withdrew to the borders of its home islands as they had existed when U.S. Commodore Matthew Perry first arrived in Japan (see page 55). Now a conquered people themselves, the Japanese seemed to face a bleak, uncertain future—one that held little promise of their regaining the status of a world power. Yet, during the brief years of the U.S. occupation, from 1945 to 1952, Japan was able to lay the foundations of the strong, dynamic economy that soon was to make it a world economic superpower.

The Launching of the Recovery.   The first postwar year saw widespread homelessness, poverty, and hunger in much of Japan. This lasted until U.S. occupation authorities were able to set up channels to distribute food, medicine, clothing, and other supplies to the people. **Inflation** brought rapidly rising prices, contributing to the hardships suffered by the people. However, as the U.S. military government headed by General Douglas MacArthur took firm control, conditions began to improve. The Americans provided nearly $2 billion in direct aid to help the Japanese rebuild their nation.

As the Cold War became more intense after 1948, the United States came to view Japan as a possible ally against the Soviet Union and other communist powers. After the Chinese communists came to power in 1949 and the Korean War started in 1950, the United States realized that a strong Japan would be to its advantage. Accordingly, the United States set about helping Japan regain its industrial strength by providing it with new technology and opening its market to Japanese products.

Japan's Economic Miracle.   By the early 1950s, the rebuilding of the Japanese economy was well under way. The nation's major industries,

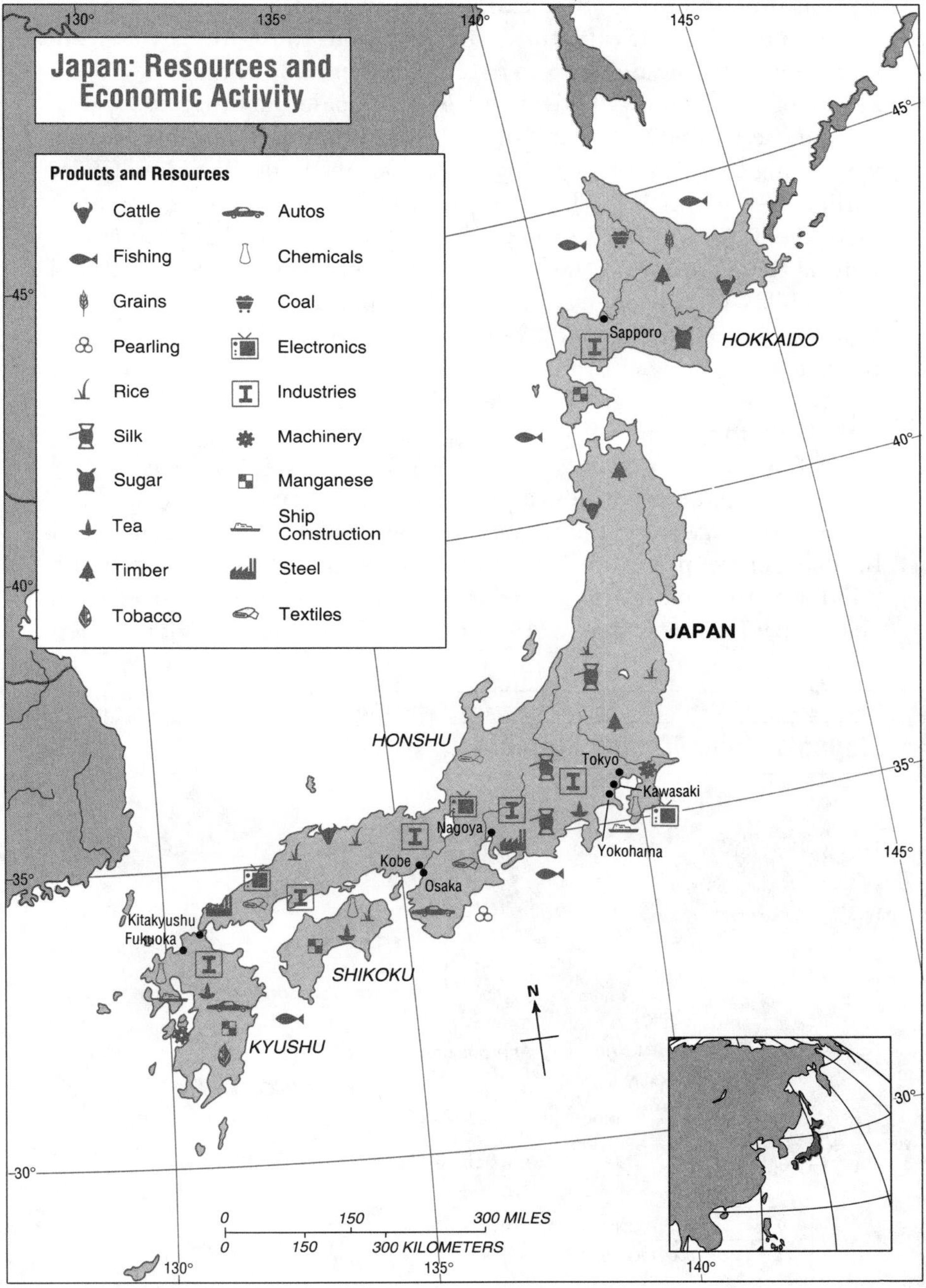
Japan: Resources and Economic Activity
Products and Resources
Cattle
Fishing
Grains
Pearling
Rice
Silk
Sugar
Tea
Timber
Tobacco
Autos
Chemicals
Coal
Electronics
Industries
Machinery
Manganese
Ship Construction
Steel
Textiles
HOKKAIDO
Sapporo
JAPAN
HONSHU
Tokyo
Kawasaki
Yokohama
Nagoya
Kobe
Osaka
Kitakyushu
Fukuoka
SHIKOKU
KYUSHU
N
0 150 300 MILES
0 150 300 KILOMETERS
130°
135°
140°
145°
45°
40°
35°
30°

such as iron and steel, chemicals, fertilizers, coal, and electric power, were rebuilt. The new factories and plants in these industries were equipped with the most up-to-date machinery and technology. This gave Japan an important advantage over the older factories and industries in the United States and other Western nations. These countries were using the technology of the years prior to World War II and even earlier. As early as 1951, Japanese industrial output had regained the high level it had achieved in 1944, during the nation's all-out war effort. During the Korean War, Japan's industrial recovery was demonstrated by its ability to provide nearly $4 billion in military supplies to the U.S. army fighting in that conflict. This achievement, however, only marked the beginning of what came to be called Japan's **economic miracle**, to describe the amazing growth of Japan's economy in the years from the early 1950s to the early 1990s.

A few statistics clearly document the remarkable expansion and growth of Japanese business and industry between the 1950s and the 1990s—the largest and fastest rate of development of any economy in history. For example, from 1950 to 1965 Japan's **gross national product** (GNP), or the amount of goods and services a nation produces each year, grew from less than $11 billion to $90 billion. This figure then

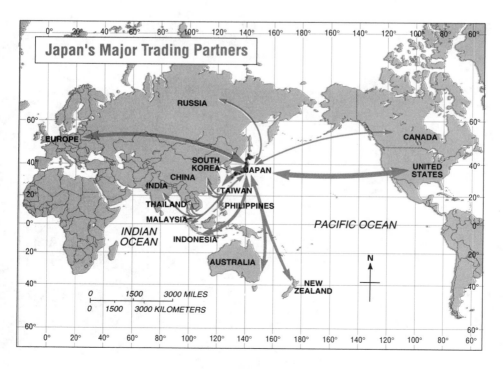

138

soared to $204 billion in 1970. During these two decades, the growth in Japan's economy as measured by GNP increased nearly 10 percent each year. During this same period, the growth rate in Western industrialized nations was less than half as great. By 1970, Japan's economy had become the third largest in the world.

In the years after 1970, Japan's economic miracle continued. The nation's GNP doubled and then more than doubled again, rising to $1.06 trillion in 1980, and then to $3.5 trillion in 1991. By the 1980s, Japan's economy had become the second largest in the world, exceeded only by that of the United States (whose GNP stood at $5.5 trillion in 1991). This economic miracle brought the Japanese people a very high standard of living, and it enabled Japan to become one of the most important and powerful nations in the world.

Adapting to Changing Conditions. Japan's economy is known not only for its incredible rate of growth but also for the impressive ability of its large businesses and industries to adapt to changing conditions. Japan's impressive economic growth depended from the start on its easy access to an enormous range of raw materials from all over the world as well as easy access to world markets. This growth came at a time when the world's trade barriers, such as tariffs, had been lowered. Thus it was possible for Japan to ship its goods freely to consumers worldwide without having to pass along high taxes in the price of goods. Although Japanese consumers provided a profitable domestic market, the rapid expansion of Japan's economy was based largely on profits on products sold to other nations. Thus, Japanese industries targeted production of those goods for which there was a widespread, worldwide demand.

In the 1950s and 1960s, for example, Japan's government worked closely with key sectors of the nation's economy to spur steel production and shipbuilding. This was a time when the nations of the world were rebuilding and expanding their economies after World War II. Japanese shipyards turned out huge tankers that carried bulk supplies of oil from the Middle East to markets throughout the world. By such effective economic planning, Japan became the leader in shipbuilding by 1956 and the world's third-largest steel producer by 1969. Its increased steel production, with an emphasis on quality at comparatively low cost, enabled Japan to move into the manufacture of automobiles. By 1969 Japan was the third-largest producer of cars in the world. With these major export products, Japan's share of world trade made significant gains, rising from 2 percent of the world total in 1960 to 9 percent of the total in 1973.

The Japanese are among the best customers for their country's varied output of electronic products. Here a couple shops in a Tokyo area of electronics stores.

In 1973, war broke out between the Arab nations of the Middle East and Israel. To punish the nations that had supported Israel, the Arab oil-producing states stopped shipping oil to these countries. The resulting sharp rise in the price of oil was a blow to Japan's economy. As a result, Japan made a determined effort to reduce its dependence on oil. It did so in two ways. It immediately set about on a program to conserve and make better use of the oil it did have access to. Further, without coal or oil supplies of its own, Japan made a major shift in its economy. It moved away from heavy industries like steel, shipbuilding, and chemicals, which used large amounts of these fuels. In their place, it concentrated on high technology industries that did not consume such large quantities of energy or depend so heavily on imported raw materials. Japan's businesses and highly skilled workforce, supported by government planning, were soon even more competitive than they had been in the older industries. Beginning in the 1970s, Japanese TVs, computers, VCRs, tape decks, camcorders, calculators, electronic cameras, and many other high-tech consumer products were sold throughout the world. Japan continued its world leadership in these products through the 1980s and into the 1990s.

Meanwhile, new markets in the expanding information services industry were emerging in these years. Japan became a leading manufacturer and exporter of computers, semiconductors, computer chips, fiber-optics, and cellular phones. However, as Japan's share of world trade increased, it caused serious problems for many Western nations and produced tensions with those nations, particularly the United States, as you will read later in this chapter.

THE GOVERNMENT–BUSINESS PARTNERSHIP

The close cooperation between big business and government in Japan has been one of the keys to the nation's great economic growth. Several ministries of government work closely with groups of business firms in different industries to help plot Japan's overall economy and plan for its future development. In a democratic society like Japan, this central planning is a joint effort by business and government. Unlike planning in socialist countries, it does not mean that the government controls the nation's economy.

The Ministry of International Trade and Industry.   In the close tie between business and government, one of the most important govern-mental ministries is the Ministry of International Trade and Industry, or MITI, as it is often referred to. MITI has helped guide the growth of Japan's economy by setting goals for individual industries and helping them acquire new technologies. It also enforces regulations and restrictions on many imported products to help protect Japanese industries. Yet, MITI encourages competition among the leading firms so that no single corporation can gain a monopoly in its industry.

When world competition or other factors force a decline in a given industry, as they did with shipbuilding in the mid-1970s, MITI assists the industry to reorganize and manufacture a product more suitable for its changing market (in this case smaller, less costly tankers). In some cases, when an industry is no longer profitable enough, MITI aids companies to shift to new businesses and helps retrain their workforce. It also provides **tax incentives** such as reductions in taxes to ease the transition. Such was the case with the chemical industry in the 1980s. MITI also sometimes encourages small companies to merge in order to form larger, more profitable businesses.

Planning the Overall Economy.   Looking ahead to the future, in the early 1980s, MITI brought together a group of major corporations to plan **artificial intelligence** computers. These would understand spoken commands, be able to recognize visual images, and reason like humans. In the event this effort is successful, Japan is expected to take the lead in developing a pace-setting new technology.

Because of the close working relationship between MITI and big business, some critics have termed their partnership "Japan, Inc.," suggesting that the Japanese government itself has become part of the nation's business enterprise. Despite such criticism, however, most of which comes from Western nations, many of these same nations are asking themselves whether such close cooperation between business and government would not benefit their own economies.

JAPANESE BUSINESS AND INDUSTRY

The organization of businesses in Japan and the way that large corporations operate reflect many of the values and traditions of Japanese society. The skill and talents of workers and management is another key part in the impressive performance of this vital part of Japan's economy.

Japan's Large Corporations. Many of Japan's businesses and industries are dominated by very large companies. As you recall, before World War II, the zaibatsu, or family-controlled business conglomerates, had a

The Economies of Japan and Other Countries						
COUNTRY	GROSS NATIONAL PRODUCT (in billions of U.S. dollars)	GNP GROWTH SINCE 1985	PER CAPITA INCOME (in U.S. dollars)	PERCENT OF LABOR FORCE IN:		
				AGRICULTURE	INDUSTRY	SERVICES
Japan	$3,500	25%	$15,000	7%	34%	59
China	2,239	58	360	68	18	14
Germany	1,570	17	19,000	5	40	46
United Kingdom	936	9	14,500	17	26	64
United States	5,520	9	16,400	2	26	72

Data covers the year 1991.

Sources: IMF International Financial Statistics; Bureau of Labor Statistics, U.S. Department of Labor

vital role in the nation's economy. The zaibatsu were giant business houses that owned powerful banks as well as shipping companies, mines, railroads, and textile, glass, and chemical factories, and often many other different businesses. A dozen or more zaibatsu controlled much of the nation's economy. After World War II, the U.S. occupation government moved to put the zaibatsu out of business. For example, the Mitsui and Mitsubishi zaibatsu were broken up into 240 separate companies.

However, as U.S. efforts to reform Japan's economy ended, large business combinations reappeared. Many of the new big business firms were part of a conglomerate of separate companies headed by a large bank or trading company. These big business firms, now called *keiretsu* (KAY-ret-soo), cooperated with the government and with one another in planning developments in their various industries. In addition, many other new giant business enterprises also developed. Many new corporations were founded in the new electronics and automotive fields and soon became world-famous, among them Sony, Honda, Toyota, Hitachi, and Sanyo. Other, smaller companies, like Sharp, Canon, Matsushita, and Toshiba, which had existed before the war, now grew into large international businesses.

The Workforce in Large Companies. Japan's workers are among the best educated in the world. The knowledge of math and science they acquire in school equips them to handle the complex technology used in the factories and offices where they work.

Workers also are willing to work very hard to develop the high degrees of skill their jobs require. They form **quality circles**, or small work-planning teams, which meet regularly to discuss ways to improve the group's performance. This strong commitment by workers to their jobs is of great benefit to businesses. It makes it possible for them to constantly seek out the latest technology, confident that their workers will use it efficiently and thus help increase the corporation's profits.

The corporation, in turn, rewards workers' efforts with bonuses that reflect the employees' contributions to their success and profits. It also provides many other important benefits, such as health care, health-insurance programs, and retirement pensions. In addition, it often makes available low-cost housing, special savings plans, low-interest loans, and company vacation resorts for workers and their families. Lifetime employment is guaranteed to a majority of workers in large companies. These are some of ways in which Japanese workers have been motivated to become the most productive in the world.

A worker at a Japanese airplane factory carefully puts the finishing touches on an engine. A high level of quality control helps account for Japan's industrial success.

Business Executives and Managers.   Japanese business executives and managers, like workers at all levels, devote their careers to achieving their corporations' success and the largest possible share of the market for its products. They regard themselves and their workers as members of a family community, whose needs each individual must serve for the common good. You read in Chapter 4 how managers solicit the workers' opinions and ideas in making important decisions. In this way, workers feel they are valued participants in most major corporate policies.

Executives themselves strive for agreement among the management of the corporation. Special efforts are made to consult with lower-level managers in formulating most business decisions. In the same fashion, managers and lower-level executives are encouraged to express their opinions and offer proposals to improve corporate operations and planning. These proposals are then sent for review to the heads of various departments for their review and approval, who pass them along to the top management. This process by which lower-level executives and managers submit proposals to top management is known as *ringisei* (ring-ee-say).

Company executives and managers enjoy high status in the company workplace hierarchy. They work hard to strengthen the feeling among the workers that everyone is a valued member of a team, sharing common goals and concerns for each other's welfare. Executives demonstrate and reinforce their close bonds with their workers in many ways. For example, they usually work in an office cubicle, not a separate private office. They may eat alongside other workers in the company restaurant, and visit the factory or office to watch employees at work. Most executives themselves have had some experience working at these factory or office jobs and are familiar with the operations and responsibilities of members of their work group. Employees usually accept these actions as sincere efforts that improve working conditions and foster solidarity between management and labor.

Not unexpectedly, Japanese executives in very high-level jobs at large companies receive much higher salaries than most lower-level workers, averaging the equivalent of between $150,000 and $200,000 a year. The heads of corporations like Toyota may receive as much as $1.3 million a year. Yet these salaries are only a fraction of those paid to executives on the same level in the United States and other Western nations. In addition to their salaries, these Japanese executives also receive the opportunity to buy company stock at low prices, generous pensions, and many other benefits. Yet Japanese executives often consider even the highest level of compensation secondary to the opportunities their job provides to serving their company. Thus, after retirement, many executives are given honorary posts in their old corporation so they can continue to contribute their ideas and advice. In this way, the company benefits from the experience of loyal members of the company group. At the same time, the retired executive is able to preserve a sense of identity and worth to society.

Many corporations also have programs designed to instill group spirit to create harmony in the workplace. A typical business day may begin with executives and workers meeting in the company recreation hall or outside the plant before work hours begin. All of them will be wearing the same uniform. After singing the company song, those present may perform exercises or aerobics to focus their energies on the work they are soon to begin. Then workers and executives move to the factory or office floor for the work of the day.

Long-Range Planning.   The success of Japan's leading corporations in turning out vast amounts of goods is due in part to their ability to plan their operations on a long-range basis. Japanese corporations raise most

Japanese manufacturers are first in world automobile output. The companies were financed in part by banks that benefitted from the high rate of savings of the Japanese people.

of their working capital by borrowing money from banks. The banks, in turn, are able to lend large sums to industry because of the huge amounts the Japanese people deposit in the banks as savings. The Japanese have long led the world in the portion of their income that they save. The rate of personal saving of the average Japanese family is three times that of a typical U.S. family.

Further, investors who do buy shares of stock in Japanese companies are satisfied to receive a much lower rate of dividends than investors in U.S. companies receive. As a result of these two factors, large Japanese companies are not subject to the pressures to produce ever-growing profits each year for stockholders, as are most U.S. and other Western companies. Thus, Japanese companies can spend greater time and effort to develop new products that may well ensure their future success as markets change. In fact, corporations in Japan spend nearly 6 percent of their total sales revenues for research and development of new products and technology. By contrast, U.S. corporations spend an average of 1 percent for this purpose. Corporations can even risk losing money in the short term in order to produce a product that is needed to gain a share of an important new market. Examples of products for which Japanese companies have done this are more powerful computer chips and high-definition television.

Japan's Labor Unions.   The organization of workers in Japan also has contributed to the continuous record-setting gains that Japanese corporations have achieved in labor productivity. In 1990, about a quarter of Japanese workers were members of labor unions. This was a record low. The reason given for the low rate of membership was that there were growing numbers of part-time workers in industry as well as young people, both groups that were not interested in joining unions.

The workers in a large corporation are members of an **enterprise union,** or a union formed within a single company. All the workers in the corporation, whatever their occupation or the kind of jobs they perform, belong to this union. Thus, the Japanese union is different from many unions in the United States, where workers in various companies in the same industry—for example, auto workers—all belong to the same union.

Japan has taken the lead in the new field of high-definition television. In 1991 Japan became the first country to broadcast daily programs in this new format.

CASE STUDY:

A Labor–Management Success Story

One of the greatest strengths of Japanese businesses has been their ability to improve their products to keep ahead of their competitors, both in Japan and in other countries. Here, Yotaro Kobayashi, the president of Fuji Xerox, describes how his company met such a challenge.

> Until 1974–75, we dominated the copy machine market in Japan. Our customers at that time used to say that Fuji Xerox is expensive, but it is the best. So, they were content with us. . . . Then the oil price crisis hit our economy. Many of our customers were caught up in this price squeeze, and they decided that they had to cut their costs . . . even if it meant giving up quality. . . .
>
> If we could give the customers a machine that would make 2,400 copies per hour and was in the price range of machines that made 1,500 copies per hour, they would want it and buy it. But other companies knew this, too, so we had to get there first. We agreed that meant getting it on the market in two years . . .
>
> Well, some of the more aggressive, risk-taking engineers came up with a new design and a development plan. . . . Everybody from top to bottom knew that this new machine was top priority, and that the company's future depended on it.
>
> There was a period when we worked through the weekends, week after week . . . for some months. And there were times when our development group stayed at the plant overnight. . . .
>
> Fortunately, this product, the FX 3500, was a success. . . . It is the best-selling machine in our company history. . . .
>
> My own feeling is that the key to our improved performance was this single-minded determination to get things right and teamwork— everybody helping everybody else . . . They all listened to each other and they worked to get the machine we needed—at the price we needed.

From Martin E. Weinstein, *The Human Face of Japan's Leadership*. New York: Praeger, 1989.

1. What did the company president believe was the reason for the company's success in creating the new product?

2. What does this account demonstrate about workers' attitudes toward their jobs and their company?

Workers who belong to an enterprise union continue to place their main loyalty in their company. They understand that the well-being of the union as well as their own well-being depends on their corporation's earning good profits. Therefore, the union works closely with corporate management to promote the welfare of the company. For example, a union is willing to cooperate with company executives in introducing new technology to increase worker productivity. Workers realize that greater productivity helps assure them of keeping their jobs under the practice of lifetime employment. Thus, the use of **robotics**, or computer-driven machinery on industrial assembly lines, to perform tasks formerly done by humans was accepted by unions. Under the system of lifetime employment, workers who are replaced by robots are retrained to perform other jobs. Similarly, when a company shifts its product line, workers are retrained to assume new responsibilities.

Members of an enterprise union also understand that their corporation must increase its earnings and profits if they are to share in them in the form of higher wages. Union members are thus concerned about their own job performance and the company's position in its industry. As you know, workers gain prestige for themselves and their families by working for the leading corporations in an industry. (See Chapter 4.) Company executives also often share information about the firm's current output and its position in its industry. Union-management relations also are close since lower-level managers often belong to the union.

Enterprise unions bargain hard with their corporations for their fair share of the profits, however. Each spring during prosperous times, a union meets with management to negotiate wage increases and improved benefits for the workers. These negotiations between the union and management have been called "the spring labor offensives." If the company is successful and earning rising profits, the union usually secures significant wage hikes for its members. For example, during the 1960s and early 1970s, when the nation's GNP was growing by nearly 10 percent annually, unions bargained successfully for increases of about 15 percent each year for their workers. In return, unions seldom engage in strikes or walkouts, as workers do in the United States and most other industrial nations. This is not to say that Japan has no strikes. In 1988, for example, there were 498 work stoppages in companies with at least 1,000 workers. About 75,000 workers were involved. However, the stoppages were quite brief, averaging less than three days each. On the whole, Japan has few labor disruptions. In this respect and in many others, enterprise unions act to strengthen the productivity of Japanese workers and their companies.

THE TWO-TIERED ECONOMY

Although large corporations now play a central role in the Japanese economy and employ about one third of the labor force, most Japanese work in smaller businesses that employ smaller numbers of people. In fact, 60 percent of the companies in Japan have 100 workers or fewer, and many small firms have a workforce of only 10 or 20 people. This sharp division between the large corporations and the many other smaller business enterprises in Japan is termed the **two-tiered system**. In this two-tiered, or dual, economy, working conditions and management styles of small businesses, small retail stores, and small farming enterprises are very different from those of large corporations.

Subcontractors and Other Small Businesses.   The largest and most important group of smaller Japanese companies consists of **subcontractors**, or those businesses that supply parts or produce other goods for the large industrial corporations that dominate the nation's economy. Subcontractors make up the majority of Japan's small businesses with fewer than 300 employees. Most large corporations receive one third of their parts from subcontractors. Some companies, like Toyota and Nissan, depend on subcontractors for as much as 60 percent of the parts they use in producing their goods.

The use of subcontractors offers Japanese corporations many advantages. They can obtain many of the finished materials they require without adding workers to their payroll. There are often several subcontractors who compete for business with a large corporation. Corporations thus often can obtain the parts they require from small firms that specialize in their field at the lowest possible prices. When conditions change and corporations need to cut back on production, they can decrease their own costs by reducing the amount of goods they purchase from subcontractors. This helps the corporation to weather business downturns more effectively.

While subcontractors help account for the efficiency and productivity that has enabled corporations to drive Japan's economic miracle, this part of Japan's two-tiered economy faces constant challenges. When their customers slow down their operations or change their products, subcontractors have to scramble for new business. As more and more Japanese companies shift part of their production to the United States, Europe, or elsewhere, Japanese subcontractors and their workers are the ones who suffer most from these moves.

There are many thousands of other small manufacturing businesses in Japan in addition to subcontractors. Nearly all of these small firms are family-owned or run by a single proprietor. They produce a wide range of products, from consumer products to sophisticated electronic equipment. In addition, there are countless other small businesses in retailing and consumer services throughout Japan, as you will read.

Workers in subcontracting firms and other small companies do not enjoy the lifetime jobs and the high wages of most workers in the large corporations. Many lack health insurance and seldom receive pensions when they retire. In addition, they have little job security, since these small firms are the most sensitive to slowdowns in the economy. As long as Japan has a labor shortage, workers who are laid off usually can find other jobs.

Retail Shops and Stores. Most Japanese do their daily shopping at small stores and shops. Even in large cities like Tokyo, most shoppers purchase many of the things they need in small shops owned and operated by a husband and wife. There are nearly 1.7 million retail stores in Japan, nearly as many as in the United States, whose population is twice the size of Japan's. Only a fraction of the retail shops are large department stores and supermarkets.

Japanese homemakers do much of their shopping for food in small local shops close to their apartments. The women shown here wear traditional costumes for their shopping outings.

The lack of space in Japanese cities and towns has greatly limited the growth of large stores and allowed the traditional small stores to continue. The average family's small apartment makes it difficult to store food or other household goods. This means that most Japanese homemakers must shop for food each day. Yet, this system has certain advantages, since it allows women to get out of their cramped apartments with their children and meet and visit with friends, who will also be shopping in these stores. As with other small private businesses, the owners of small stores lack the job security and benefits enjoyed by those employed by corporations.

Japanese Farmers.   Japanese agriculture, with its declining workforce, is also part of the nation's two-tiered economy. As Japan's businesses and industries expanded dramatically beginning in the 1950s, agriculture as a source of employment sharply declined. As noted in Chapter 1, farmers make up only 7 percent of the workforce, and more than three fourths of them engage in farming on a part-time basis, also working at other jobs.

Japan's farms have remained small, averaging only 2.5 acres (about 1.1 hectares), but they have been heavily mechanized with small but efficient farm machinery that has increased their productivity. New, improved types of seeds and fertilizers have also vastly increased the size of the crops produced by Japanese farmers. Japan's farms, together with its fishing and dairy industries, produce nearly 70 percent of the nation's food supply. Yet, this achievement is made possible only by large government **subsidies**, or payments, to farmers.

Each year the Ministry of Agriculture purchases the nation's entire rice crop, sells whatever is needed by consumers, and then stores the rest. Without these subsidies, which cost the government about $20 billion annually in the 1980s, many of Japan's farmers would not survive. At the same time, the government keeps the tariff on imported rice at a high level. As a result, Japanese consumers must pay five times as much for rice as imported U.S. rice would cost if it were available. This increases the cost of living in Japan, where families often must spend nearly one third of their income on food.

However, most Japanese regard farmers as an important group and support the government's agricultural policy. Many Japanese themselves come from farm families who moved to the cities only in recent decades. Moreover, they believe that it would be dangerous for Japan to become even more dependent on imported food. They remember the hardship caused by the cutoff of soybean exports to Japan by the United

Farmers use machinery adapted to the small size of their property. The rice harvester shown here, not much bigger than a lawn mower, helps this farmer raise his output.

States in the early 1970s when that country had a shortage of that crop. As the head of a consumer group in Japan put it,

> We cannot turn over our lives to the United States just because [its] food is cheaper. Even if we have to pay high prices for self-sufficiency, we will have to bear it.

JAPAN'S FOREIGN TRADE

In recent decades, Japan's trade with the United States, the nations of Southeast Asia, and many other countries has grown dramatically. Japanese products are seen in the homes and offices and in parking lots of New York City; Jakarta, Indonesia; and Montreal, Canada. The United States is still the leading export nation in the world, but Japan is rapidly closing its lead.

Trade as Japan's Lifeline. Japan depends on trade with other nations. It does so for two reasons. It must import the raw materials used by its industries as well as the oil and coal to power its factories and businesses. Lacking these vital resources in its own nation, Japan's remarkable economic growth has depended on importing these items. In return, these imports have required Japan to become an exporting nation in order to pay for the goods it imports. In doing so, Japan has achieved a

Major Japanese Exports and Imports

PRODUCT EXPORTED	EXPORTS (in thousands of U.S. dollars)	PERCENT OF TOTAL EXPORTS
Machinery	$125,108,690	37.7%
Electrical Equipment	56,217,640	18.0
Passenger Cars	44,712,595	14.2
Transport Equipment	31,310,506	10.0
Industrial Chemicals	17,195,281	5.5
Toys and Musical Instruments	16,243,823	5.2

PRODUCT IMPORTED	IMPORTS (in thousands of U.S. dollars)	PERCENT OF TOTAL IMPORTS
Mineral Fuels	$54,756,348	23.1%
Food and Direct Consumers	34,698,137	14.7
Machinery	27,419,324	11.6
Crude Materials	24,644,751	10.4
Industrial Chemicals	16,909,947	7.1
Metals	15,078,356	6.4

Data covers the year 1991.

Source: U.S. Department of Commerce; "Summary of Trade", Japan Tariff Association, January 1992.

favorable **balance of trade**, meaning that it exports more than it imports. Today, Japanese industrial products and high-tech goods are sold in all parts of the world.

The United States became Japan's largest **trading partner** after World War II and has kept this role ever since. During the 1960s and 1970s, Japan greatly expanded its trade, especially with the nations of Southeast Asia as well as with Australia and Canada. In the years since then, Japan's trade has continued to grow, especially with the other industrialized nations. Japan has become a leading world exporter of industrial products like steel and heavy machinery, tankers, and machine tools. It also has been the largest exporter of electronic consumer goods such as TVs, CD players, compact stereo systems, camcorders, cellular phones, and VCRs. Today, Japan also sells more cars abroad than any other country. It also is one of the largest producers and exporters of products for the information industry, such as computers, fiber-optics, semiconductors, and computer chips.

Tensions with Other Nations.   As Japan rapidly increased its exports, tensions developed between Japan and other industrial nations. Many of these nations, including the United States, also manufactured many of the products that Japan exported. They became concerned when their citizens favored Japanese products over their own. In some cases, Japan's success came at the expense of important industries in these nations. For example, U.S. steel companies were unable to compete with less costly and superior Japanese steel. U.S. car manufacturers also suffered declining sales at home as smaller, less expensive, better built Japanese cars captured a growing share of auto sales in the United States. European nations, too, were unhappy at the threat posed by Japanese exports.

Japan has attempted to reduce tensions produced by the success of its exports by agreeing to limit its annual exports of certain products. For example, in the early 1980s, Japan's car manufacturers had the capacity to produce 12 million cars each year. Of this amount, 5 million vehicles were sold annually in Japan and the rest were marked for export. But, under pressure from the United States, Japanese automobile makers agreed to export no more than 1.7 million cars to the United States. They reduced their exports to Germany as well.

Nevertheless, the ill feeling caused by Japan's huge sales of goods in the United States and other nations continued. Japan's great success in increasing its export trade lies at the heart of this problem. By 1960, Japan's exports had reached a total of $4.1 billion. But the great surge in

Japanese exports was only beginning. During the next three decades, Japan's exports to other nations increased at an annual rate of almost 19 percent. In 1970, exports totaled $19.3 billion. By 1980 they had exceeded $129.8 billion. By 1991, Japanese exports had climbed to more than $314 billion. This represented an increase of about 700 percent in 30 years. No other nation had ever increased its share of world trade by such a vast amount in such a short period.

During these same decades, Japan's imports also greatly increased, but at a slightly slower rate than did its exports. In 1960, Japanese imports stood at $4.5 billion. This figure grew to $18.9 in 1970 and reached $140.5 billion in 1980 (much of the increase due to rising oil prices). By 1991, Japan's imports stood at more than $236 billion. However, during the 1980s, Japanese imports grew at a noticeably slower rate than its exports. As a result, Japan began to have a **trade surplus,** or an excess of exports over imports. In other words, Japan was selling more to other countries than it was buying from them. As this surplus remained substantial each year, frictions with these countries, especially the United States, were heightened. In 1980, Japan was buying more from the United States than it was selling to them. The tide turned in the later 1980s. In 1983, Japan was selling the United States $20.5 billion worth of goods more than it was buying. By 1991, the trade imbalance with the United States had reached more than $38 billion.

Japanese Investments Abroad. Japan's trade surplus caused enormous amounts of capital to flow into the nation during the 1980s. Japanese corporations used this money to expand Japan's investments overseas, especially in the United States and Great Britain. For example, many Japanese auto makers like Toyota and Honda set up plants and subsidiaries in the United States to manufacture cars there. By 1992, Japan had established more than 600 plants to produce electronic products and machinery as well as automobiles in the United States. Other Japanese firms paid a total of nearly $100 billion between 1980 and 1990 to buy such famous U.S. properties as Rockefeller Center in New York City and the Pebble Beach golf course in California. Japanese companies also acquired several major movie studios in Hollywood as well as large U.S. record companies. Further, the Japanese government and private investors bought huge amounts of the bonds sold by the U.S. government each year to finance its enormous national debt.

Relations between the United States and Japan were often strained as some Americans and members of Congress worried about what they termed the "Japanese takeover" of the United States. They also charged

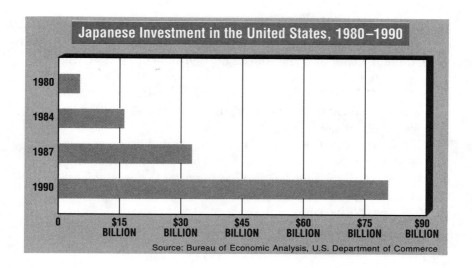

Japanese Investment in the United States, 1980–1990

1980	
1984	
1987	
1990	

0 — $15 BILLION — $30 BILLION — $45 BILLION — $60 BILLION — $75 BILLION — $90 BILLION

Source: Bureau of Economic Analysis, U.S. Department of Commerce

that Japan used unfair restrictions to keep U.S. products out of Japan and to discourage U.S. investments there. They pointed out that the Japanese bought only about 16,000 U.S. cars a year, compared with the 5 million cars purchased in the United States that were made in Japan. They blamed this on the red tape and complicated regulations on auto imports imposed by the Japanese government.

Other Americans believed that these charges were unfair. They pointed out that U.S. manufacturers made little or no effort to fit their product to the Japanese market. For example, in Japan, people drive on the left side of the road, yet U.S. car manufacturers did not modify their cars to take this into account. Defenders of Japan also noted that there is little outcry when European companies buy U.S. real estate or businesses. They claimed that the critics were engaged in "Japan-bashing." By the early 1990s, relations between the two nations seemed to be growing steadily worse. They reached a low point in January 1992, when President George W. Bush and the heads of three U.S. car companies went to Tokyo to try to persuade Japanese officials, unsuccessfully, to open Japan to U.S. car exports.

Both nations continued to try to resolve their differences and reduce tensions. In the early 1990s, there were signs that the world's two economic superpowers were trying to smooth out some of the difficulties posed by their trade and investment imbalances. Japanese investments in the United States declined significantly and Japanese purchases of U.S. companies slowed. The Japanese government agreed to double the amount of auto parts imported from the United States, from $7 billion in 1991 to $15 billion in 1994. It also continued to limit the number of Japanese cars exported to the United States. President Bush resisted the demand by some Americans that the United States impose trade restrictions on Japanese products and repeated the U.S. commitment to free trade. Moreover, U.S. exports to Japan continued to increase in volume, nearly doubling from $16 billion in 1987 to more than $53 billion in 1991.

Despite these problems, Japan and the United States remain each other's largest trading partners, and each continues to value this special relationship. This relationship also has important consequences for all the nations of the world, since Japan and the United States together create 40 percent of the world's total economic output.

CLOUDS ON JAPAN'S ECONOMIC HORIZON

The phenomenal growth of Japan's economy after the 1960s was not a complete success story. This growth was accompanied by many serious problems. The pressure from other countries for a fairer trading system, just discussed, is only one of these problems.

The Environment and Worker Safety. On Japan's homefront, pollution of the environment accompanied its economic expansion. Factories belched smoke into the air and discharged their wastes into water supplies, threatening the health of Japan's citizens. As noted in Chapter 5, in the 1960s and 1970s, thousands of people were poisoned as a result of the dumping of chemical wastes into Minamata Bay. The noise level of the already overcrowded cities was deafening.

In the workplace, the early years of economic expansion saw many workers exposed to dangerous and unhealthful conditions. Those who became ill were not paid for their loss and suffering. Factory owners opposed corrective legislation, claiming that they would take care of their workers, a promise most of them did not keep. The Japanese people became increasingly aware of these problems and organized protests. Slowly, steps were taken to improve conditions. Anti-pollution laws were passed and social security and welfare measures were enacted. By the 1970s, the days of "production first" seemed to be over.

Problems with the Economy. For over three decades, continuing rapid growth of the Japanese economy was taken for granted. While other industrialized countries suffered periodic recessions and depressions, the Japanese economy steamed ahead virtually without a pause. But in the early 1990s, at a time when industrial nations in the West were experiencing recessions, Japan was forced to realize that it was not immune from economic illness.

Between January 1991 and January 1992, Japan's industrial output fell by 12 percent. For the first time since 1974, its GNP shrank. Beginning in January 1990, the stock market started a fall that resulted in a loss of 50 percent in the value of stocks by March 1992. Bankruptcies, even of large corporations, increased. Savings by families declined sharply and demand for consumer goods slackened. Consumer debt rose to new heights and banks were awash in bad debts from consumer loans. Concern arose that businesses would find it difficult to raise the capital needed to grow. Profits of giant corporations like Matsushita, Sony, Toshiba, Fujitsu, and Nippon Steel fell. Businesses were forced to slash their budgets for new plants. The value of real estate plunged. For the first time, the fear of unemployment haunted the Japanese economy.

The Japanese were stunned at this turn of events. Unaccustomed as they were to even temporary economic slowdowns, they now faced the prospect that their economy might go into a long-term decline. Economists, bureaucrats, and businesspeople desperately sought ways to stem the tide.

Chapter 6:
CHECKUP

REVIEWING THE CHAPTER

I. Building Your Vocabulary

Match the terms with the correct definitions below.

economic miracle	two-tiered system
gross national product (GNP)	subcontractors
keiretsu	subsidies
quality circles	balance of trade
enterprise union	trade surplus
robotics	*ringisei*

1. an excess of exports over imports

2. the amazing growth of Japan's economy since 1945

3. a union formed within a single company

4. the amount of goods and services a nation produces each year

5. division in the economy between large corporations and many small business enterprises

6. businesses that supply parts or produce other goods for large corporations

7. big business companies in Japan

8. process by which lower-level executives and managers submit proposals to top management

9. small work-planning teams that strive to improve the work group's performance

10. payments made by the government to producers

11. the use of computer-driven machinery to perform assembly-line operations

12. balance between the amount of goods a nation imports and exports

II. Understanding the Facts

Write the letter of the best conclusion to each sentence next to its number.

1. By the 1920s and 1930s, Japan had developed its economy and had become:
   a. an economic superpower.
   b. the third-largest economic power in the world.
   c. the most industrialized nation in Asia.
   d. Europe's largest trading partner.

2. During the U.S. occupation of Japan after World War II, the United States:
   a. aided Japan and helped its economy recover.
   b. allowed Japan to rebuild its economy on its own.
   c. encouraged U.S. businesses to dominate Japan's economy.
   d. broke up the zaibatsu and kept Japan's economy weak.

3. The Ministry of International Trade and Industry (MITI) has helped guide the growth of Japan's economy by:
   a. outlawing unions and subsidizing foreign businesses in Japan.
   b. setting goals for Japanese industries.
   c. forming new government-owned corporations.
   d. banning unions of workers.

4. Workers who belong to Japan's unions continue to work closely with the management of their company because:
   a. they believe their well-being depends on the company's earning good profits.
   b. the government rewards union members who achieve high productivity.
   c. each union is part of a nationwide union.
   d. companies fire workers who go out on strike.

5. One reason Japan's favorable balance of trade has caused tensions with the United States in recent years is that:
   a. a flood of U.S. products has been exported to Japan.
   b. exports of Japanese rice and other farm products have reduced the crops U.S. farmers can sell abroad.
   c. Japanese companies have used the trade surplus to buy well-known U.S. firms and famous properties.
   d. Japanese electronics goods, cars, and other products have become too expensive for Americans to buy.

III. Thinking It Through

Write the letter of your correct conclusion to each sentence next to its number.

1. In the 1980s and early 1990s, as Japan's economic miracle continued:
   a. the nation's GNP reached the highest in the world.
   b. the Japanese people enjoyed one of the highest living standards in the world.
   c. Japan sold most of its manufactured products to the countries of Asia.
   d. the *keiretsu* lost their importance.

2. Executives and managers of Japan's corporations strive to strengthen workers' loyalty and devotion to their firm by:
   a. paying outstanding workers much higher salaries than other workers.
   b. keeping their own salaries low and limiting the influence of enterprise unions.
   c. making all workers feel they are valued members of a team who share common goals and concern for each other's welfare.
   d. contributing part of their own salary to the workers' pension fund.

3. The use of computer-driven machinery is more widespread in Japan than in any other nation because:
   a. Japanese workers' rapid gains in productivity have made such machinery essential to the nation's survival.
   b. Japan has a surplus of skilled workers.
   c. Japan's labor unions cooperate with management for their common good and have agreed to their use.
   d. Japan lacks coal, iron ore, and most other industrial raw materials.

4. The limited space in Japan's cities and in people's homes affects the way people shop in which one of the following ways?
   a. Most families have to shop in large supermarkets and eat at fast-food chains.
   b. Subcontractors set up food markets where families do their daily shopping.
   c. Most stores and shops are in huge shopping malls where housewives take their children for their daily shopping.
   d. Most families must shop in small local stores.

5. Each of the following is a major reason why Japan achieved its economic miracle *except*:
   a. The Japanese people were united in their determination to rebuild after World War II and help their country become an economic superpower.
   b. The low rate of savings by the Japanese meant that the large amounts of money they spent provided good markets for businesses.
   c. The government worked closely with business and industry to strengthen and shape Japan's economy.
   d. The skill and efficiency of Japan's industrial corporations helped the economy to grow rapidly.

DEVELOPING CRITICAL THINKING SKILLS

1. Explain how the policies of the U.S. occupation helped Japan after World War II.
2. Describe the partnership between Japan's government and big business and explain how it affects the nation's economy.
3. Discuss how Japanese corporations contribute to the continuing economic miracle in Japan.
4. Explain how Japan's two-tiered economy affects Japanese farmers.
5. Describe the tensions between Japan and the United States and how the two nations are trying to ease their differences.

INTERPRETING A GRAPH

Study the graph on page 157. Then answer these questions.

1. Which three-year period saw the greatest increase in Japanese investments in the United States?
2. By about how many times did Japanese investments increase from 1980 to 1990?
3. From what you have read in this chapter, explain how Japan was able to make these large investments.

ENRICHMENT AND EXPLORATION

1. One small Japanese company that makes gloves has printed the following on the back of its executives' business cards:

COMPANY RULES

1. *For self*
   Are you carrying out your mission?

2. *For society*
   Are you rendering service to society?

3. *For the world*
   Are you acting without shame as an international businessman?

Now, imagine that you are a student in a Japanese high school. Using this business card as a model, write a set of three rules that you think should guide all students in your class.

2. Review the reasons for Japan's economic miracle. Decide which of these were directly due to actions by the United States and write a brief paragraph explaining how these actions benefited Japan's economy.

7 Japan and the World (1945–Present)

Throughout Japan people expressed their profound sense of grief and great personal loss. They attended ancient ceremonies and rituals at Shinto shrines and Buddhist temples to mourn. The death of Emperor Hirohito (hee-roh-HEE-toh) in January 1989 brought to an end the longest imperial reign in the nation's history. It also demonstrated the remarkable transformation that Japan had undergone during the 63 years of Hirohito's reign. Much of Japan's remarkable development as an urban and industrial nation had come while he was Japan's emperor. He had seen Japan change from a nation disgraced by military aggression and total defeat to a respected world power.

When the state funeral for the late emperor was held in Tokyo on February 24, 1989, the eyes of the world were focused on this event. The leaders of 154 nations were gathered there to attend the ceremony and express their sympathy to the emperor's family, the Japanese people, and their government. Presidents, prime ministers, and monarchs from nations throughout the world were in attendance at Emperor Hirohito's funeral. The newly elected President of the United States, George Bush, was there, as were British prime minister Margaret Thatcher and other prominent world leaders. In fact, never before had so many heads of state and government been present on such an occasion. Even more important, this impressive event was a clear demonstration of Japan's role as a great world power.

JAPAN'S DEALINGS WITH OTHER NATIONS

When World War II ended in 1945, Japan was a conquered nation, for the first time in its history. Then, during the U.S. occupation and the

165

JAPAN AND THE WORLD

1945–Present

1945	World War II ends. U.S. military occupation of Japan begins. Cold War begins.
1947	New Japanese constitution goes into effect.
1949	*Communists come to power in China.*
1950–1953	*Korean War*
1958	Japan begins to aid Asian nations.
1960s	*Many African nations become independent.*
1962	*Cuban missile crisis.*
1971	Japan pledges to reduce textile exports to the United States.
1973	*Arab oil embargo.*
1977	Japan agrees to limit exports of color TVs to the United States.
1978	Japan signs peace treaty with China.
1979	Japan agrees to begin joint defense planning with the United States.
1981	Japan pledges to limit car exports to the United States.
1983	*Democratic government is restored in Argentina.*
1991	*Persian Gulf War* *Soviet Union becomes Commonwealth of Independent States.*
1992	*South Africa moves toward a multi-racial government.*
	President George Bush visits Japan on a trade mission.
	Japan authorizes use of its troops in UN peacekeeping efforts.

years that followed, the nation devoted its full energies to its economic recovery and firmly committed itself to a peaceful future. Without an army of its own, Japan had to depend on the military forces of the United States for its protection. As a result, Japan's **foreign policy**, or its relations with other nations, was based on trade and commerce, not military power. Thus, Japan did not return to a policy **of isolationism**, or withdrawal from contacts with other nations, as it had done twice earlier in its history. (See Chapter 3.) As events developed, Japan's new foreign policy served the nation well.

Japan and the United States.   As the occupying power, the United States at first fostered the building of democracy in Japan. Later it also encouraged economic rebuilding. Japan's own postwar leaders generally welcomed these policies. The Japanese favored a "low posture" in world affairs. By this they meant seeking good relations with all nations and focusing on economic growth.

During the occupation, the U.S. army built military bases in Japan and stationed a force of 60,000 there. This force acted as a domestic police for the nation as well as a defensive army. The Japanese government and a majority of the people willingly accepted this arrangement, though the Japanese Communist and Socialist parties opposed it as what they termed "American imperialism." The Security Treaty that Japan signed with the United States in 1952 (see Chapter 3), allowed U.S. bases and military forces in the nation to remain there. In this way, Japan continued to depend on the United States for its protection. Under this treaty, in 1992 about 56,000 U.S. troops were still stationed in Japan. It was expected, however, that it would be only a matter of time for this number to be reduced to a largely symbolic force.

Despite its desire for neutrality and peace, Japan worked closely with the United States to ensure its own security as well as the growth of its economy. Thus, Japanese industries produced large amounts of the supplies needed by the U.S. forces fighting in the Korean War. The $4 billion that Japan earned in this way, in turn, strengthened Japan's economy. Japan began to regard its former enemy as its ally, though it was determined not to become involved in the Korean War or any other conflict. During the postwar decade, this policy proved to be a great success for Japan. Its reliance on U.S. military forces for its security freed Japan from the huge costs of providing for its own defense. It was thus free to devote its money and resources to expanding the nation's industrial base and building up its overseas trade.

Japan's Overseas Trade

EXPORTS FROM JAPAN TO:	VALUE (in thousands of U.S. dollars)	PERCENTAGES OF TOTAL EXPORTS
United States	$91,537,637	29.0%
Germany	20,605,352	6.6
South Korea	20,067,881	6.4
Taiwan	18,254,581	5.8
Hong Kong	16,314,613	5.2
Singapore	12,213,087	3.9
United Kingdom	11,039,528	3.5
Thailand	9,431,136	3.0
China	8,593,143	2.7
Malaysia	7,634,605	2.4
Total (all countries)	$314,525,461	100.0%

IMPORTS TO JAPAN FROM:	VALUE (in thousands of U.S. dollars)	PERCENTAGES OF TOTAL IMPORTS
United States	$53,317,255	22.5%
China	14,215,837	6.0
Australia	13,011,325	5.5
Indonesia	12,769,673	5.4
South Korea	12,339,218	5.2
Germany	10,738,726	4.5
United Arab Emirates	10,524,336	4.4
Saudi Arabia	10,080,950	4.3
Taiwan	9,492,501	4.0
Canada	7,698,426	3.3
Total (all countries)	$236,736,729	100.0%

Data covers the year 1991.

Source: "Summary of Trade," Japan Tariff Association

Japan's close relationship with the United States benefited the nation in other ways as well. This growing friendship made it easier for the United States to fulfill its promise to return all the Japanese territory it had occupied after the war. In 1968, Japan regained Iwo Jima and the Bonin Islands, and in 1972 Okinawa again became part of Japan. U.S. efforts to ensure free trade and end tariff barriers among the Western nations also greatly aided Japan's trade. In addition, the United States itself soon became the largest market for the export of Japanese goods. By the mid-1960s, Japan's success in selling to the U.S. market had resulted in a trade surplus with the United States. (See Chapter 6.)

Cold War Tensions. In the setting of the Cold War, the close relations with the United States were not an unmixed blessing. This relation presented problems for the Japanese, and these were based mainly on the fear that its security treaty with the United States would draw Japan into war again. For this reason the presence of U.S. forces in Japan, possibly armed with nuclear weapons, and U.S. pressure to build up its Self-Security Forces disturbed the Japanese people. In addition, the U.S. role in the Vietnam War, which was highly unpopular, raised the fear that it might escalate and become a nuclear war. Left-wing groups in Japan even attempted to prevent the United States from using its military bases in Japan to help wage this war. Demonstrations were held to protest the presence of U.S. warships armed with nuclear weapons in Japanese ports. Because these feelings ran so deep, Japan and the United States quietly extended the security treaty in 1970 without any changes, an action that sidestepped the need for a debate in the Diet. In this way, Japan avoided the possiblity that the debate would touch off new anti-military protests in Japan.

President Richard Nixon's 1972 visit to China and the United States' later recognition of the Chinese Communist government without consulting Japan was regarded as an insult. To the Japanese these moves were a signal that they were still regarded by the United States as junior partners. The "Nixon shock," however, turned into an important advantage for Japan. It made it possible for Japan to proceed with its goal of establishing diplomatic and trade relations with Communist China. It did so later in the year of Nixon's trip to China, ending nearly a century of hostility and conflict between the two nations.

With peaceful relations with China restored, Japan began to provide machinery, machine tools, and technology to the Chinese government. Japan's trade with China grew rapidly, reaching $6.6 billion by 1979 and

$8.5 billion by 1991. The reopening of relations with China was a major step in establishing Japan once again as an Asian power in its own right. It was a forerunner of improved diplomatic contacts with other nations of Asia as well. These in turn were followed by a growth in trade with these nations. Eventually, as a group, the Asian countries became Japan's second-largest trading partners, after the United States.

The "Oil Shock," 1973.   Probably the most important international development affecting Japan in the 1970s was the **embargo** on oil by the Arab nations of the Middle East during the Arab-Israeli War of 1973. The embargo banned all oil shipments to the West and its partners. Japan's economy depended on imported oil for nearly 80 percent of the fuel its businesses and factories consumed. While the oil embargo created oil shortages in Japan, in the long run it demonstrated Japan's resourcefulness in erecting cushions against the possibility of being hit by another oil crisis. First, Japan made fundamental changes in its economy. It shifted from heavy industry, such as steel and chemicals, which requires large amounts of energy, to lighter high technology industries that consume less energy. Second, Japan also began an intensive effort to reduce its energy needs and even to develop nuclear-powered plants to produce electrical energy, despite the Japanese people's deep dislike of nuclear power. The memory of the nuclear blasts of Hiroshima and Nagasaki during World War II was still fresh in the minds of the Japanese.

At the same time, Japan acted to ensure future oil supplies from the Middle East after the oil embargo was ended. Japan began to make loans to Iraq and other Middle East nations. It also vastly increased its exports of machinery and industrial plants to the region in order to develop closer economic links to these oil-rich nations. As a result, the nations of the Middle East soon became another of Japan's major trading partners.

The 1970s clearly demonstrated how vulnerable, or open to injury, Japan was to sudden developments on the international scene such as the oil crisis. Equally disturbing to the Japanese was the country's inability to influence the course of world events. This fact underscored Japan's own lack of power and its dependence on the U.S. military. Yet, the Japanese government and the people alike were not prepared to abandon their commitment to the "low posture" peaceful policy that had enabled their nation to avoid becoming involved in conflicts in any of the world's many trouble spots.

Moving Toward Self-Defense. After the Vietnam War ended in 1975, the United States began to urge Japan to increase its role in its own defense. With that costly and unpopular war over, the U.S. government wished to cut back on its huge outlays for military spending. It therefore pressed Japan to assume greater responsibility for its own self-defense and to begin to play a more active part in international affairs. The United States asked Japan to build up its military and naval power by spending a larger part of its budget on defense. The United States pointed out that the Japanese government spent less than 1 percent of its total GNP on defense. This was in contrast to the 25 to 30 percent of the annual U.S. budget devoted to military spending each year.

Japan resisted much of this pressure and continued to limit its Self-Defense Forces to 250,000 men. Nevertheless, the enormous annual increases in its GNP meant that even by keeping to its 1 percent commitment it would have enough funds to make impressive increases in its military expenditures. Thus, military spending rose significantly, from $3 billion in 1974 to over $40 billion by 1992, and Japan bore an increasingly larger share of the cost of U.S. military bases there. Soon Japan ranked seventh among world nations in defense spending.

In 1979, the Japanese government agreed to begin joint defense planning with the U.S. government. During the 1980s, the two nations held joint military exercises as well. Japan also agreed to accept responsibility for its own defense within an ocean zone of 1,000 miles (1,610 kilometers) from its shores.

Yet, though most Japanese accepted the need for sharing more of their defense burden with the United States, they drew back from any formal alliance. Thus, when the Japanese prime minister referred to the United States and Japan as "allies" in a 1983 speech, many Japanese were upset. They still did not wish to acknowledge that Japan had abandoned its long-standing neutral role in favor of even an unofficial alliance with the United States. In the Persian Gulf War of 1991, Japan supported the United States' successful effort to oust Iraq from Kuwait, but it did not provide forces to serve in the international military coalition. Japan did, however, contribute to paying for the cost of that conflict. Once more, the Japanese had relied on the United States to safeguard their vital interests in the world—this time, Japan's oil lifeline.

New Tensions with the United States. Although Japan's unofficial alliance with the United States seemed to become stronger during the postwar decades, a serious problem developed that intensified as the years went by. Japan's success in rapidly expanding its industries and increasing its trade with the United States after 1965 was at the root of the problem. The U.S. government became concerned about the resulting loss of jobs and even the elimination of some domestic industries. As a result, it began to press Japan to agree to voluntarily limit the amount of certain products it exported to the United States. In 1971, after lengthy negotiations, Japan pledged to reduce its textile exports to the U.S. market. In 1977, Japan signed a similar agreement to limit exports of color TVs. In 1981, after Japanese cars had flooded the U.S. market, the United States pressured Japan to limit its exports to this country to no more than 1.7 million cars a year.

The U.S. government also complained that while Japan was flooding the United States with exports, it was putting restrictions on U.S. exports to Japan. The United States pointed to Japan's restrictions on imports of oranges and beef, which kept U.S. farmers from selling these products to the Japanese. Finally, in 1978, Japan agreed to increase its imports of these U.S. products. Imports then rose very sharply, and by 1989 Japan was buying 76 percent of all U.S. exports of beef and 53 percent of its citrus exports. By 1992, Japan was importing over 20 percent of the farm products exported by U.S. farmers. Nevertheless, Japan

In early 1992, President Bush traveled to Japan to try to persuade the Japanese to buy more U.S. products. Later that year, the Japanese complained about U.S. restrictive import policies.

would not agree to increase imports of rice from the United States because of its long-standing program of subsidizing Japanese rice growers. Even with the concessions that it did make, Japan's trade surplus with the United States reached $5.4 billion in 1976 and continued to grow spectacularly in the years after that. (See Chapter 6.)

Despite such an uneasy relationship with the United States and a distrust of the United States, a poll in 1992 revealed that the Japanese people still regarded the United States as their closest friend in the world. Some Japanese go so far as to say that the United States may be Japan's only friend in the world.

Japan and the Soviet Union and Its Successors. Almost since the end of World War II, Japan had been unhappy and fearful about Soviet policies. Despite its policy of not becoming involved in any of the conflicts stemming from the Cold War, Japan was opposed to Soviet aggression in many parts of the world.

In addition, Japan was involved with the Soviet Union in a dispute close to home. The Soviet Union had occupied Japan's Kurile Islands north of Hokkaido at the end of World War II and refused to return these territories after the war. Japan learned in 1979 that Soviet forces were building up their military strength there and that Soviet naval forces in the area were being increased. Not until the collapse of the Soviet Union in 1991 did negotiations take place with its successors about the return of the islands to Japan. Also aggravating Japan's relations with the Soviet Union was that country's opposition to Japan's new improved relations with Communist China, now one of the Soviet Union's major foes. Japan had good reason, therefore, to join the United States in condemning the Soviet invasion of Afghanistan in 1979. It did so by backing the U.S.-led boycott of the 1980 Olympic Games in Moscow.

During the rest of the 1980s, however, when the Soviet Union abandoned its aggressive foreign policy after Mikhail Gorbachev came to power, Japan tried to improve relations. However, its efforts to negotiate trade and export agreements with the Soviet Union were not successful. Japan's trade with the Soviet Union and its Eastern European satellites was barely 10 percent of its total world trade. After the collapse of the Soviet Union in 1991, Japan provided $700 million in loans for food, medicine, and other purposes. However, in the light of its territorial dispute over the Kurile Islands, Japan was not expected to become involved in bolstering the economy of Russia and the other countries in the Commonwealth of Independent States.

In 1991, these Japanese protested against Soviet leader Gorbachev's visit. They demanded the Soviets return the Kurile Islands, occupied by them since World War II.

Japan and Southeast Asia and the Pacific.   After World War II, Japan worked hard to build good relations with the countries of Southeast Asia and the Pacific. During the war, it had pursued particularly brutal and destructive policies in these regions. With peace, Japan was eager to overcome the hostility with which the people of many Southeast Asian and Pacific lands still regarded it. During the 1950s, the Japanese provided large amounts of aid to countries it had conquered in the war. In 1958 alone, it contributed $200 million to Burma (now Myanmar), $550 million to the Philippines, and $320 million to Indonesia in 1956.

In that year, Japan also began a program to assist Asian nations to develop their economies and thus increase their markets for Japanese goods. These efforts gradually helped to reduce some of the Asians' deep feelings of hostility toward Japan. Japanese industries soon developed an important and growing trade with those countries. Indonesia and Malaysia, which have valuable deposits of oil, soon played a major role in Japanese trade. By the 1970s, the nations of Southeast Asia accounted for nearly 25 percent of Japan's imports and purchased nearly 25 percent of its exported goods. As early as the mid-1960s, over 30 percent of Japan's growing overseas investment was in Southeast Asia. This region continued to be a major area for Japanese investment in the following decades.

Japan continued to strengthen its economic and political ties with Southeast Asia in later decades. It worked closely with Southeast Asian nations to promote economic cooperation among them by founding the Asia Development Bank to make intergovernmental loans. Japan also sharply increased its aid program to these nations, which were soon receiving the largest share of Japanese foreign aid. By 1992, Japan had become the world leader in providing foreign aid to **developing nations,** or nations that were striving to become industrialized. Japan's grants of aid to the developing nations reached more than $10 billion in that year. Indonesia, the Philippines, Thailand, Bangladesh, Myanmar, and India received the largest amounts of this aid.

Japan also had built up close economic relations with Taiwan, South Korea, Hong Kong, and Singapore during the 1970s and 1980s. By then these small nations had developed industrial economies, second only to Japan's in Asia. Japanese banks had made large investments in these newly industrialized countries, and Japanese businesses had set up manufacturing plants there. South Korea became an especially significant trading partner for Japan. However, deep political strains between the two nations remained, dating back to Japan's conquest of Korea during the first half of the 1900s. In Southeast Asia, too, some of the old

Prime Minister Miyazawa met with South Korea's President Roh in 1992 in an effort to heal the decades-old wounds that Japan had inflicted on its East Asian neighbor.

hostility toward Japan remained. It was inflamed by the feeling in the countries there that Japan's great economic success was due in no small measure to the oil and other raw materials it imported from Southeast Asia. The depth of this resentment toward Japan had been revealed in 1974 when a visit by the Japanese prime minister led to riots there.

Japan and Western Europe. Japan's relations with the nations of Western Europe also became more difficult. Throughout the postwar years, European nations maintained more trade barriers, such as tariffs and import quotas, against Japan than any other region of the world. The industrialized nations of Europe, such as West Germany and France, manufacture automobiles and many of the electronic products that make up Japan's leading exports. Even so, Japan signed trade agreements with individual nations to encourage greater free trade and a reduction of European trade barriers. Since the formation of the European Community (EC) by the 12 major nations of Western Europe, many of these restrictions have eased, and the EC now has become one of Japan's largest trading partners.

International Cooperation. Japan joined the United Nations (UN) in 1956, and the Japanese people enthusiastically supported the work of this world body of nations dedicated to peace. Japan actively participated in the programs of various UN agencies to promote the social and economic welfare of the world's developing nations. However, as the Cold War rivalry between the Soviet Union and United States grew in the 1950s and 1960s, the effectiveness of the UN's role in world affairs was reduced. Like many other nations, Japan was forced to accept this growing weakness of the international body.

Japan received a significant setback in the UN in 1978 when its effort to gain a seat in the UN Security Council was defeated. The Security Council is the major policy-making body of the UN. This action was particularly humiliating for the Japanese because the opposition was led by another Asian nation, Bangladesh. This provided new evidence of the continuing suspicion with which many Asian nations still viewed Japan. Many Japanese had not recovered from the shock of this rejection even after Japan was elected to the Security Council in 1980.

In the early 1990s, there was considerable discussion in Japan over whether it should apply for a permanent seat on the Security Council of the UN. After all, it was pointed out, countries with far less economic power sit on the Security Council. Yet, the Japanese government did not openly seek such a seat. One reason may have been that, once on the Security Council, it might have little to say about the international matters that come before that body. This would be a reflection of Japan's decades-long concentration on its own economic growth.

Japan, however, did become a member of most of the international trade and financial organizations established by the industrialized Western nations after World War II. Japan joined the International Monetary Fund (IMF) and cooperated in its work to stabilize world currencies. As a member of the World Bank, it helped provide loans and assistance programs for the developing nations. It became a member of the General Agreement on Tariffs and Trade (GATT), the organization that supervises the international trade policies that are so vital to Japan's growth. Its membership in the Organization for Economic Cooperation and Development (OECD) in 1966 recognized Japan's role as one of the world's seven leading industrialized nations. Japan's prime minister regularly attends the annual summit meeting of the leaders of the OECD nations, where these nations coordinate their economic policies.

JAPAN'S ROLE IN WORLD AFFAIRS TODAY

Japan's enormous economic success not only represents the reward for decades of sacrifice and hard work but also has been a source of growing national pride and confidence. Yet, it has also thrust Japan into the international spotlight. There the world's nations are focusing their attention on Japan's role in world affairs. In this unaccustomed position, Japan's leaders are feeling their way, not always sure how to respond to the new challenges.

Japan in a Changing World. Historic events in the late 1980s and early 1990s brought fundamental changes of importance to Japan. The collapse of communism and the establishment of democracy among the nations of Eastern Europe touched off a series of events that ended in 1991 with the breakup of the Soviet Union. Removing the decades-old threat of world communism also brought an end to the Cold War. With the former Soviet Union split up into many separate states, the United States was now the only world superpower. The United States, relieved of the great burden of the Cold War, began to redefine its role in world affairs. It began to reduce its military power and devoted more of its attention to domestic problems and the strengthening of its own economy. To the United States of the early 1990s, stalled in a lingering reces-

sion, or slowdown in business and industry, Japan's growing trade surplus and investments in the United States seemed, now more than ever, to pose a serious challenge to its economy. Western Europe, also hit by a recession, was no less concerned with Japan's trade policies.

Japan's Dilemma.   Even before these dramatic world events, Japan had been seeking to define its proper role in international affairs. Japan's leaders and its people alike had been exceedingly cautious and uncertain about what that role might be, however. Despite Japan's status as an economic superpower, it was not eager to take on a formal role as a world leader. There were, of course, many reasons for this reluctance.

The Japanese recalled their nation's efforts to become a leading world power during the 1930s and 1940s and the disastrous ending of that dream in defeat. Moreover, most Japanese had long accepted Japan's reliance on the United States for its military defense, thus allowing Japan to concentrate its efforts on achieving the economic miracle that dazzled the world. In this way, without the necessity of becoming a military power, Japan had achieved unparalleled prosperity for its people and increasing dominance in the world economy. Not surprisingly, most Japanese were far from eager to change this successful formula. Indeed, many were fearful that changing Japan's role might even endanger its great economic achievement. In many ways, most Japanese believed it therefore was easier, perhaps even wiser, to continue to follow its "low posture" policy in world affairs.

Many other elements contributed to the dilemma faced by Japan in the early 1990s. Most of these had deep roots in Japanese history and the culture of its people. As an island nation, the Japanese had long been accustomed to relying on themselves for their own well-being. As you have read, even as late as 1600, the nation's leaders had made a conscious decision to isolate themselves from the world. Only when forced by the Western nations in the mid-1800s did Japan emerge from its isolation. Many Japanese are comfortable with the limited role their nation has played in world affairs since 1945, and they continue to believe it is in Japan's best interest not to abandon it for some unknown role of future leadership.

The Japanese view of themselves as a homogeneous and unified people with a unique culture also made it difficult for them to think of assuming a role of greater world leadership. In dealing with other nations, Japanese business people, for example, often consider themselves to be representatives of Japan, their nation, not simply the leaders of large companies. Even in sports, Japanese athletes display this same attitude. For example, Japan's leading woman figure skater formally apologized to her nation for winning the silver medal for second place in the 1992 Olympic Games instead of the first-place gold. Although other countries may find it difficult to understand such behavior and attitudes, the Japanese see it as a recognition of their individual responsibilities to their nation. This focus on Japan as the center of people's lives makes it very difficult for the nation to think about the concerns of the world at large or to consider what role it might play as a world leader.

The sense of being a special people is sometimes interpreted by outsiders as a feeling of superiority toward the peoples of other nations. This attitude is another reason why the Japanese find it so difficult to think in terms of other peoples. Feelings of superiority present a powerful obstacle to Japanese efforts to become active in world leadership.

Another reason the Japanese hesitate to assume world leadership responsibilities is what they consider Japan's increasing vulnerability, or possibility of being weakened. They point out that Japan must depend on importing nearly all the minerals and other raw materials its industries use in making its manufactured products. It also depends on imported oil and coal to provide the power that drives these industries. Moreover, it must import a significant part of its food supply. In these circumstances, the Japanese feel they are at the mercy of world events beyond their control. Further, if as a world leader they should make a move or support a program that would injure one of their major trading partners, they would suffer severe economic consequences. It is very difficult for the Japanese to view the nations of the world as other than trading partners. Accepting the greater and very different responsibilities that international political and moral leadership involves would be an overwhelming challenge for many Japanese.

Despite all these factors, Japan's government and its people reluctantly realize that they must begin to take more responsibility in world affairs. They understand that it is no longer possible to focus solely on their economic development at home and overseas. Many Japanese even have come to accept the fact that many of the reasons that have just been discussed here are, in reality, rationalizations, or arguments used to convince themselves that their present policy is justified. They see that they have been using such rationalizations in order not to have to give up their present policy of limited involvement in world affairs. Equally significant, they now realize that such a policy is no longer appropriate for a nation with the fastest-growing economy in the world.

Moreover, the Japanese know that the profound international changes brought on by the collapse of the Soviet Union and the end of

CASE STUDY:

"Leave Us Alone"

Many Japanese now are debating what Japan's role in the world should be, to what extent it should **internationalize,** or become part of the world community. Toyoo Gyohten [toh-yoh gyoh-ten], an official in the Ministry of Finance, points to some of these problems.

> The Japanese as a group have been amazingly flexible, versatile, and quick to respond to outside influences. In the 7th century, we imported Buddhism and much of Chinese culture. In the 19th century, we responded quickly to a massive encounter with Western culture and absorbed enormous changes. After our defeat in 1945, we again responded effectively to major outside influences. These . . . major encounters and adaptations to the outside world were our experiences in internationalization. But in these . . . cases, we responded as a group. Our leaders, our elite, saw the need for change, assimilated [absorbed] what they thought was necessary to adapt effectively, and transmitted it. The group below remained intact. . . . That was how internationalization worked up until recent years.
>
> Now . . . our interaction with the outside world is becoming so widespread, so diversified, that I don't think the process can be controlled and directed from above, the way it used to be. We may have to learn how to respond in a more individual way. . . .
>
> I am not sure whether we will be flexible and adaptable enough in this phase. . . . Japan's dilemma, now, is that we seem to have gotten big enough and strong enough, so that most Japanese think we can deal with foreigners pretty much on our own terms. . . .
>
> So, I've noticed that . . . in recent years, many Japanese are moving away from internationalization. Some of our businessmen have become quite . . . arrogant [overbearing]. . . . Their attitude toward the outside world is "Leave us alone. Don't bother us with your complaints."

From Martin E. Weinstein, ed. *The Human Face of Japan's Leadership.* New York: Praeger, 1989.

1. According to Toyoo Gyohten, how did Japan respond to other nations before 1945?

2. Why does Toyoo seem to be concerned about changes he sees taking place in Japanese attitudes today?

the Cold War are forcing Japan to redefine its place in the world. This was brought forcefully home to Japan in May 1992 in a speech before the UN General Assembly by Chancellor Helmut Kohl of Germany. He bluntly accused Japan of not doing its share to help the former Soviet Union and the nations of Eastern Europe. "Now especially," he said, "it is time for Japan, an exporting nation, to assume a larger share of the West's common responsibility and, in keeping with her economic strength, to help insure the success of the reforms in Central, Eastern and Southeast Europe and the Commonwealth of Independent States."

Japan's Future in the World.   One important recent change in Japan's international policy has been its new focus on the nations of the **Pacific Rim**. These Pacific Rim nations, forming an arc from China to Korea and Southeast Asia to Australia, also include a larger group of nations stretching from the Philippines across the Pacific to the west coast of the United States and Canada. Japan views this region as a major world economic region whose members can work together in the future to promote free trade for the common welfare of their people. As you have read, Japan now supplies capital and technology to China and newly industrialized Asian nations and also has greatly increased its foreign aid to many other Asian nations. Japan also has increased its trade with Australia and New Zealand, and signed a treaty of friendship with those nations. The United States, which already sells more products to Pacific Rim nations than it ships across the Atlantic, is expected to share with Japan in the forging of new advances in this region. Such a shared effort also would serve to lessen rivalry and competition between them.

Japan also has taken the initiative to try to reduce some of the growing pressure from other industrialized nations to change its economic policies. In 1986, Japan formulated a plan to devote more of its huge trade surpluses to supplying aid to developing nations. In 1987, the Japanese government announced a new five-year plan to help reduce the imbalance of its trade with Western nations. Japan agreed to adopt new policies designed to lessen exports of manufactured goods to the United States and other industrial nations and to encourage the Japanese to buy more foreign-made products.

By the early 1990s, *kokusaika* (koh-koo-SEYE-kah), or internationalization, was a word heard very often throughout Japan. This Japanese word means building closer ties to other nations. Yet, the changes this might bring about in Japan itself and in its position in the world were still unclear. Japan had only begun to consider seriously the possible roles it might play on the world scene.

Chapter 7:
CHECKUP

REVIEWING THE CHAPTER

I. Building Your Vocabulary

Match the definitions with their terms.

developing nations	isolation
foreign policy	recession
"low posture"	embargo
Pacific Rim	*kokusaika*

1. seeking good relations with all nations without aligning militarily with any side

2. a policy of internationalization

3. a ban on exports

4. nations that are striving to become industrialized

5. arc of nations from China to Korea and Southeast Asia to the Philippines and across the Pacific to the United States

6. being cut off or separated from other nations

7. a nation's relations with other nations

8. a slowdown in business and industry

II. Understanding the Facts

Write the letter of the correct answer to each statement.

1. After World War II, Japan's foreign policy was based on:
   a. military power. b. trade and commerce.
   c. imperialism. d. foreign aid.

2. The Arab oil embargo of 1973 affected Japan more than some other nations because:
   a. Japan exported oil to the Middle East.
   b. the United States also cut off oil shipments to Japan.
   c. Japan depended on oil from the Middle East.
   d. Japan's electronic industries consumed more energy than had its heavy industry.

3. During the 1970s, Japan began to assume greater responsibility for its own defense when the United States:
a. pressed Japan to increase its defense spending.
b. withdrew its military forces from Japan.
c. signed a treaty of alliance with Japan.
d. refused to sign a new defense agreement with Japan.

4. The growing tensions between Japan and the United States during the years after the 1970s were mainly caused by:
a. Japan's increasing exports and investments in the United States.
b. trade restrictions and regulations on Japanese exports to the United States.
c. the lack of free trade policies among the world's nations.
d. disputes over Okinawa and Iwo Jima.

5. In recent years Japan has been seeking to define its proper role in world affairs because:
a. the Japanese know they must abandon their insularity and feelings of superiority.
b. Japan wishes to continue to focus its attention on the economic development of its own nation.
c. the nations of Southeast Asia have become its major trade partners.
d. Japan's growth as an economic superpower requires it to accept greater responsibility.

III. Thinking It Through

Write the letter of your correct conclusion to each sentence next to its number.

1. Japan's 1947 U.S.-sponsored Constitution, which pledged the nation never to go to war and not to build up its military forces:
a. clearly expressed the Japanese people's determination to avoid war.
b. was a provision that the Japanese people deeply resented.
c. was designed to save the United States the expense of monitoring Japan's security forces.
d. became a major source of tension between Japan and the United States.

2. During the Cold War, Japan's strong commitment to peace and neutrality was shown by:
   a. its support of the United States in the Vietnam War.
   b. its willingness to allow the United States to keep the Pacific islands captured during World War II.
   c. giving aid to developing nations.
   d. its hesitation in taking sides with either the United States or the Soviet Union.

3. During the 1970s and 1980s, events like the Arab oil embargo, the Vietnam War, and the Soviet invasion of Afghanistan:
   a. made the Japanese even less willing to take greater responsibility for their own defense.
   b. convinced many Japanese that their nation should sign a treaty of alliance with the United States.
   c. demonstrated how vulnerable Japan was to sudden developments in the world.
   d. made many Japanese urge their government to withdraw from the UN.

4. Japan agreed to voluntarily limit its exports of certain products to the United States in order to:
   a. increase the price of those products in the United States.
   b. ease growing tensions with the United States over trade.
   c. reduce the regulations and restrictions on U.S. exports to Japan.
   d. increase the power of Asian nations of the Pacific Rim.

5. Japan was slow to assume its world responsibilities as an economic superpower because:
   a. it did not wish to risk the possibility of being a rival of the United States in foreign policy.
   b. the European nations and the Soviet Union opposed such an effort by Japan.
   c. Japan feared this would increase tensions with its Asian trading partners.
   d. it did not wish to risk offending the nations with which it traded.

DEVELOPING CRITICAL THINKING SKILLS

1. Explain why the death of Emperor Hirohito in 1989 demonstrated that Japan's position in the world had changed greatly since its defeat in World War II.

2. Describe some of the ways Japan's "low posture" policy has benefited the nation in its foreign relations.

3. Explain why Japan is vulnerable to sudden changes in world events such as the "oil shock" of 1973 and the Gulf War of 1991.

4. Describe some of the steps Japan has taken to increase its role in its own defense.

5. Explain some of the reasons Japan faces a dilemma as it seeks to define its proper role in international affairs.

ENRICHMENT AND EXPLORATION

1. Choose a small group of your classmates to role play delegates to the 1978 session of the United Nations at which Japan was defeated in its effort to be elected to a term on the Security Council. Divide the group into four pairs of students. One pair will represent Japan, a second pair will represent the United States, the third pair will represent the other Western industrial nations, and the last pair will represent the developing nations of the world. As each pair casts its vote, it should state the reasons why it is voting for or against the proposal. Do research to compare the votes of the class members with the actual votes of the UN members. Discuss any differences and why they occurred.

2. Reread the discussion in your text on "Japan in a Changing World." Then select the two or three factors you think best explain why Japan hesitates to become a leader in world affairs. Using your own words, write a short summary of these reasons and conclude it with a brief statement of what you believe Japan's role should be in the future.

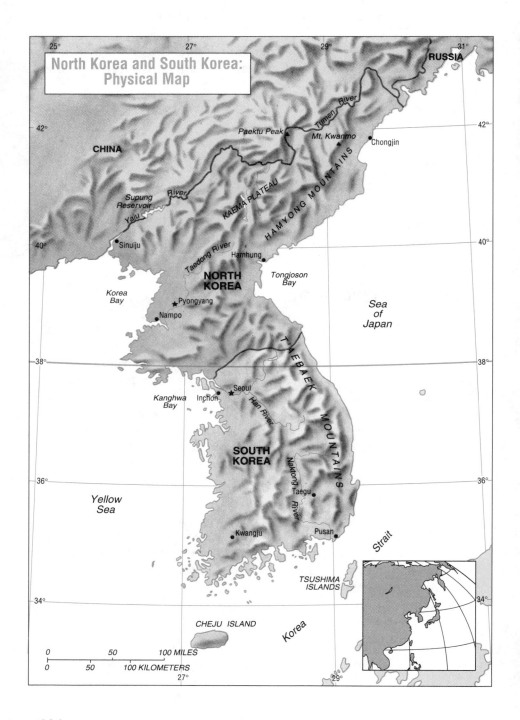

North Korea and South Korea:
Physical Map

RUSSIA

CHINA

Paektu Peak ▲   Turmen River
                Mt. Kwanmo ▲   ● Chongjin

Supung
Reservoir   River
        Yalu   KAEMA PLATEAU   HAMYONG MOUNTAINS

● Sinuiju

                        Taedong River
                                    Hamhung ●
                        NORTH
                        KOREA   Tongjoson
                                     Bay

Korea
Bay   ★ Pyongyang   Sea
        Nampo ●   of
                                                    Japan

Seoul
Kanghwa   Inchon ★
Bay   Han River   T A E B A E K

                SOUTH   M O U N T A I N S
                KOREA

                            Naktong River

Yellow   Taegu ●
Sea

            Kwangju ●   Pusan ●
                                            Strait

                                    TSUSHIMA
                                    ISLANDS

CHEJU ISLAND   Korea

0   50   100 MILES
0   50   100 KILOMETERS

8 Korea: The Land and the People

The U.S. visitors to Seoul, the capital city of South Korea, were struck by the same two things about the city that impress most visitors. They were awed by the great beauty of Seoul, with its towering mountains in the background and the amazing contrasts to be seen in its buildings and monuments. Here were tall modern office buildings, banks, and hotels like those in New York or Chicago or any other large U.S. city. The sleek glass exterior of a structure like the Lotte Hotel contrasted with a lovely park across the way that was reached by an underground connection. There were so many cars and buses on Seoul's wide avenues that pedestrians had to cross them through underground tunnels. Once in the park, the travelers were astonished to see a majestic palace, the Toksu (tahk-soo) Palace, the residence of Korea's last king, which was built in the 14th century.

As they continued along Sejong-ro (say-jahng-roh), Seoul's main street, the Americans passed the city hall, several foreign embassies, and tall office buildings. Then, they walked through a large ancient city gate and were standing before another royal residence, the Changdok (chahng-dahk) Palace, which was the home of Korea's rulers before Toksu Palace was built. After visiting the palace museum, they decided to spend some time in the vast gardens near the palace, where people often stroll for hours down paths bordered by flowers and ponds and cross over streams by footbridges. In this peaceful setting it was hard for the visitors to remember that they were in a city of 11 million people.

It would have taken much more time to visit the Buddhist temples, the city gates, the royal tombs, the churches, and museums of the capital. Yet, the visitors had already discovered that in Korea the nation's ancient history and its modern society exist comfortably side by side.

KOREA'S GEOGRAPHY AND CLIMATE

Korea is located on an East Asian peninsula that juts down from the Chinese mainland and lies between China and Japan. It occupies an area of land roughly the size of the state of Minnesota. Its southern half has a temperate climate, much like that of New York State. Its northern part has a harsher climate, like that of Quebec, Canada. Since 1948, Korea has been divided into two separate nations, North Korea and South Korea.

Geography and Landscape. To the east of the Korean peninsula is the Sea of Japan, which the Koreans call the East Sea. To the west lies the Yellow Sea. To the south is the narrow Korea Strait, which separates Korea from Japan, less than 120 miles (192 kilometers) away. Nearly 3,400 offshore islands border the peninsula.

The Korean peninsula is a rugged, beautiful land consisting largely of mountains and high hills. In fact, Korea is one of the most mountainous areas in the world—the name Korea itself means "land of high mountains and sparkling streams." It has a relatively small land area, extending about 620 miles (1,000 kilometers) from north to south and averaging about 170 miles (250 kilometers) from east to west.

Korea's major mountain chain, the Taebaek (te-bek) Mountains, extends from north to south along the eastern coastline, forming the backbone of the Korean peninsula. Mountains and hills also cover most of the southwestern area of the peninsula. Altogether, nearly 70 percent of Korea is mountains and steep hills. Since farming there is difficult, only about 25 percent of the population lives in this rugged terrain. Most Koreans live in the low-lying plains found along the western coast as well as in the northeast and near the southern coast. The major Korean cities are located in these coastal plains, including Seoul, the capital of South Korea, and Pyongyang, North Korea's capital city. The most fertile soil and the principal farming areas also are in these lowland plains and river valleys. Thus, even though South Korea has only 45 percent of the total land area of the peninsula, compared to 55 percent for North Korea, South Korea's far larger area of plains enables it to sustain a population twice that of North Korea.

Korea's location in East Asia has had a profound effect on the land throughout its history. With the huge Chinese empire to the north and Japan not far off its eastern coast, Korea has often been a battleground for invading armies. At the same time, its mountainous landscape served as a shield that allowed the Koreans to forge their identity as a homogeneous people.

Because of Korea's location so close to China, Chinese culture spread to Korea early in its history and had a major role in shaping the culture of the Korean people. Korea also served as a bridge by which China's rich culture spread to Japan. (See Chapter 2.) Its location also influenced Korea's destiny in yet another way. Surrounded by water on three sides, with a 6,000-mile (9,600-kilometer) coastline, Korea has been able to depend on fishing as a major source of its food supply. The ocean currents in the East Sea provide an abundance of many varieties of fish, shellfish, and edible seaweed.

The Climate of Korea.   Most of the Korean peninsula has a temperate climate, though conditions vary somewhat from north to south. In the north, summers are hot, rainy, and relatively brief, while winters are dry and very cold. In the south, winters are also dry but milder, and summer lasts longer and brings even more rainfall. The milder climate in South Korea makes possible a longer growing season there. As a result, South Korean farmers are able to plant two crops of rice, soybeans, and barley annually, while North Korean farmers generally can raise only one crop each year. The greater agricultural productivity of South Korea is another key reason why it has been able to sustain a much larger population than that of North Korea.

Energy, Minerals, and Human Resources.   The Korean peninsula's most abundant resource is its rivers. There are several major rivers as well as many other swift-flowing rivers and streams in Korea. Most of them flow westward from the Taebaek Mountains toward the Yellow Sea. Many of these rivers have been harnessed by dams to provide **hydroelectric power,** which is a major source of energy. Both North and South Korea rely on the electric power generated by these dams to fuel their growing industries and provide for their expanding cities.

Nature has not endowed Korea with an abundant supply of natural resources. Most of the minerals and other resources are in the northern part of the Korean Peninsula. Fairly large amounts of coal, iron ore, copper, tungsten, lead, and zinc are mined in North Korea and used in manufacturing there. South Korea has far fewer resources. In recent years, however, new deposits of iron ore and coal have been discovered there and now make an important contribution to that nation's newly industrialized economy. Yet, South Korea lacks the natural resources

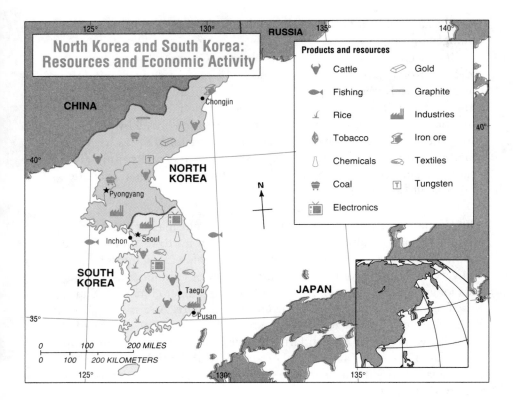

North Korea and South Korea: Resources and Economic Activity

Products and resources

Cattle		Gold	
Fishing		Graphite	
Rice		Industries	
Tobacco		Iron ore	
Chemicals		Textiles	
Coal		Tungsten	
Electronics			

that today give North Korea an important advantage in the development of its heavy industries like steel, cement, and chemicals. As a
result, South Korea's manufacturing base has turned more to the production of electronics and other high-technology products which use
fewer such raw materials and depend more on the skills of its highly
educated workforce.

The workforce of both North Korea and South Korea, which is liter-
ate and highly motivated, is perhaps the most important resource in
both countries. The Korean people are among the best educated and
highly skilled in the world. Their culture places a high value on education and hard work, making them efficient and productive workers. In
North Korea, as you will read, the communist government tirelessly
bombards workers with propaganda about the importance of their labor
and the contribution they must make in building a strong communist
nation there. By contrast, in democratic South Korea, the workforce is
more highly motivated by the traditional Confucian values of the worth
of hard work as one of the elements of a harmonious society.

THE KOREAN PEOPLE

Koreans are an ancient people who trace their civilization back thousands of years. Over these many centuries, the Korean people forged a strong sense of common identity. Koreans see themselves as a people with a proud heritage that sets them apart from their Chinese and Japanese neighbors. Their pride has helped them endure foreign conquests and the division of their country after World War II.

The Early Koreans.   Although Koreans have been divided into two parts—North Korea and South Korea—for nearly half a century, they still consider themselves to be one people. Indeed, they are a single, homogeneous people. The origins of the Korean people are still being investigated by archaeologists and historians. While they have not yet discovered all the facts, they do know that the early peoples of Korea arrived there from Central Asia about 10,000 years ago. Over a long period of time, other small bands of hunting people from Mongolia and North China moved into the Korean Peninsula. Some of these same groups also reached Japan and became the ancestors of the modern Japanese people.

By about 2000 B.C., small groups were located along Korea's coastal plains, where they now lived by fishing as well as by hunting. Gradually, they developed more settled ways of living as they learned to plant rice and make pottery. Stone tools and weapons eventually gave way to ones

North Korea and South Korea

COUNTRY	POPULATION	AREA	RURAL / URBAN RATIO	LIFE EXPECTANCY	INFANT MORTALITY (per 1,000 live births)	LITERACY RATE
North Korea	22,627,000	46,540 sq. mi . 120,570 sq. km.	38 / 62	67 M 73 F	32.0	99%
South Korea	43,545,000	38,025 sq. mi . 98,510 sq. km.	32 / 68	66 M 73 F	25.5	92

M = Male
F = Female

Source: *World Almanac, 1992;* UN Population Division

made of iron and bronze. These groups probably lived together in dwellings built in pits in the ground as well as in hillside caves. By about 500 B.C., these ancestors of the present-day Korean people had settled throughout the peninsula. They established three early kingdoms that were gradually united into a more powerful Korean state. This state then ruled Korea for the next 1,000 years, as you will read in the next chapter.

The Family and Society.   The family occupies a place of central importance in Korean society. Harmonious family life has been viewed as necessary to the peace and prosperity of the nation. Thus, family members view their family relations as the central element in their lives and place great value on the social status of their family. The traditional extended family, including grandparents as well as parents and their children, is, however, being replaced by the smaller nuclear family of husband and wife and their children. Crowded housing conditions in urban areas are, in large part, responsible for this change. Along with the growth of the urban nuclear family is the growing participation of women in the workforce.

A Korean mother carries her young child on her back while doing her farm work. Such closeness strengthens Korean children's strong sense of family and family obligation.

Growing numbers of Koreans live in cities today. Even under the new conditions of city living, however, Koreans observe the traditional ideals of family living stressed by the ancient Chinese philosopher Confucius in the 6th and 5th centuries B.C. These include the importance of respect for the family's ancestors, the authority of the father, and proper relations between parent and child, husband and wife, and older brother and younger brother. Children are expected to display filial piety, the Confucian ideal of showing respect for one's parents and elders and devotion to the family's welfare.

In Korea, marriage is a matter that concerns the entire family. The traditional practice of arranged marriages is still carried on, although this custom is fading. However, even in marriages that are initiated by the young people themselves, they usually seek the approval of their parents. The importance of continuing the family line unbroken from generation to generation still has a strong hold over Koreans. This is reinforced by a law that forbids marriage between a man and a woman who are even distantly related on their fathers' side. The family kinship link from generation to generation is more important to most Koreans than the relations between husband and wife.

Family roles have been changing in recent years. Fathers have less absolute authority than in the past. Mothers have assumed greater independence and equality as they carry on their traditional role of caring for and raising the children.

In the past, following Confucian tradition, at the ages of six or seven, boys and girls were separated. They were not even allowed to sit in the same room. Boys went to school, while girls were trained to perform household tasks, marking the beginning of their role as inferiors in society. Today, however, children of both sexes attend school and they are treated more equally within most families.

Nevertheless, in society at large, segregation of men and women still is widely practiced. Men and women seldom mingle in social groups. Instead they usually join together with friends of the same sex. Men often spend their evenings with male friends whom they have known from school or with whom they work. Korean men generally spend little time with their families, leaving most family responsibilities to women. The social separation of the sexes still makes it difficult for Korean women to achieve equality in society. For example, it is a huge obstacle to equal job opportunities for women. Women find it difficult to enter the professions and many other fields of work or even to secure equal wages at less skilled jobs, as you will read.

CASE STUDY:

Families in Korea

The following selection, written by a U.S. professor who has studied Korean society, clearly shows the importance of the family in Korean society and the values and traditions it represents.

> Most Koreans . . . would not agree that they, as individuals, should think of themselves as separate from their parents and families. The close family ties and dependencies valued so highly in Korea might seem unhealthy to us; to Koreans . . . "a life in which egos [individuals] are all autonomous, separate. . . . and self-sufficient [is] too cold, impersonal, lonely and inhuman."
>
> Children [in Korea] incur a debt to their parents who gave birth to them and raised them. This debt lies behind the idea of filial duty: treating parents respectfully at all times, taking care of them in their old age, mourning them well at proper funerals, and performing ceremonies for them after their deaths. Even fulfilling these duties, however, is not enough to repay the debt to one's parents. The full repayment also entails [requires] having children and maintaining the continuity of the family line. The continuity of the family line is thus a biological fact which human society, in accordance with natural law, should reflect. . . .
>
> Koreans incorporate the fact of biological continuity into their family life according to the ancient ideas of birth and conception. Mothers traditionally were thought to produce the flesh of their children, and fathers to provide the bones. As bone endures longer than flesh, kinship through males was thought more binding than through females. Even today men pass on membership in their clan [group] to their children, while women do not. Thus, although maternal second cousins may marry, no one with any degree of kinship through males, no matter how remote, can.

From Clark W. Sorensen, "The Korean Family," in *Korea.* New York: The Asia Society, 1986.

1. What is the reason traditionally given for the fact that in Korea the family line passes down from the father rather than from the mother?

2. What duties are expected of a Korean child?

The Importance of Education. The age-old tradition of scholarship and learning found in both Buddhist and Confucian teachings continues to be strong in Korean society today, especially in South Korea. Families there willingly make great sacrifices so that their children can receive the best possible education. In South Korea, as in Japan, education is most important in determining a person's future career and position in society.

Today, all South Korean children are required to attend school for nine years. After they finish elementary school, students usually spend three years at a middle school and then three years studying in high school. Although attending the upper grades is not compulsory, most students complete high school. However, parents must help pay some of the costs of their children's education in the middle school and high school.

The government of South Korea supervises public education and plans the curriculum and textbooks for all courses. While Korean education is formally modeled on that of the United States, it has been shaped by Korean values. The subjects taught in high school are similar to those studied by U.S. students—math, science, geography, music, physical education, and art. Korean history and culture are regarded as especially important subjects of study, since they help inspire students' pride in their nation and their cultural heritage. Special courses in moral education also are designed to strengthen traditional values, such as filial piety and loyalty. In recent years, many students have been attending vocational and technical high schools where specialized training and job skills are a major part of the curriculum. The transformation of Korea into an industrialized nation has spurred this trend.

More than half of all of South Korea's high school graduates go on to college. To gain admission to a college or university requires rigorous study, since students first must pass a difficult entrance exam. Competition for admission to the leading universities is extremely keen, since graduates of Seoul National, Koryo, and Yonsei universities enjoy enormous prestige and are often recruited for careers in government and the professions. The most promising high school students try for these schools, and, as in Japan, attend after-school private tutoring schools to prepare for their college entrance examinations. There are, however, many national universities in the provinces as well as private universities and engineering and vocational colleges.

The pressure on students to obtain the best possible education has been so great that the government attempted in the 1980s to curb special tutoring to pass college entrance exams. It also tried to eliminate the

An art student painting the scene in the yard of an historic palace in Seoul. Koreans have a strong sense of identification with the monuments of their nation's past.

examinations given for admission to the best high schools. However, graduating from a good high school and then being admitted to a leading university still remains the goal of most families for their children. This is true even though striving to reach that goal is often stressful for both children and parents and a burden on the family budget.

In North Korea, public education is directed by the government to serve the needs of the state. All students must attend school for 11 years, with 5 years of elementary and 6 years of secondary education. Education is used primarily as a means of implanting communist ideology in students' minds and strengthening their loyalty to the government. The content of education also is geared to the skills needed by the nation's workforce. Technical and vocational training is stressed in North Korea's schools. Many cities also have technical schools that provide special training for adults. The best secondary school graduates may attend Kim Il-Sung University or one of the 140 other colleges in North Korea. Most university students are trained as engineers, scientists, and technology specialists whose skills are needed to continue North Korea's ambitious program of industrialization.

Religious Traditions. The early people of Korea worshiped spirits and demons that they believed dwelled in nature and controlled their lives. In those ancient times, people constantly faced life-threatening dangers from floods, failure of their food supply, and sickness and disease as indications of nature beyond their control. They therefore devised a system of rituals, or ceremonies, to satisfy the spirits that brought about these calamities. **Shamans**, or priests, held ceremonies in which they appealed to their ancestors to drive out evil spirits. This early religion, known as **shamanism,** is still found among some rural people in the more isolated villages of North and South Korea. Traces of shamanist belief sometimes are still seen even in today's cities. For example, public ceremonies may be held to pray for the end to a series of traffic accidents or to invoke good fortune for the future when a major new building is dedicated. Also, many people who want help with their personal problems or who wish to learn about the future consult fortune tellers. This is thought to be a heritage of shamanism.

Buddhism. Buddhism, which spread to Korea from China in the 4th century A.D., remains a strong religious tradition in South Korea. The imposing Buddhist temples and shrines found today throughout South Korea include some of the country's most beautiful works of architecture. Giant statues of the Buddha also dot the landscape and add to its beauty. In North Korea, by contrast, the government officially discourages religion and has converted many Buddhist temples to other uses.

Buddhism's teachings and its emphasis on the attainment of enlightenment through meditation have held great appeal for Koreans, as they have for other peoples of Asia. For many South Koreans, Buddhism also provides a strong symbolic link with Korea's past and a sense of stability at a time when their own lives are undergoing rapid change. Buddhist monks and nuns continue to conduct traditional religious ceremonies today much as they did centuries ago. Buddhism remains the leading religious faith in South Korea, with the largest number of followers.

Confucianism. Confucianism is a moral and ethical system that has greatly influenced the lives and beliefs of Koreans. Brought to Korea from China in the 14th century A.D., Confucian ideals were soon incorporated into government, education, and many other aspects of Korean society. (You have already read about the role of Confucian ideals in family life on page 193.)

Confucianism taught that all human relationships were fixed and determined in order to promote harmony in society. All relationships were said to be based on the concept of subordination, or the relation-

197

ship of superiors and inferiors. These relationships ranged from the ruler, at the top of the scale, who held the position of greatest power, to the humblest subject, who was powerless. Each member of society had to recognize his or her proper role and behave in ways that were suited to it.

Confucianism also stressed the importance of learning and scholarship in people's lives. Those who were well educated and pursued scholarly study were judged superior to those who remain uneducated and ignorant. These Confucian beliefs were carried out by Korea's monarchs through an official examination system for government offices as well as by their view of their own proper moral duties as rulers.

Today, Confucianism has fewer practitioners than Buddhism or Christianity in South Korea. Still, its beliefs are strongly reflected in many aspects of daily life, as you have read. The most visible signs are the traditional rituals performed at weddings and during mourning for the dead. Other ceremonies honoring families' ancestors are still widely practiced, especially during the festival of *ch'usok* (choo-sahk), or the moon festival, celebrated in mid-September.

Christianity. Christianity has been an important religious influence in modern Korea, although it did not reach Korea until fairly recent times. Roman Catholicism, the first Christian faith introduced, was brought to Korea in 1783 by Korean envoys to China. They brought back with them writings on Christianity by Catholic missionaries who had tried to convert the Chinese. However, Catholicism met strong resistance from the government, which feared that the new religion's opposition to Confucian reverence for and worship of people's ancestors would weaken Korean society. Thus, Korean Catholics were persecuted severely. The Catholic Church did not gain real strength in Korea until the late 1800s. Protestant missionaries from the United States first brought their faiths to Korea in the 1880s. Various denominations of Protestantism spread rapidly during the next century.

These were years of conflict and foreign occupation in Korea, and Christianity, with its promise of redemption and a future life, gained widespread appeal among many Koreans. Christian missionaries built schools and played an important role in Korean education. Some of Korea's leading universities were founded as Christian colleges. In recent years fundamentalist Christian sects, which stress belief in the literal interpretion of the words of the Bible and the assurance of salvation through faith, have gained believers. As a result, Christianity is the second-largest religion in South Korea, with more than 7 million worshipers.

An Urbanized Society. Despite Koreans' long history, the last 50 years have brought social change that has been more rapid and remarkable than most developments in the past. Both North Korea and South Korea have become urbanized. That is, they have become nations in which most of the people live in cities. Since the 1950s, farming villages and towns have declined as more and more of their people have moved to cities. Since Korea's major cities are located on the coastal plains, which make up only 20 percent of the land, this has meant that a larger and larger portion of the population has been crowding into a small area of the peninsula. The result has been that South Korea, especially, has one of the highest rates of population density of any nation in the world. You will recall from Chapter 1 that population density is the number of people per square mile or square kilometer in a country.

A few statistics will show how rapidly the population pattern of Korea has changed. Before the 1930s, Korea was an agricultural nation and nearly all its people made their living as farmers. In 1930, less than 6 percent of Koreans lived in cities. Then, as industries were developed, the number of Koreans living in cities reached 12 percent by 1940 and

Modern Seoul houses the factories, banks, and other businesses that spark South Korea's industrial economy as well as many buildings from its centuries-old past.

nearly 20 percent by 1950. Yet, in 1950, the vast majority of the people still lived as farmers in rural areas in both North and South Korea. However, all this quickly changed in the next few decades, the years following the Korean War. This change was more rapid in South Korea than in North Korea.

From 1960 to 1991, South Korea's urban population more than doubled, from 29 percent to 68 percent of the total population. Thus, in just 31 years, South Korea's society was transformed by the nation's industrialization and the continuous growth of Seoul, Pusan, and other cities. Today, the population of South Korea's cities continues to grow as the number of people living in the countryside continues to decline. The population of Seoul has reached 11 million, making it the home of nearly one fourth of South Korea's population and one of the largest cities in the world. Pusan, the nation's second-largest city, has a population of 3.8 million. In addition, the population of Taegu (teh-goo) has grown to 2.2 million, and there are three other cities with populations of more than 1 million each.

Few nations in history have seen so dramatic a shift take place among their population in such a brief span of years. Even Japan, which experienced urbanization and industrialization later than most other nations, needed more than a century for this development. The sudden, accelerated pace of change in South Korea produced strains and great hardships both among the farming population and the growing numbers of newcomers to the cities. Yet, despite these fundamental changes in its society, Korean culture and traditions survived and were adapted to the new urban landscape of the late 20th century. One of the forces that made this possible was the Saemaul Undong (say-mah-ool oon-dahng) movement.

Saemaul Undong.   The New Community Movement, which is what *Saemaul Undong* means, was launched by the South Korean government in 1971 to help smooth the transition from a farming nation to an industrialized power. In the following years, it helped Korea modernize and change from a developing nation into a newly industrialized country.

Until 1971, the government had paid little attention to agriculture, and farm production lagged far behind industrial growth. Most South Korean farmers lacked agricultural machinery and knowledge of improved farming technology. Thus, farmers' incomes remained low, often amounting to less than half of the wages earned by city workers. As the farmers suffered increasing hardships, more and more young people left their family farms to seek jobs in cities. Yet, they lacked

These farmers, on the island of Cheju, were among those who were helped to modernize and increase their output by the South Korean government's New Community Movement.

training and skills for the jobs in the new factories and industries being established in the nation's rapidly expanding urban centers. At the same time, the departure of workers from farms caused a severe labor shortage in industry.

To remedy this situation, the South Korean government set the goal of the third five-year plan, introduced in 1972, as "balanced growth between industry and agriculture." In farming communities, the new plan encouraged villagers to learn to work together in a spirit of self-help to modernize their farms. Government aid was provided to purchase farm machinery, new seeds, and fertilizers. Farmers were taught how to store and market their crops more efficiently. The nationwide program was a success and clearly strengthened farmers' self-reliance and self-confidence.

In the rapidly growing cities, the Saemaul Undong movement helped industrial workers adjust to city life with its often-bewildering crowded environments. It encouraged them to retain the feeling of kinship and belonging that had marked their lives in the villages before moving to the cities. It fostered cooperation and practical action to improve urban conditions. It encouraged people to form friendships with their neighbors, volunteer to help keep their neighborhoods clean, and plan community action programs to benefit all families. In these ways, Saemaul Undong helped ease some of the painful shifts that have been taking place in South Korea's society.

REVIEWING THE CHAPTER

I Building Your Vocabulary

Match the terms with the correct definitions below.

urbanized   filial piety
population density   shamanism
Saemaul Undong   hydroelectric power

1. the Confucian ideal of respect for one's parents and elders

2. the "New Community Movement" launched by South Korea in 1971

3. describing a nation in which most of the people live in cities

4. the number of people per square mile or square kilometer in a country

5. early Korean religion that worshipped spirits and demons in nature

6. energy derived from the flow of water

II. Understanding the Facts

Complete each of the following statements.

1. The _____ climate of South Korea makes it possible for farmers there to plant two crops of rice each year.

2. The Korean people are a _____ people who share a common culture and ethnic background.

3. Since Korea is a mountainous peninsula, most of its major cities are located on the plains along the _____ .

4. As part of their Confucian heritage, Koreans regard the _____ as the central element in society.

5. The leading religions in South Korea are Buddhism and _____.

III. Thinking It Through

Write the letter of your correct conclusion to each sentence.

1. The Korean people are the most important resource in their nation because:
   a. they have developed the abundant natural resources and raw materials found in both North and South Korea.
   b. they are among the best educated and highly skilled in the world.
   c. they must make up for the lack of other forms of power.
   d. they are devout believers in both Confucianism and Buddhism.

2. The government of South Korea has made a special effort to:
   a. improve agriculture while the country has industrialized.
   b. relocate people from farms to the cities.
   c. build large office buildings in Seoul and other cities.
   d. discourage people from following any religion.

3. One great difference between North Korea and South Korea is that North Korea:
   a. does not believe in educating its people.
   b. has little industry.
   c. urges its people to work for the good of the communist state.
   d. has more people than South Korea.

4. Improvement in the position of women in South Korea is shown by the fact that:
   a. most marriages are no longer arranged.
   b. women may now marry men who are distantly related to them.
   c. working women are paid the same as men for the same jobs.
   d. women have greater independence in the home.

5. The lasting influence on education of Korea's Confucian and Buddhist heritage is shown by the fact that:
   a. great value is placed on scholarship and learning.
   b. religion is required to be the focus of all education.
   c. the leading universities are supported by religious groups.
   d. students are given vocational and technical training.

DEVELOPING CRITICAL THINKING SKILLS

1. Describe the main geographical features of the Korean peninsula and explain how they have influenced Korea's history.

2. Explain how the Saemaul Undong movement has attempted to ease the great strains and hardships faced by South Koreans as their nation has rapidly changed from a rural to an urbanized society.

3. Describe the Korean family and the responsibilities of children to their parents.

4. Explain why Koreans regard education as such an important part of their lives.

5. Describe some of the ideals and beliefs of Confucianism.

ENRICHMENT AND EXPLORATION

1. In your library, consult a tourist's guidebook on South Korea. Study its description of the capital city of Seoul and then make a list of key places in Seoul that you would like to visit and learn more about. Write a one- or two-sentence description of each place, including when it was built, its purpose, its size, and how it looks today.

2. Make a chart comparing the religions of Korea with the religions of Japan. Under separate headings for each country, list each religion that its people practice and some of the main beliefs of each religion. Indicate the two most widely practiced religions in each country, the earliest religion in each, and the religion introduced most recently in each.

9 Korea: A History of Unity and Division (Prehistory–1953)

At first it seemed that nothing could stop the Japanese invaders. They had landed in southern Korea in the spring of 1592 and quickly forced the small Korean army to retreat. The large, well-armed Japanese force of 160,000 men pushed steadily north. In less than a month, the Japanese had captured the Korean capital at Seoul and overrun the Korean peninsula. Then, just when things seemed hopeless, the Korean navy launched an attack against the Japanese ships that were bringing supplies and reinforcements from Japan. From May to July, the Korean navy, commanded by Admiral Yi Sun-sin (ee soon-sihn), fought fiercely against these Japanese supply ships, sinking nearly 250 vessels. Then Admiral Yi attacked the Japanese fleet at Pusan and sank over half the ships there. This daring sea campaign was one of the major reasons why Japan's invasion of Korea ended in failure.

Korea's great naval victory against Japan in 1592 was one of the first sea battles in which armored ships were ever used. Admiral Yi's fleet of 80 ships included a number of the armored vessels, or "turtle ships," that moved more quickly and skillfully than the Japanese ships. Japanese sailors were astonished when the weapons they fired bounced harmlessly off these Korean vessels. Mysterious, dense clouds of smoke also surrounded the turtle ships. The crews on the few Japanese ships that got near them could hardly believe what they saw. The turtle ships were covered with iron plate and pointed objects and were armed with heavy guns. Most astonishing of all, they were decorated with large carved turtle heads that gave off thick sulfur smoke to conceal their movements.

Korea was able to defeat another attempted Japanese invasion in 1597. Yet, Korea was not always as fortunate throughout its long history. Earlier, during the 13th century, Korea had been con-

A HISTORY OF UNITY AND DIVISION

Prehistory–1953

c. 900 B.C.	Early Koreans use bronze weapons and tools.
c. 400 B.C.	Early state of Choson is established.
104 B.C.	China attacks Choson.
100–668	The Three Kingdoms rule Korea.
676–982	Silla rules a unified Korea.
918–1392	The Koryo dynasty rules Korea.
1261	Mongols complete conquest of Korea.
1392	Yi Song-gye starts his dynasty's five-century rule of Korea as a Confucian state.
1592	Japanese ruler Hideyoshi Toyotomi invades Korea.
1615–1867	*Tokugawa period in Japan*
1868	*Meiji Restoration begins in Japan.*
Late 1700s	Catholicism is introduced to Korea.
1876	Korean ports are opened to Japanese ships.
1894	Tonghak Revolt against the Japanese in Korea takes place.
1896	*Ethiopians defeat invading Italian army.*
1910–1945	Japan rules Korea.
1910	*Revolution in Mexico*
1917	*Communist Revolution in Russia*
1919	March 1 Movement is crushed.
1939–1945	*World War II*
1945	38th parallel dividing line is set up.
1949	*Communist rule starts in China.*
1948	Republic of [South] Korea and Democratic People's Republic of [North] Korea are set up.
1950–1953	The Korean War is fought.
1953	Demilitarized Zone (DMZ) is set up.

quered by Mongol invaders from China. Later, in the 20th century, Japan again attacked Korea and conquered it, occupying it for several decades, as you will read.

THE EARLY HISTORY OF KOREA
(PREHISTORY–A.D. 668)

Korea is one of the oldest nations in the world, with a history covering many thousands of years. Our knowledge of the early period of Korea's history is based on the remains of tools and weapons, pottery and clay figures, and ancient burial tombs that archaeologists have found. Written records, both Korean and Chinese, enable historians to begin to reconstruct the later development of the first ancient Korean kingdoms.

The Earliest Korean People. The ancestors of present-day Koreans were hunters who arrived on the Korean peninsula from northern China and Manchuria. Small groups of them, probably in search of food, first began to move into Korea about 40,000 to 50,000 years ago. These early people hunted small animals and were also fishers and gatherers. Archaeologists have found remains of the stone weapons, flint fish hooks, and crude stone tools used by these early people. These discoveries have enabled historians to begin to reconstruct Korea's early history. Although study by these experts still continues to uncover new evidence, we now know the main outlines of this early civilization.

The migration of people from northern China and Manchuria into Korea continued over a long period of time. Gradually, the people living in Korea learned how to plant crops, a practice that enabled them to lead more settled lives. They lived in dwellings dug into the ground equipped with fireplaces and, it is believed, covered with thatched roofs. Evidence suggests that people lived together in **clans**, or families believed to have common ancestors. By about 900 B.C. the early Koreans had learned to use bronze to make weapons and tools. Farming also became more widespread, and rice was now cultivated. By about 400 B.C., small states, each of which consisted of members of the same tribe, began to emerge throughout the Korean peninsula. Warfare among these tribal states was common. One of the first and most powerful of these states was Choson.

Choson (400-104 B.C.). Choson was established along the lands in the northern part of the Korean peninsula bordering the Yalu River and eastern China. From China, this tribal state learned how to farm with iron plows, harvesting tools, and horses. Its power also was based on wars of conquest that used iron weapons and horse-drawn chariots in battle. In 194 B.C., Choson was at the peak of its power, controlled by a strong ruler named Wi Man (wee mahn). However, China attacked Choson in 104 B.C. and destroyed it, replacing it with four Chinese military colonies. China's culture continued to spread into Korea during the following centuries through these Chinese military colonies. Choson and later Korean kingdoms also borrowed the Chinese writing system as well as Chinese forms of religion and government. Thus, early in its history, Korea's culture was profoundly influenced by China, though Koreans adapted this heritage in ways that best fitted their own society.

The Three Kingdoms (A.D. 100-668). In about A.D. 100, a strong Korean kingdom named Koguryo (koh-goo-ryoh) conquered the Chinese military colonies and expanded its rule over much of northern Korea. Two other powerful Korean kingdoms emerged soon after this—Silla (sihl-lah), in southwestern Korea, and Paekche (pek-cheh), in southeastern Korea. Each was ruled by a series of kings who were also military leaders. The rulers of the Three Kingdoms commanded strong armies and fought endless wars of conquest. They were supported by a small tribal aristocracy, or an elite group who held great power as large landholders. The members of the aristocracy helped the rulers of the Three Kingdoms administer their powerful centralized governments. This aristocracy was to remain the most important group in the later history of Korea, as you will read. All those who were not members of the privileged aristocracy had to pay taxes and provide their labor when the kings required it.

The Three Kingdoms were bitter rivals and fought to control all of the Korean peninsula. In the early 400s, Koguryo pushed south, attempting to conquer the two neighboring kingdoms. However, Paekche and Silla united to halt this invasion and by 500 repelled Koguryo. Koguryo then allied with Paekche to attack Silla. After a long struggle, Silla turned for help to neighboring China, and, aided by Chinese armies, Silla conquered Paekche in 660. Eight years later, it invaded and took control of Koguryo. Then, in 676 Silla gained control of all of Korea by driving out the Chinese. The Three Kingdom period, which had lasted for nearly 600 years, now gave way to a unified Korea under Silla.

THE UNIFICATION OF KOREA (676-1392)

Silla now extended the power of a single state throughout the Korean peninsula. Under the leadership of Silla's rulers and the Koryo (koh-ryoh) dynasty, the Korean people forged a common pattern of culture.

Silla Unification (676-982). After conquering its rivals, Silla rapidly consolidated its power throughout the Korean Peninsula. For the first time, Korea was under a single ruler. Silla's king now established his power as absolute monarch over all of Korea. He reduced the authority of the powerful aristocrats by granting them salaries and forcing them to recognize the state as supreme owner of all the land. The aristocracy, at least in theory, now held its land as a grant from the king. Silla's kings built impressive palaces, residences, and royal tombs as evidence of their great power. Silla's economy also grew as Korea began to trade with both China and Japan. The rulers of the kingdom also borrowed China's tax system and ways of governing, dividing Silla into provinces administered by appointed officials. Chinese culture spread into nearly every phase of Korean political, social, and economic life. This was the most important legacy of the great Silla kingdom.

Cultural Borrowing from China. Buddhism, now at its height in China, also flourished in the Silla kingdom. Silla kings believed that Buddhism would protect their kingdom and its people better than the ancient shamanist religion. (See Chapter 8.) Thus, majestic Buddhist temples and shrines were established in all parts of the peninsula, and Korean monks traveled to China to study Buddhist texts. Some of the beautiful works of Buddhist sculpture and religious paintings executed in Silla still survive today. Korean literature and other writing used the Chinese writing system. Silla also set up a national university and started a system of examinations for government offices, practices that, again, were borrowed from China.

However, it is important to note that in Silla, as in Japan, most of the cultural borrowing from China was adapted to the nation's needs. For example, in the Silla examination system only members of the aristocracy were allowed to gain government office, whereas in China scholars from all classes achieved positions based on merit.

By 780, the power of the Silla kingdom and its impressive culture began to be undermined by struggles among rival aristocratic families from the provinces. These aristocrats, based in provincial castle towns,

This Buddhist temple dates from the 800s. With its statue of Buddha, it is a striking example of cultural borrowing from China at this time in Korea's history.

grew more powerful than the king and conspired to place their supporters on Silla's throne. During the late 800s, the kingdom was in constant turmoil as civil wars were waged and peasant rebellions broke out to protest crushing taxes and widespread famine. By 890, Silla was near collapse. Finally, in 918 a general named Wang Kon (wahng kun) defeated his rivals and Silla surrendered to him shortly afterwards.

The Koryo Dynasty (918–1392). Wang Kon founded the Koryo dynasty, from which Korea takes its name. By 936 he had established a unified kingdom in the Korean peninsula. However, the Koryo dynasty found it difficult to reestablish order and stability in the kingdom. The aristocrats regained their power and retook control of their land. They asserted that this property belonged to them, not the state. Land was now the source of both wealth and power in Korea.

The rulers persuaded the powerful aristocracy to move their families from their provincial castle towns to the capital at Kaesong. However, this group continued to resist royal authority. As a result, successive Koryo kings were weakened until they became no more than pawns in the hands of rival aristocratic factions.

Under the Koryo rulers, Buddhism was made the official state religion. The government built huge Buddhist temples, which soon gained vast properties and wealth. Buddhist leaders, too, built up their own military forces to protect their wealth. Increasingly, they became involved in power struggles as allies of rival factions among the aristocracy. As a result, Buddhism as a religious force was weakened.

During the 11th and 12th centuries, under a series of weak Koryo kings, the aristocracy occupied all high government positions and systematically excluded military men from these posts. Bitterly resentful of their treatment as inferiors, the military leaders staged a revolt and seized power in 1196. Led by General Ch'oe Ch'ung-hon (choh choong-whahn), a military government was set up, with the Koryo ruler remaining as a figurehead. Ch'oe and his son and other family members continued to wield all real power for the next 50 years. At the same time, the heavily taxed peasants revolted against the harsh landowners.

The Mongol Conquest. Even greater dangers faced Korea during the Koryo dynasty in the form of foreign invasions. While Silla had enjoyed relatively peaceful relations with China, new Chinese dynasties now launched attacks against Koryo rulers. During the 11th and 12th centuries, China invaded Korea several times. Then, in 1231 the Mongols, who had completed their conquest of China, sent their armies into Korea. The people successfully supported the Ch'oe struggle against the Mongols, but after 30 years of resistance, the superior Mongol forces were victorious. The Mongols then occupied Korea for the next 100 years. They turned Korea into a virtual Mongol state by intermarrying with Koryo princesses and subduing the aristocracy. Koryo's rulers became puppets of the Mongol army.

Korea was now part of the vast Mongol Empire, which stretched from China to the Middle East and early Russia. While the Mongol invasion caused widespread devastation throughout the Koryo kingdom, it also had other, unexpected results. Most importantly, it opened Korea to many of the new developments in technology and culture that were taking place throughout the huge Mongol territory. Thus, during the dark days of the Mongol conquest, Koreans learned to grow cotton, and gunpowder was introduced. New knowledge in mathematics and astronomy also spread to Korea. Korean artisans, too, made important cultural contributions by producing exquisite pale-green porcelainware called celadon. Korean scholars also compiled two great histories, which remain the most important source of ancient Korean history.

However, the Mongol conquest fatally weakened the Koryo dynasty, which had been beset with uprisings and military revolts even before the arrival of the Mongol armies. In addition to the destruction suffered during the Mongol invasion, Mongol forces used Korea as their base to launch the two unsuccessful invasions of Japan in the late 13th century that you read about in Chapter 2. Meanwhile, rival aristocratic factions fought civil wars throughout the kingdom. By then, the Koryo dynasty was so weakened that it now depended on the support of the Mongol armies to keep it in power. Finally, the mighty Mongol Empire itself collapsed and the Ming dynasty that had gained power in China sent its army into Korea to subdue this former Mongol ally. The general who was sent to repel the Chinese, Yi Song-gye (ee sung-geh), instead seized power from the Koryo ruler and in 1392 took the throne, thus founding the new Yi dynasty.

KOREA, A CONFUCIAN STATE (1392–1910)

Korea had adopted many features of China's impressive cullture during the period of the Three Kingdoms and even earlier, as you have read. However, during the long rule of the Yi dynasty Korea's cultural borrowing from the Chinese Empire had an even more profound influence on the development of Korean society.

A Confucian scholar studies ancient texts in Hahoe, a village famous for its celebration of old Korean traditions. The architecture of Hahoe dates back to the Choson period.

The Yi Dynasty (1392–1910).   Yi Song-gye was the first of 26 kings of the Yi dyasty who were to rule Korea for the next five centuries. From the beginning, Yi displayed his intention to be a more forceful ruler than the Koryo kings. He moved the capital city from Kaesong to Seoul, in the center of the kingdom. He limited the power of the old aristocracy by reviving the old policy that all land was owned by the state and would be used to reward those who were loyal to the ruler. As a result, much of the provincial land around Seoul was given to Yi's supporters. Yi and his successors modeled Korea's government and society on China, even more than the Silla and Koryo rulers had done. Under the Yi dynasty, Korea became more of a Confucian state than China itself.

Korea's Confucian Heritage.   Yi Song-gye diminished the influence of Buddhism and replaced it with the moral and ethical teachings of Confucianism. The traditional Confucian emphasis on the virtue of knowledge and scholarship again helped shape the new government. A new, more rigorous examination system for all government offices was instituted. Success on the examinations required years of disciplined study of Confucian texts and writings. Special Confucian schools called *sowon* (soo-wun) were established throughout the land for this purpose. Serving the government became the most highly valued goal in Korean society. Members of the government bureaucracy were accorded the highest status and often gained great wealth. Similar examination systems also were required for the military and the professions. While this Confucian system of government examinations seemed to work efficiently under Yi Song-gye, it proved to be less effective under later Yi monarchs.

The old aristocracy gradually regained its strength, and its members soon once more dominated the government and the military. This small elite aristocracy, which now became known as the *yangban* (yahng-bahn), achieved this by monopolizing the examination system. The *yangban* also were granted large land holdings by Yi Song-yge's successors. They turned these grants, no longer owned by the state, into estates that they could pass on to their heirs. In this way, the leading *yangban* families soon controlled nearly all the wealth and power in the kingdom. The stage thus was set for a renewal of bloody factional strife, which began in earnest in the early 1500s.

The transformation of Korea into a Confucian state during the Yi dynasty was modeled on China's system of centralized government, land ownership, taxation, and class ranking. Yet, in many ways these borrowings prevented the development of native Korean institutions

This delicate white vase is a product of the Yi dynasty, a period of many cultural achievements.

and ideas. For example, the low status of merchants and traders in Confucian thinking hindered Korean commerce and trade and the growth of Korea's economy. The doctrine of honoring ancestors and continuing the family line resulted in many child marriages. The Confucian belief that the military should be controlled by civil authorities led to many unqualified government officials holding important ranks in the army.

Yi Cultural Achievements. The early Yi monarchs were the most successful rulers of the dynasty, and during the 1400s Korea's culture flourished. Royal scholars prepared a history of the Koryo dynasty, an encyclopedia of knowledge, and a collection of Korean music. These works, as well as many Confucian texts, were published using moveable metal type. This method of printing helped strengthen scholarship throughout Yi Korea.

Even more important was the invention of ***han'gul*** (hahn-gul), the first Korean phonetic alphabet, by King Sejong in 1443. Although complex Chinese characters and writing continued to be used by all educated Koreans, *han'gul* was employed as well and today is used in all Korean writing. Fine examples of Korean art and calligraphy also were executed by scholar-officials of the *yangban* in the 15th century. However, these cultural advances were soon overshadowed by the renewal of political struggles.

214

CASE STUDY:

Attending a Korean Confucian School

The most talented young men in most *yangban* families attended Confucian schools, where they had to study hard and were under very strict discipline. A modern Korean professor has described student life at one of the schools, Song-gyun-gwan (soong-gyun-gwahn).

> Those students who indulged in tall tales [lies] and heresy [dissent], spoke ill of [criticized] those who studied harder, talked [about] wine and women, and fawned upon [played up to] the rulers as a means of getting state appointment were punished. . . .
>
> Those students who traveled often at the expense of the state treasury . . . not writing compositions and not reading books but going around on horseback and violating curfew were punished.
>
> The students were allowed to go home every eighth and twenty-third day to wash and change clothes; but those who . . . went shooting arrows, played cards, went hunting or fishing . . . were also punished.
>
> During the first ten days of every month, the minister of the board of rites [ceremonies] and the president of Song-gyun-gwan met to review the academic records of each student . . . and selected five excellent students. . . to apply for the civil service [government] examination. For the students in the lower dormitories [grades] and in the four schools in the capital, [certain officials] met during the first ten days of each month in one of the schools to test the students on the Four Books [Confucius's *Analects*] and selected [the] ten most excellent students, allowing them to apply for the preliminary examination to become first-degree licentiates [officials]. . . . Those who were lazy and could not finish the courses . . . were punished.

From Russell Warren Howe, *The Koreans*. San Diego, CA: Harccourt Brace Jovanovich, 1988.

1. What were some of the things students did that caused them to be punished?
2. Why do you think the school was so strict with its students?

The Hyangwonjong Pavilion in Seoul is part of a complex of old buildings where feasts for royal ministers and diplomatic delegations were held.

Weakness of the Yi Dynasty.   In 1498, court officials began to quarrel over the interpretation of Confucian teachings about the proper role of the monarch and the duties of the bureaucracy. These quarrels soon led to a series of bloody purges against high government officials. *Sowon* scholars in the provincial Confucian schools allied themselves with the rival *yangban* factions at court as they vied for power. This factional strife, called ***tangjaeng*** (tahng-jeng), grew worse, and by the late 1500s had undermined the Yi dynasty's power. It was just at this point of greatest weakness that Korea was attacked by Japan.

Korea had enjoyed nearly two centuries of peace under the Yi dynasty following the Mongol invasion of the 13th century. During those years, Korea had again turned to China and its culture, as you have just read. Yet, this dependence on China and its view of the superiority of Chinese culture made Korea increasingly vulnerable. In these 200 years, Korea effectively cut off its relations with all other nations except China, which led Korea to be regarded as the **Hermit Kingdom.** Thus Korea was totally unprepared when Japan's new ruler, Hideyoshi Toyotomi, launched a massive invasion in 1592. (See Chapter 2.)

Japan's Invasions of Korea. Hideyoshi's goal was to conquer China, using Korea as his base and then moving his forces northward up the Korean peninsula. At first the Japanese forces advanced rapidly, reaching Seoul within three weeks of their landing at Pusan. From Seoul they pushed on as far as Pyongyang. By then, the Yi ruler had appealed to China, which sent an army to help halt Japan's advance. At sea, as you read in the introduction to this chapter, Admiral Yi Sun-sin, the commander of the Korean navy, defeated the Japanese in a great naval victory, using his new armored "turtle ships." The Korean people now united to drive out the Japanese.

Hideyoshi launched another attack in 1597, though this time his army failed to reach as far north as Seoul before it was forced back. Then, when Hideyoshi died suddenly and Admiral Yi attacked Japan's invasion fleet, the Japanese withdrew their army from Korea. Although the invasion had failed, it caused great destruction everywhere and nearly bankrupted the Yi government. Conditions grew worse still when armies from Manchuria occupied Korea in 1627 and again in 1636.

Korea in the 1700s. During the 18th century, however, stability returned to the court. Royal scholar-officials studied the problems that Korea faced and drafted proposals for reform. This effort was known as *sirhak* (seer-hahk), or the "practical learning" movement. Many of these proposals highlighted the weaknesses in Korean government and society and recommended drastic changes. Although the entrenched powerful *yangban* resisted, many proposals to develop the economy were carried out. Local industry and trade were encouraged. Merchants established networks of fairs throughout Korea where manufactured goods and other products were traded, and the government issued coins and money to promote trade and commerce.

With the growth of the merchant class, the old class system weakened. Many merchants and traders became well-to-do. Many *yangban* families also engaged in commerce to add to their wealth. Many *yangban* also became farmers. At the same time, many ordinary citizens bought the rank of *yangban* from impoverished members of that class.

Improvements in agriculture placed further strains on the class system. Wet rice farming and better irrigation systems came into widespread use. Many farmers now were able to raise two crops a year, rice in summer and barley in winter, increasing their incomes. New crops like tobacco and ginseng, a plant used as a medicine, also brought farmers more income. These gains in agriculture also brought

Seesaw jumping during the New Year's holidays is one of many traditional activities that Koreans still carry on as reminders of their country's past.

an increase in Korea's population, which grew from about 5 million in 1669 to over 7 million in 1750.

THE END OF KOREA'S ISOLATION

Korea's retreat from relations with other nations except China, which had lasted since the end of the Japanese invasions in the 16th century, was brought to a sudden end in the late 1800s. The arrival of the Western nations with their navies and merchant ships soon changed the course of Korea's history.

The Arrival of the Western Powers.   The early 1800s marked the beginning of bitter years for Korea. A series of famines, droughts, and peasant uprisings challenged the Yi dynasty. It also faced a chronic shortage of money as landholders and peasants alike tried to avoid paying taxes. The government even lacked funds for its military forces. Again, as in other periods of great weakness, Korea was called on to deal with decisive challenges from foreign powers.

As you recall, the Western powers sent navies and merchant ships to East Asia in the mid-1800s to open Japan and China to Western trade and commerce. Though Koreans were fully occupied with their own internal problems, they, too, were drawn into this web of imperialist politics. After its long period of isolation, Korea was unprepared and ill-equipped to deal with these outside powers. Its chief support in earlier foreign crises, China, was itself threatened and thus unable to help its client-state.

Catholicism in Korea. The Catholic religion, which had been brought to Korea by the late 1700s, became one of the early points of friction between Korea and the imperialist nations. During that period, some leading court officials of the *sirak* movement were converted to Catholicism. Catholicism spread and gained other followers among the common people. As more ships from Western nations began to arrive along the Korean coast, Catholic missionaries often accompanied them. However, Yi rulers refused to accept the Catholic religion. They opposed this Western faith that taught that the Confucian reverence of ancestors was a form of idol worship. Thus, during the first half of the 1800s, the government persecuted converts to Catholicism as disloyal subjects and executed French priests who had secretly entered Korea.

Efforts at Reform. In 1864, a remarkable figure in Korea's history took control of the government when Taewon-gun (tay-wahn-goon) became regent for his young son, the Yi monarch. Taewon-gun was determined to resist the Western nations by restoring the power of the monarch. Therefore, he set about reducing the power of the *yangban* and forcing them to pay taxes for the first time to help increase revenue for the army. At the same time, the regent lowered the tax burden of the peasants to gain their loyalty. He also reformed the examination system and opened it to all factions. To lessen factional rivalry, Taewon-gun closed the Confucian schools in the provinces. He also effectively built up the power of the military, armed it with modern weapons, and built defensive fortresses.

The Power Struggle over Korea. Taewon-gun failed in his efforts to keep the Western nations out of Korea, however. In 1866 he drove away a French force sent to avenge the murder of French priests. In 1871, he repulsed U.S. warships that had been sent to retaliate for the burning of a U.S. merchant ship. But these successes were short lived. Though the regent believed he had ended the foreign threat, Korea soon became a prize that was fought over by China, Russia, and Japan. The regent himself became so unpopular for the tax burden he had imposed to strengthen the nation that he was forced from office in 1872.

The ruler who succeeded Taewon-gun, Queen Min (meen), undid his reforms but was weak and ineffective. Japan then took advantage of the situation by sending a fleet to Korea to force it to sign a trade treaty that opened its ports to Japanese merchant ships. Under the treaty, Pusan and two other ports began to receive Japanese ships in 1876. Korea was forced to sign a similar trade treaty with the United States in 1882 and with Britain, Germany, Russia, and France soon after.

Chinese and Japanese Rivalry over Korea.   China and Japan were locked in a battle to gain influence over Korea. China was alarmed at the prospect of losing Korea as a client-state, hoping to keep Korea out of the Western sphere. China itself had been forced to sign unfavorable treaties with the Western nations. Japan was even more resolved to prevail over Korea. It wished to prove that in foreign relations, as in modernizing its nation at home, it had learned the effective use of Western models. In Korea itself, the government was deeply divided over which policy to follow. Reformers, who argued that Korea must adapt to Western ways in order to survive, believed Japan offered their nation the best model. Others, who still opposed any compromise with Western influences, turned to China for aid. This lack of national unity only added to the difficulty that Korea faced in maintaining its independence. The struggle between China and Japan to win Korea grew more bitter still during the 1880s.

The Tonghak Revolt of 1894.   Meanwhile, the condition of the Korean people became steadily worse, as poverty and hunger became widespread. A new religion called *Tonghak* (tahng-hahk), based in part on ancient shamanism, recruited many followers with its condemnation of Western learning and Catholicism. When the Korean government banned Tonghak and executed its leader, fearing he might stir up revolt among the peasants who had embraced the new religion, rebellion broke out in 1894.

The Korean government, unable to suppress the rebellion, welcomed the help of Chinese troops. But Japan eagerly seized upon the Tonghak Revolt as an excuse to send its army into Korea. The Chinese and Japanese clashed, leading in 1894 to the Sino-Japanese War. Japan won a swift, decisive victory in this conflict. In the peace treaty, Japan gained control over Korea.

Japan's Growing Influence.   In 1895, Japan forced the Korean government to accept a series of reforms and to introduce Western institutions. The examination system for government officials was ended, Korea's currency was standardized, and discrimination based on class ranking was forbidden. Although these reforms might have helped modernize the nation, most Koreans opposed them as a dangerous threat to their culture and traditions. To overcome this opposition, which it believed the government shared, the Japanese helped plot the murder of Queen Min late in 1895. The king then fled to the Russian embassy in Seoul, where he remained for over a year.

During this period, a group of young Koreans founded a movement called the Independence Club to arouse their nation to the grave danger it faced and to institute democratic reforms. At their urging, the king returned to his palace and proclaimed himself emperor of Korea. However, the king soon was overshadowed by his conservative court officials, who opposed the reform program. These officials then acted to ban the Independence Club and jailed its leaders, including young Syngman Rhee (sing-mahn ree), who would head South Korea's government a half century later.

Japan's only rival for control of Korea was now Russia. In 1898 those two nations signed agreements not to intervene in Korea, but Russia secretly encouraged the Koreans to resist any Japanese takeover of their nation. Then in 1904 and 1905 the two nations fought in the Russo-Japanese War (see Chapter 3). The 1905 treaty that ended the war recognized Japan's supremacy in Korea. That same year the Japanese forced Korea to become its **protectorate**, or a nation controlled and ruled by Japan.

Koreans tried to undo this action by appealing to the world powers to act to prevent Japan's takeover, but this proved to be fruitless. After Japanese forces arrived in Korea in 1905, armed resistance broke out in the southern part of the country. Japan then moved swiftly to depose the emperor, crush the resistance, and disband Korea's army. In 1910, Japan annexed Korea as part of the Japanese Empire.

JAPANESE RULE OF KOREA (1910–1945)

Under Japan's rule during the next 35 years, Korea was modernized and reformed to serve the needs of the Japanese. These years were decades of harsh foreign domination. The efforts of Koreans to reform their own government and institutions that had barely begun were abruptly halted. Korean nationalism, or the people's feelings of shared pride in their nation, was suppressed by force. The Japanese established a military government in Seoul to rule the nation, with Japanese-appointed governors in all the provinces. All important government positions were held by Japanese officials, with Koreans allowed to serve only as minor bureaucrats and clerks. A large Japanese-manned police force, backed by the army, enforced Japan's rule and hunted down those Koreans they considered dangerous nationalists.

Korea's Economy Under the Japanese.   One of Japan's major goals was to develop Korea's economy. It did so in order to use Korea's resources and raw materials to fuel Japan's own rapidly growing industries and businesses. Since Korea had barely begun to build its economy, Japan's efforts here were impressive. Japan built up Korea's system of transportation and communication, constructing modern roads, building railroad networks, setting up a postal system, and enlarging harbors. The Japanese developed hydroelectric power to fuel new Korean factories and the iron- and coal-mining operations that were begun in the north. Korea also was turned into a major market for Japan's textiles and other manufactured goods. But while Japanese trade with Korea was encouraged, Koreans were not permitted to trade with Japan.

All of this economic development was financed by Japanese banks and businesses, and Koreans did not share in the profits. In fact, the Koreans were not allowed to play a role in the economic development of their own country. Nevertheless, Koreans did benefit from some of Japan's efforts. Its rule brought an end to the turmoil of past centuries. Japanese modernization also brought better health care and improved living conditions, especially in the larger cities.

Korean farmers, the vast majority of the population, faced special hardships throughout Japan's occupation of their country. Japan took control of much of Korea's farmland and sold it to Japanese owners. Korean farmers then were forced to work for the Japanese. In this way, Japan ensured that Korea's rice crop would be used to feed the people of Japan. As a result, the Koreans now had to depend on other cereals for food. Some of the Korean farmers who had lost their lands were allowed to go to Japan to work at unskilled jobs there. The descendants of those immigrants make up part of the minority Korean population in present-day Japan. (See page 17.)

Efforts to Suppress Korean Culture.   In the process of ruling and modernizing Korea, Japan ignored Korea's ancient heritage and traditions. Instead, Japan set out on a program to suppress Korea's culture and forcibly impose Japanese ways on the people. The Korean school system was used by the Japanese in an attempt to achieve this goal. Students were required to learn the Japanese language as well as to study the history and culture of Japan. Korean history and language were ignored. All Koreans were forced to adopt new Japanese names and to worship at Shinto shrines built by the Japanese throughout the country. At the same time, all political activity was outlawed to prevent efforts to resist this "re-education" program. However, Japan's effort to suppress Korean culture had precisely the opposite effect—it inspired the development of strong feelings of nationalism among the Koreans.

The Rise of Nationalism.   The death of the Korean emperor in early 1919 showed the depth of Korea's hatred of Japanese rule. Nearly 1 million Koreans attended the emperor's funeral held in Seoul on March 1, 1919. There the strength of the nationalist movement was clearly shown when a group of Korean leaders staged a massive, peaceful demonstration at which they read a "Proclamation of Independence." The Japanese police then attacked the demonstrators, killing 2,000 and imprisoning 19,000 others. This **March 1 Movement** was quickly crushed, and its leaders fled to China and other nations. The leaders of the March 1 Movement now split and formed rival groups. One group, based in Shanghai, was led by Syngman Rhee. Another nationalist group, based in Manchuria and led by Kim Il-Sung, organized armed bands against Japanese forces there. These rival nationalist groups would later play a dominant role in Korea at the end of World War II, as you will read.

During the 1920s, Japan's rule in Korea became somewhat less harsh to avoid provoking new nationalist resistance. More Koreans were allowed to join the government and the police force, though still only in the lower ranks. A few Korean newspapers and magazines were allowed for the first time. Still, Korean nationalism had not died out, and a nationwide student uprising occurred in 1929. Japan then reimposed harsh military rule on the Korean people. By the 1930s, when military leaders had gained the upper hand in the Japanese government, Korea was again treated as a conquered nation. Several hundred thousand Koreans were forced to serve in the Japanese army as well as to work in mines and factories in Japan. Then World War II, which brought defeat to Japan, finally ushered in the prospect of liberation and independence for Korea.

KOREA AFTER WORLD WAR II (1945–1953)

After the years of harsh Japanese rule, Korea welcomed the defeat of Japan in World War II and anticipated regaining its role as an independent nation. Instead, World War II ended with the division of Korea into two separate nations and a bloody war that brought suffering and destruction throughout the Korean Peninsula.

The 38th Parallel Dividing Line. During World War II, the United States, Great Britain, and China had agreed in the Cairo Declaration in 1943 that "in due course Korea shall become independent." However, the Allies had prepared no plan for the establishment of an independent Korea after the war. The sudden collapse of Japan in 1945 limited the Allies' ability to decide on a course of action. The Soviet Union had promised to carry out the Cairo Declaration pledge when its troops entered the war against Japan on August 8, 1945. Soviet troops occupied northern Korea just a few days before Japan surrendered on August 15, 1945. The United States then proposed that Japanese forces south of the 38th parallel in Korea surrender to the U.S. army and Japan's forces north of that line surrender to the Soviet Union. This is the plan that was carried out when the war was over.

The U.S. goal was to reestablish an independent Korea. For this reason it may have proposed the 38th parallel as a temporary measure for carrying out the Japanese surrender and at the same time preventing the Soviet Union from occupying all of Korea. The Soviet Union, for its part, considered the 38th parallel as a permanent dividing line separating the Korean people.

Elections in Korea. After nearly two years of talks, the Soviets and the United States were unable to reach an agreement on establishing a government for all of Korea. In 1947, the United States then asked the United Nations to help settle the issue of Korean independence. The UN then recommended that elections be held nationwide in Korea under UN supervision. The United States then carried out elections in South Korea in May of 1948 and ended the American military government there soon after. The newly elected national assembly then drafted a constitution, and Syngman Rhee was elected as the first president of the Republic of South Korea (ROK). However, the Soviet Union refused to allow the UN to supervise the election in North Korea. Instead, North Korean elections were carried out by the Soviets, and the Democratic People's Republic of Korea (DPRK) led by Premier Kim Il-

Syngman Rhee, South Korea's first president, proudly displays his country's flag at his headquarters after U.S. troops repelled a heavy attack by North Korean forces.

Sung (kim eel sung) was established as a communist-ruled nation. Soon after, the Soviets withdrew their armies from North Korea.

A Divided Korea. Koreans, after years of Japanese occupation, now found themselves a divided people. Families were uprooted and split apart by the creation of two rival Koreas. The ancient Confucian Korean state in which family kinship ties were the basis of society now faced the terrible shock of families and relatives separated by an artificial border at the 38th parallel. Koreans also were deeply divided now by opposing forms of government and political doctrine. North Korea proclaimed itself a communist nation and was ruled by a militant dictator who viewed South Korea as a reactionary regime created by U.S. imperialists. Although South Korea had a government modeled on U.S. democratic institutions, under Syngman Rhee it seemed more intent on carrying on the authoritarian rule of Korea's earlier Confucian-inspired aristocracy. In this uncertain and increasingly alarming situation, about 1.8 million Koreans fled from North Korea into South Korea and several thousand fled from South Korea to North Korea. These migrations led to still more family separations and hardships in this troubled land.

North Korea vs. South Korea. Compounding Koreans' bitter postwar legacy, both North and South Korea refused to recognize the other as a legitimate nation. Thus, both sides began to build up their armed forces, fearing an attack from the other. By 1950, North Korea actively supported armed communist groups in South Korea. That same year, Syngman Rhee expelled left-wing members in the newly elected South Korean general assembly, where opposition parties now held 60 percent of the seats. This growing hostility between North and South Korea and Kim Il-Sung's belief that North Korea could easily defeat its weaker foe, finally prompted him to launch an invasion into South Korea in June 1950. North Korea had turned to war to unify Korea under its rule.

The Korean War (1950-1953). When North Korea attacked across the 38th parallel, it enjoyed great military superiority. Its army was much larger and better trained and equipped than South Korea's. Further, it had received weapons and money from both Communist China and the Soviet Union. By contrast, South Korea's smaller army consisted largely of untrained, poorly equipped recruits with few modern weapons. In just five days, North Korean troops swept everything before them and occupied South Korea's capital of Seoul. Only the Cold War rivalry between the United States and the Soviet Union saved South Korea from certain defeat.

The U.S. government had watched with alarm as communism advanced in the nations of Eastern Europe and Asia after World War II. Then, in 1949, the Chinese Communists had seized power in the world's most populous nation, which bordered Korea. Thus, when the North Korean invasion began in June 1950, President Harry S. Truman saw this act as yet another communist move to extend its empire. He promptly requested the United Nations act to end the aggression. Under pressure from the United States, the UN agreed to send an army to defend South Korea.

Largely composed of U.S. troops, and led by General Douglas MacArthur, the UN forces halted the North Korean advance, which had reached Pusan by September 1950, and then drove the communist forces back north. MacArthur counterattacked, forcing the North Koreans to retreat to the northern border with China along the Yalu River. The UN army entered North Korea's capital of Pyongyang on October 20.

The war took another dramatic turn when Chinese Communist troops crossed the Yalu and stormed into North Korea. Now the UN forces were pushed southward across the 38th parallel as China continued its troop buildup, which eventually reached 1.2 million men. However, the fighting then seesawed back and forth until a military stalemate was reached by early 1951.

The war finally ended in a truce in 1953, after lengthy negotiations. The border between North and South Korea was established near the

Rail traffic is blocked at the DMZ. The sign reads, "The train wants to keep running northbound," indicating South Korea's long-cherished hope for reunification.

38th parallel, where an unoccupied demilitarized zone, named the **DMZ,** was set up. When South Korea refused to sign the truce, fearing that it would still be open to another invasion, the United States signed a security treaty pledging to defend South Korea against any future attack and to provide aid to help rebuild that nation. North Korea received similar pledges of support from the Soviet Union and Communist China. Thus the war had settled nothing. Korea remained divided and its people still separated. Only now the entire peninsula had suffered death and destruction on an almost unimaginable scale.

The Legacy of the Korean War.   The devastation and loss of life in Korea was one of the tragedies of modern history. More than 4 million people were killed in the fighting. Of these, South Korea lost over 1.3 million people, including 1 million civilians and over 300,000 soldiers. North Korea lost 1.5 million people, with 1 million civilian deaths and the loss of more than 500,000 soldiers. Communist Chinese casualties numbered nearly 900,000. The property damage was nearly as terrible. Nearly one third of all homes were destroyed and as much as 40 percent of all industry in both Koreas was wiped out. In addition to this devastation, more than 500,000 people fled from North Korea into South Korea during the conflict.

In this awesome conclusion to the bloody Korean War, which in many ways resembled a civil war among the Korean people, few observers in 1953 could have predicted the rapid changes that were to occur in the next few decades. You will read about the incredible recovery and rebuilding of this war-torn land and the amazing growth of the economies and political systems of the two Koreas in Chapter 10. You will also read about the efforts of the Korean people to achieve their dream of again becoming one nation.

227

REVIEWING THE CHAPTER

I. Building Your Vocabulary

Match the definitions and the terms.

aristocracy   *sirhak*   protectorate
han'gul   DMZ   *tangjaeng*
yangban   nationalism   March 1 Movement
Hermit Kingdom   *sowon*

1. the first Korean alphabet

2. name given to Korea when it cut off relations with all nations except China after the Mongol invasion

3. an elite group which held great power as large landowners

4. the military zone separating North Korea and South Korea

5. the small aristocracy that monopolized the examination system in Korea

6. the "practical learning" movement

7. a nation controlled and ruled by another nation

8. a people's feelings of shared pride in their nation

9. factional strife among the Korean court aristocracy

10. schools that taught Confucian texts and writings

11. demonstrations against the Japanese occupation of Korea

II. Understanding the Facts

Write the letters of the correct answers.

1. The earliest people living in the Korean peninsula came from:
   a. Japan.
   b. southern China and India.
   c. northern China and Manchuria.
   d. Indonesia and Japan.

2. One of the most powerful of the early states that began to emerge in the Korean peninsula in about 400 B.C. was:

a. Koryo. b. Choson.

c. Silla. d. South Korea.

3. Korea was first unified under a single ruler by:

a. the kingdom of Silla. b. Queen Min.

c. the Yi dynasty. d. Taewon-gun

4. Under the Yi dynasty, which ruled Korea from 1392 to 1910, Korea:

a. was conquered by the Mongols.

b. was divided into North and South Korea.

c. became a Confucian state.

d. rejected all Chinese influences.

5. During the years when Japan occupied Korea, from 1910 to 1945:

a. Korean nationalism grew stronger despite efforts to suppress Korean culture.

b. Korea's economy remained weak, although Koreans achieved impressive cultural advances.

c. Korea's economy was strengthened, and most Koreans enjoyed an improved standard of living.

d. Japan did not succeed in using Korea's resources to help Japanese businesses and industries.

III. Thinking It Through

Write the letter of your correct conclusion to each sentence next to its number.

1. Under the Yi dynasty, Korea became a Confucian state because:

a. it adopted Buddhism as the official state religion.

b. King Sejong invented *han'gul* to write down the teachings of Confucius.

c. it adapted China's system of government examinations, land ownership, centralized government, and code of conduct.

d. Korean merchants and missionaries opened Korea to a new religion.

2. In becoming the Hermit Kingdom during the two centuries after Korea defeated two Japanese invasions in the late 1500s, the following took place:
   a. Korea cut off all relations with other nations except China.
   b. Buddhist monks gained control of the government and turned Korea into a religious kingdom.
   c. the March 1 Movement failed to bring Western reforms to Korea.
   d. the Western powers forced Korea to open its ports to their ships and traders.

3. Foreign nations' struggle over Korea began as a rivalry among China, Japan, and Russia and ended in:
   a. the division of Korea between Japan and China.
   b. the Japanese occupation of Korea.
   c. the growth of Korea's culture.
   d. the Korean War.

4. The division of Korea into two nations after World War II and the splitting up of families caused a profound shock because:
   a. Korea had never been invaded by Chinese armies.
   b. most Koreans expected the UN to prevent this from happening.
   c. Buddhist beliefs began to replace Confucian teachings.
   d. family kinship ties were the basis of Korean society.

5. The Korean War, which lasted for over three years and brought widespread death and destruction, was a tragedy for Koreans because:
   a. it prevented Korea from becoming an industrial country.
   b. the Korean people still were divided into two rival nations.
   c. fighting continued for many years.
   d. it ended with the Chinese communists in control of South Korea.

DEVELOPING CRITICAL THINKING SKILLS

1. Describe the early people who lived in Korea and explain how historians have learned about them.

2. Explain why the aristocracy was such an important group in Korea's history and what some of the results of their power were.

3. Describe how Confucian teachings influenced the development of Korea for more than 500 years during the Yi dynasty.

4. Explain the rivalry among China, Japan, and Russia over Korea in the late 1800s and early 1900s and the outcome of this struggle.

5. Describe the causes of the Korean War and the consequences of this conflict for the Korean people.

ENRICHMENT AND EXPLORATION

1. Imagine that you are a high school student in Korea during the Japanese occupation. You have been keeping a secret diary describing how your education and your life have been changed by the Japanese takeover of your nation. Write an entry in which you tell about a typical day at school.

2. Contact the American Legion, the Veterans Administration, or some other veterans' organization in your community to set up an interview with someone who fought in the Korean War. Have some of your classmates help you prepare in advance a list of the key questions you plan to ask about the veteran's impression of the Korean people and their country. Tape the interview or write down the person's answers to your questions. Then share your findings with the class.

MODERN KOREA

1953–Present

1948	South Korea establishes the Republic of Korea.
	Syngman Rhee is elected president.
	Kim Il-Sung comes to power in North Korea.
1950s	Rhee establishes authoritarian rule in South Korea.
1950–1953	Korean War
1954	South Korea and the United States sign a defense treaty.
1957	*European Common Market is established.*
1960	Rhee wins rigged election and is forced to flee South Korea.
1961	Park Chung Hee seizes control of South Korea, establishes a junta.
1963	Park is elected president of South Korea.
1965	South Korean troops are sent to aid U.S. forces in Vietnam.
1967	*Arab-Israeli war is fought.*
1960s–1970s	South Korea experiences an "economic miracle."
1975	*Portugal, last large colonial power, gives up African colonies.*
1981	Chun Doo Hwan is elected president of South Korea.
1987	Roh Tae Woo is elected South Korea's president.
1985	North and South Korea allow some separated families to reunite.
1990	*Civil war ends in Nicaragua.*
1991	North Korea and South Korea begin negotiations on peaceful reunification.
1992	North Korea agrees to allow inspection of its nuclear capability.

10 Modern Korea: Two Nations or One? (1953–Present)

The large crowd waited expectantly as the barefoot runner climbed the stairs of the huge stadium. Carrying a fiery torch, he continued to the top, where he lit a giant flame—the symbol of the Olympic Games. A mighty roar, loud cheering, and waves of applause greeted the parade of young athletes from the nations of the world who had come to Seoul to compete in the 1988 Summer Olympic Games. These handsome young men and women runners, jumpers, swimmers, divers, and gymnasts marched around the stadium, each group carrying the flag of its country. Hundreds of millions of people around the world watched this spectacular opening ceremony on television. For the next two weeks, South Korea was the center of much of the world's attention.

The South Korean government and its people had worked hard for several years building new sports arenas and stadiums preparing for this great event. The excitement and anticipation of South Koreans clearly reflected the prestige and recognition that the nation now enjoyed as host of the Olympic Games. Yet, one dark cloud continued to mar the joy of this great occasion. North Korea had refused to take part in the 1988 Olympics and had asked the other communist nations to join in its boycott. Although only Cuba had joined North Korea's action, South Koreans once more were bitterly reminded that their land was still divided, as it had been for more than four decades.

KOREA, A DIVIDED LAND

At the end of World War II, Korean nationalists who had fled their nation during the Japanese occupation returned home. They hoped to build a modern state based on the ancient culture and traditions of the

Korean people. Instead, as you know, Korea was split into two nations, each with a very different political and economic system.

South Korea Under Rhee, 1948-1961. The new South Korean constitution guaranteed the people basic freedoms, provided for regular elections, and granted considerable power to the National Assembly, South Korea's legislature. Soon after the constitution was adopted, U.S. troops withdrew from now-independent South Korea. However, the new nation faced grave problems. A series of communist-led uprisings rocked South Korea in 1949. Though they were suppressed, they deepened the growing distrust and enmity between South Korea and North Korea.

President Syngman Rhee became convinced that North Korea intended to weaken and eventually overthrow his government. It would do this, Rhee feared, by supporting a communist guerrilla movement in South Korea or by an outright armed invasion. In 1950, as you read in Chapter 9, Rhee's fears were realized. Kim Il-Sung, the North Korean communist leader, ordered his army to invade South Korea, and for three years the Korean War ravaged the peninsula. After the peace that came in 1953, South Korea and North Korea were farther apart than ever, and regarded each other as deadly foes.

Rhee's government in South Korea was convinced that it must dedicate all its efforts to rebuilding the nation and increasing its military power to prevent another North Korean attempt to reunify Korea by force. Rhee also believed that he must take strong measures to unify the people of South Korea behind his government even if he had to weaken the nation's new democracy. During the 1950s, Rhee resorted to **authoritarian rule**, governing as a strongman and often ignoring constitutional limits on his executive powers. Thus, Rhee often jailed those he termed communist conspirators as well as any political opponents. He allowed friends to take over many of the business enterprises the Japanese had developed, and he appointed supporters, many of whom were unqualified, to government offices.

Yet Rhee's strong-willed determination was accepted by most Koreans as necessary to rebuild the devastated country and to meet the threat posed by North Korea. To them, authoritarian rule seemed to be in keeping with the Confucian tradition of the people's duty to respect and obey the ruler.

The United States continued to back Rhee despite its misgivings about his authoritarian policies. In 1954, it signed a defense treaty to help protect South Korea from attack. It also continued to station a sizable U.S. military force along the DMZ border with North Korea. It also provided $3 billion in aid to help rebuild South Korea.

Economic and Social Problems. The South Korean economy was slow to recover from the destruction of the war, however. Preoccupied with protecting South Korea from attack from the north, Rhee seemed unable to focus on economic recovery as one of the nation's top priorities. Even by 1956, South Korea's industrial and agricultural production had barely returned to the level it had attained during World War II. Rhee's most important economic achievement was the redistribution of the nation's farmland. The large estates that had been held by the Japanese were divided among South Korean farmers, who now became owners of their own small plots of land.

Rhee and his Liberal party did little to cope with the vast social problems that the country faced, however. Many thousands of women had been widowed by the war and were without adequate means of support. Unemployment figures were staggering. Despite the land programs, farmers by the thousands were leaving the countryside to find work in the cities.

The Korean War widowed many South Korean women, who then could not support their children. The children were placed in homes while their mothers were being trained for work.

The Park Regime, 1961-1971.   Realizing how unpopular their regime was, Rhee and his party resolved to win the 1960 elections by any means, legal or illegal. Only by rigging the election did they win. Immediately, a nationwide protest spread across the nation. South Koreans were no longer willing to accept Rhee's authoritarian rule, especially when it was the result of illegal election practices. University students protested, and people held demonstrations throughout the nation. Rhee was forced to flee the country, and a new, more liberal government was elected.

However, the new government was based on factions that were badly divided. Unrest continued as new protests and demands for reform were heard. The new government was further weakened by radical groups that insisted that it negotiate with communist North Korea on unifying the nation. Then, in May 1961, a group of army officers led by General Park Chung Hee (pahrk chung hee) seized control of the government of South Korea.

General Park Chung Hee ruled South Korea with an iron hand to protect it, as he claimed, from attack by North Korea. He suppressed critics of his regime harshly.

Park declared martial law and established a **junta,** or a military government controlled by army officers. The National Assembly was dissolved, all political parties were banned, and the Korean Central Intelligence Agency was established to strengthen the government's power. South Koreans had little choice but to accept the new government. Nevertheless, many hoped that Park's government would lead to stability and an end to the political turmoil that had gripped their nation. Park played on these hopes, declaring that he would end military rule as soon as the economy was strengthened and corrupt business and political leaders had been removed.

A New Constitution.   In December 1962, Park drew up a new constitution for South Korea. It called for a strong president elected directly by the people. He had wide powers to appoint a prime minister and government officials without the approval of the National Assembly. Park said he would withdraw from politics as soon as a new presidential election was held. Then in March 1963 he shifted his position, declaring that the army should rule South Korea for four more years, until conditions improved enough to have a civilian government. At this point, the U.S. government's opposition and growing resistance at home forced Park to back down, and he agreed to hold the election in October. Park then resigned from his position in the army and announced he would be a candidate for the presidency.

Park won the 1963 election, but under his presidency South Korea had an even more authoritarian government than it had known during the Rhee regime. During Park's rule, South Korea built up its armed forces. Beginning in 1965, it sent troops to Vietnam to support U.S. forces fighting there. This move helped reduce the U.S. government's criticism of Park's harsh rule at home. In that same year, 20 years after the end of World War II, Park negotiated a peace treaty with Japan. However, Park's rule grew even more authoritarian in the early 1970s. In 1971, after having been reelected president, he declared a state of national emergency, outlawed opposition political parties, closed down the universities, and imposed strict censorship. During the remainder of the 1970s, Park ruled South Korea by force, often using martial law. Opposition leaders were forced into exile, student protestors were arrested, and the press was heavily censored.

However, during the 1960s and 1970s, South Korea experienced dramatic economic growth. As in Japan, this growth was dubbed an "economic miracle." The harsh policies of the Park government were easier for the Korean people to live with when incomes were rising, new housing was built, and living standards were rising substantially.

Assassination of President Park.   In October 1979 President Park was assassinated by the head of the Korean CIA. During the months that followed, South Korea seemed headed for greater freedom. Then in May 1980, army officers working behind the scenes regained control of the government. Chun Doo Hwan (chun doo whahn), an army officer and follower of President Park, assumed power, putting down student protests and declaring martial law. In September 1980, Chun dissolved all existing political parties. He then established the Democratic Justice party, made up of military officers and some civilian leaders. Chun then lifted martial law and called for a presidential election. A new constitution increased the power of the National Assembly and limited the president to one seven-year term in office. In February 1981, Chun was elected South Korea's new president.

President Chun's Administration, 1981-1987.   In the early 1980s, President Chun proclaimed a "new era" in national politics. South Korea entered a period of relative peace and stability for the first time in many years. Chun showed himself to be a capable leader who loosened many of the harsh controls established by the Park regime. His policies also successfully ended a steep downturn in the economy that had lasted from 1980 through 1982.

By the mid-1980s, new opposition political parties had gained strength under Chun's less authoritarian rule. They demanded more freedom and confronted Chun's government on a growing number of issues. Their challenge won strong support among university students, who staged widespread protests. Chun then pledged to voluntarily step aside when his term of office ended in 1988.

In the presidential election held in December 1987, Chun kept his pledge, making his regime the first ever in South Korea to transfer power peacefully. The Democratic Justice party turned to a new leader, Roh Tae Woo (roh teh woo), who won a narrow victory against the divided opposition parties. President Roh then moved to build his support among the people by allowing greater freedom of the press, permitting students to organize and workers to form labor unions, and releasing political foes from prison. In 1990, the Democratic Justice party joined with two of the opposition parties to form a new united political party, the Democratic Liberal party (DLP). South Koreans hoped that President Roh would finally be able to bring political stability to their nation and that the long era of authoritarian rule was coming to an end.

South Korean students, wearing masks to protect them from tear gas, protest in Seoul against President Roh's labor policies and demand that he resign.

NORTH KOREA, A COMMUNIST NATION

After World War II, Korean communists led by Kim Il-Sung gained control of North Korea during the Soviet occupation. Then in the decades that followed, Kim Il-Sung established a one-party totalitarian state that controlled every aspect of its people's lives.

The Rise of Kim Il-Sung. At the end of World War II, Soviet troops liberated northern Korea from Japanese rule. Groups of Korean communists who had been in exile and had fought against Japan in China and Manchuria returned to their homeland. Kim Il-Sung, who had been imprisoned by the Japanese for leading guerrilla resistance forces in Manchuria, soon won out in a struggle for power among returning exiles. With the backing of the occupying Soviet army, Kim became head of the Korean Communist party in 1946. In 1948 he came to power as absolute ruler of the new communist nation of North Korea, a position he has held for over 40 years.

Kim Il-Sung moved quickly to build up the military power of North Korea. With military aid from his Chinese and Soviet allies, Sung's army grew to 200,000 troops by 1950, nearly twice the strength of South Korea's forces. However, when he launched his invasion of South Korea in 1950, even this force was not large enough to win once the United States had come to South Korea's rescue. Communist China had to enter the war on Kim's side to save him from defeat. After 1953, China became even more important than the Soviet Union as North Korea's ally. Even with the war ended, North Korea continued to maintain a huge military force, spending more than 20 percent of its GNP annually on weapons and defense.

Building a Totalitarian State.   Under Kim Il-Sung, North Korea became a totalitarian state, or a nation in which the ruler has absolute control over the people. The North Korean people were indoctrinated with the ideals of communism, and public education was used to develop citizens loyal to communism—and to Kim Il-Sung. The secret police suppressed all attempts at opposition.

Under Kim Il-Sung, the government took over the ownership and operation of all factories and businesses, private property was abolished, and farms were controlled by the state. The government drew up a series of five-year plans to develop North Korea's industry and agriculture. This total **planned economy** was designed to serve the needs of the state. The North Korean people now had no choice except to obey their communist rulers. During the 1950s and 1960s, as you will read, North Korea successfully rebuilt its wartorn economy and made major advances in developing its heavy industry and in increasing its agricultural production.

The Cult of the "Great Leader."   As Kim Il-Sung became absolute ruler of North Korea, he was depicted as a near superhuman figure. He was called the "Great Leader," who looked after the needs of his people at home and protected them from their deadly enemies in South Korea. Kim was constantly praised in the press, and his speeches and writings were discussed in factory and farm group meetings. Korean history as taught in the schools emphasized Kim's and his ancestors' role in building North Korea as a nation. Giant statues of Kim and posters with his picture were installed in cities and villages across North Korea. The largest university and many government buildings were named after Kim. In Pyongyang, a 105-story hotel, the tallest building in Asia, was dedicated to him.

Kim Il-Sung being greeted by his supporters. Responding to the campaign to portray him as a "Great Leader," many of them were overcome with emotion in his presence.

The communist Korean Workers party headed by Kim was referred to as the "mother" party, and North Korea itself was called a harmonious "family." As this clearly demonstrated, Kim skillfully used Korea's Confucian tradition to strengthen his regime. Systematically, he replaced Confucian loyalty to family and the family's ancestors with loyalty to the state and the Communist party. Thus people were taught that a society based on harmony among its members—the Confucian ideal—was now being achieved in North Korea under Kim's totalitarian regime.

The following quotation from a North Korean government newspaper is typical of North Korean **propaganda**, or information used to indoctrinate Kim Il-Sung's totalitarian philosophy.

> Kim Il-Sung . . . is the great father of our people. . . . Long is the history of the word "father" being used here as a word representing love and reverence . . . expressing the unbreakable blood ties between the people and the leader. Father. This familiar word represents our people's single heart of boundless respect and loyalty. . . . The love shown by the Great Leader of our people is the love of kinship. Our respected and beloved leader is the tender-hearted father of all the people.

> His heart is the traction [pulling] power attracting the hearts of all
> people . . . uniting them as one. . . . Kim Il-Sung is the great sun and
> the great man. . . . Thanks to his great heart, national independence
> is firmly guaranteed.

The reality, however, was very different from the benevolent society depicted by North Korean propaganda. North Korean society, in fact, was based on the power of a totalitarian state administered by a communist government backed by powerful military forces. All of the nation's men and some women had to serve in the army, where loyalty and self-sacrifice were taught together with communist ideology and praise of Kim Il-Sung.

In keeping with the personality cult of the "Great Leader," Kim Il-Sung began to groom his son, Kim Jong Il (kim jung eel), to be his successor. He appointed Kim Jong Il to several powerful government posts in the 1970s, and the son also served in the second-highest position in the Korean Workers party. North Korea's propaganda machine worked overtime praising the writings and the achievements of the "Dear Leader," as Kim Jong Il was being called by the 1980s. By 1992, however, the "Great Leader" was still firmly in power, though he was now 80 years old. It remained to be seen whether he would realize his wish to establish a communist dynasty in North Korea.

The Policy of *Chuch'e*. During the 1970s, Kim Il-Sung tried to become less dependent on aid and support from other communist nations. He then followed a policy that concentrated on strengthening North Korean nationalism. This new policy, called ***chuch'e*** (choo-cheh), stressed the nation's need for self-reliance and independence. This meant that North Korea had to develop an economy that was self-sufficient and less dependent on imports. It meant that North Korea had to make its own defense forces more powerful and depend less on military alliances with China and the Soviet Union. It also indicated that North Korea did not wish to be drawn into the growing rivalry between these two communist powers. The *chuch'e* policy led to an even greater buildup of North Korea's armed forces and military might in the 1970s and 1980s. However, *chuch'e* was a failure in improving North Korea's economy, which faced increasingly serious problems in these years, as you will read.

Kim Il-Sung's new policy was also unsuccessful in its attempt to open diplomatic relations with non-communist nations. Some of North Korea's crude efforts to weaken South Korea alienated other countries.

For example, in 1983, North Korean terrorists attempted to assassinate Chun Doo Hwan. A bomb they planted during a visit by Chun to Burma (now Myanmar) killed several members of his cabinet, though Chun himself was unhurt. Later, in 1987, another bomb destroyed a South Korean airliner in an effort to undermine South Korea's role as host of the 1988 Olympic Games. These actions repelled nations that might have been inclined to view North Korea in a more favorable light.

SOUTH KOREA'S ECONOMIC DEVELOPMENT

South Korea's economy has been based on the free-enterprise system combined with centralized assistance and guidance from the government. South Korea's "economic miracle" has transformed it from a **developing nation** dependent on farming into an industrialized power and a leading trading nation. Today, South Korea's economy is one of the fastest growing in the world.

Industrial Growth in the 1950s and 1960s. When Korea was divided, South Korea's population was twice as large as North Korea's, but it had far fewer resources and industries. The Japanese had built steel mills and machine factories in northern Korea, but had kept southern Korea a largely agricultural area. South Korea not only lacked iron ore, high-quality coal, and other minerals needed to develop its industries, but it also had few energy sources. Therefore, when peace returned after the Korean War, South Korea began to establish industries that used less energy and required little in the way of natural resources. It turned to the manufacture of textiles, radios, calculators, and transistor boards. Enterprising business people also imported technology from other nations to introduce new methods of manufacturing. The Rhee government helped by establishing tariffs and other trade restrictions to protect the developing industries from imported products. During these years, South Korea was barely able to produce enough goods to meet the needs of its people. It imported far more goods than it exported, and its economic growth was financed largely by foreign aid provided by the United States and international lending agencies.

During the 1960s, South Korea began to build a strong industrial base. Under President Park's regime, the government drew up a series of five-year economic plans to guide the development of the nation's economy. All of this planning had as its major goal the modernizing of Korea's manufacturing plants to produce goods for export to other nations. Much of this centralized planning was undertaken by the Economic Planning Board (EPB) established by the Park government. The EPB provided tax advantages, low-cost loans, and many other incentives to promote the growth of industries. In doing so, it usually favored large manufacturers and big businesses, since only large enterprises would be able to compete in world export markets.

With such help, South Korea's GNP rose from $2.3 billion in 1962 to $6 billion in 1965, then expanded even more, reaching $25 billion by 1970. A large part of South Korea's success in these years was due to its skilled labor force. The introduction of compulsory education and technical and vocational schools helped produce a highly literate workforce committed to a high level of productivity. Many returning veterans of the Korean War also were now experienced in handling electronic equipment and complex machinery. In addition, many South Koreans who had studied business methods, engineering, and scientific technology in the United States and other Western nations now had returned to South Korea to help their nation modernize. In the nation's relatively large population, workers also competed for jobs, thus keeping wages low.

South Korean workers' commitment to high quality work and their hard work helped South Korea make great strides toward industrialization. By the mid-1960s, South Korea's industrial production was growing at a rate of 25 percent a year, one of the highest growth rates in the world. Manufacturing employees worked a six-day week and often put in overtime hours without extra pay. Women filled many jobs, especially in the textile industry, though they received lower pay than men and were expected to leave their jobs when they married.

South Korea's *Chaebol*.   Another reason for South Korea's economic success and a central feature of its modern economy was the ***chaebol*** (cheh-boh). The *chaebol* were large business conglomerates that controlled many of the nation's large industries. The *chaebol* conglomerates received low-interest loans from the government, foreign-aid funds, and other assistance during the 1950s. They worked closely with the Economic Planning Board to help produce the goods and exports called for in the government's five-year plans. Many of the original founders of the *chaebol* still head these businesses, and members of their family hold top positions in their operations.

Each *chaebol* usually owns and operates factories and plants in many different kinds of businesses. Today, for example, one *chaebol*, Samsung, operates in such varied businesses as consumer electronics, textiles, construction, shipbuilding, heavy machinery, computers, aircraft, and finance. Another *chaebol*, Hyundai, owns shipyards, manufactures cars, produces steel and heavy machinery, and runs financial institutions. Still another, Lucky-Gold Star, produces an equally wide range of goods, from chemicals to VCRs.

Because of their key role in developing the nation's economy, the *chaebol* have achieved a dominant role in South Korea. By 1977, the top ten *chaebol* were producing goods whose total value was nearly half of the nation's annual GNP. Today, the five largest *chaebol* account for nearly half of the nation's annual GNP. Most of the *chaebol* compete against one another. They have vast resources that enable them to employ advanced technology and achieve economies that come with large-scale manufacturing. The *chaebol* recruit many of their executives and managers from South Korea's leading universities, and they employ nearly half of the nation's industrial workforce. Many small South Korean businesses and factories also are subcontractors for the *chaebol*. As you can see, there are many similarities between big business in South Korea and Japan.

Changes in Agriculture. Until the 1960s, South Korea's economy was still based largely on agriculture. Over half of the population still made their living by farming their own land, usually small plots that averaged less than 2.5 acres (1 hectare). Most of South Korea's 1.5 million farmers cultivated rice. Yet, during the 1950s, the nation had to import rice and other grains to feed its people. During the 1960s, farm productivity increased as more small machinery was being used and improved strains of seed and fertilizer were introduced. The Saemaul Undong movement also helped farming communities to cooperate in improving rural life. (See Chapter 8.)

The five-year plans of the Park government targeted improvements in agriculture as a high priority. During the 1960s, government loans helped farmers modernize rice production, and government crop price guarantees encouraged farmers to increase their output of rice. The Park government also supported a national system of farm cooperatives to provide credit, insurance, and storage facilities, all designed to improve farmers' productivity. In addition, the government brought electricity to rural areas and greatly improved rural roads so that farmers could get their crops to market readily. Nevertheless, in the 1960s and increasingly in the 1970s, large numbers of people, especially younger family members, continued to leave rural areas and migrate to the cities seeking jobs in South Korea's new industries.

In the 1970s, with a declining farm population, some small farms were merged. Using improved irrigation, hybrid seeds, and new types of fertilizer, these larger farms produced some of the highest yields of rice in the world. By 1977, South Korea's farmers were growing enough rice to feed the nation. However, the standard of living among the nation's farmers had fallen below that of workers in the industrialized cities. To remedy this situation, the government embarked on a new course. It increased its imports of rice and other food from abroad, mainly from the United States. This permitted Korean farmers to shift to raising livestock, fruits and vegetables, and other crops that could be sold at higher prices than rice. This brought a larger income to most South Korean farmers, making it possible for them to buy cars, live in better homes, and share in the higher standard of living enjoyed by the nation's urban population. Today, only 21 percent of the population earns its living by farming, a little more than half of what it was in 1977. Agriculture now accounts for only 10 percent of the nation's GNP, as opposed to 24 percent in 1977.

The Shift to Heavy Industry.   By the 1970s, South Korea's economy was beginning to shift from light industries to heavy industry such as steel, chemicals, shipbuilding, and construction. International developments, President Park and officials of the Economic Planning Board realized, would force the nation to become more self reliant. The U.S. recognition of Communist China and the withdrawal of U.S. forces from Vietnam would make South Korea more dependent on its own military power for defense against North Korea. Thus the development of heavy industry was vital to enable South Korea to produce more of its own weapons and military needs.

At the same time, these new industries were used to build the modern **infrastructure**, or basic facilities of a nation, needed in Korea's rapidly expanding cities and industrial centers. Highways, bridges, airports, and railroads were modernized, and harbors and port facilities were expanded. Electrification, sewers, and water systems improved living conditions in South Korea's cities and rural villages alike. South Korea also became a world leader in doing construction work for other countries, building more than $21 billion worth of pipelines, buildings, docks, and other facilities in the Middle East alone. The income from this work was a great help in enabling South Korea to cope with the "oil-shock" of the 1970s, when world petroleum prices quadrupled. South Korea's economy, largely dependent on imported oil, thus managed to continue its rapid growth throughout the decade. The nation's GNP

This automated steel mill in Seoul dates from the period when South Korea was building up its heavy industries to make the country less dependent on other nations.

more than doubled in the 1970s, increasing from $25 billion in 1970 to $58 billion by 1980. During this period, South Korea had a record GNP growth rate of between 11 and 12 percent each year. The nation's exports also grew at an annual rate of nearly 50 percent during most of these years.

A Newly Industrialized Country. By the 1980s, South Korea's economy had been transformed. It had become a modern industrial nation. South Korea, together with Taiwan, Singapore, and Hong Kong, was now regarded by the nations of the world as a **"newly industrialized country."** At this time, also, South Korean industries and government planners had begun to make basic shifts in the economy to meet changing conditions. Rising world oil prices and increasing wage costs in South Korea now favored industries that required less energy and fewer workers. As a result, the United States and other nations began to buy computers and semiconductors, VCRs, TVs, camcorders, microwave ovens, cars, running shoes, and clothing produced by South Korean

South Korea has turned to the manufacture of television sets and other electronic products and is now a strong competitor of Japan and other East Asian countries.

chaebol companies. The people of South Korea also became a major market for many of these new consumer goods as their incomes and standard of living rose.

In less than 30 years, South Korea's exported goods have skyrocketed from a total of $50 million in 1962 to more than $71.5 billion in 1991. Its largest customers are the United States and Japan. In addition, more than half of the raw materials and products South Korea imports come from these two nations. South Korea continues to maintain its close political ties with the United States, and it has improved its political relationship with its former enemy, Japan. Large Japanese investments, manufacturing facilities, and loans have also played a major role in South Korea's economic miracle. South Korea's dynamic economic growth still continues.

However, South Korea may find it difficult to maintain its record economic growth. In recent years, workers have demanded and received higher wages, and this added cost may make South Korean products less competitive. The nation's labor unions, weak in the past, have been growing in strength. World markets for some of the nation's products are becoming flooded with high-quality goods from many other countries. South Korea's huge spending on its military defense also has become a deep drain on its economy, with nearly 40 percent of the nation's annual budget devoted to defense. But perhaps the most serious and most unpredictable challenge South Korea faces is its future relations with North Korea after Kim Il-Sung passes from the scene. After many years of failed efforts, in 1991 the two Koreas signed a series of agreements pledging to work for reunification and to settle all disputes peacefully, as you will read. Whether these agreements will be carried out and what will happen when a new North Korean regime takes power remain open questions.

NORTH KOREA'S ECONOMY

Although North Korea is very secretive about the details of its economy, it is possible to piece together a general picture of how the economy has developed and what some of its main features are. Like South Korea, North Korea has made great progress in industrializing the country.

A Planned Communist Economy.   North Korea is a communist state in which all businesses, farms, and factories are owned and operated by the government. All decisions about what goods to produce and how much to produce are made by North Korea's communist government. In this **command economy**, the government of Kim Il-Sung dictates that all the nation's human and natural resources be made to serve the purposes of the communist state.

When North Korea was established in 1948, it set about capitalizing on the important advantages it had over South Korea's economy. Most of the peninsula's coal, iron ore, and other mineral resources were in North Korea, and most of the nation's sources of hydroelectric power were there as well. In addition, during their occupation of Korea, the Japanese had developed a mining industry and had built steel plants, a chemical industry, and tool factories there. Thus, North Korea had a base on which to build its industrial economy.

Emphasis on Heavy Industry.   Kim Il-Sung was determined to undertake the expansion of heavy industry in North Korea, giving it top priority over agriculture and the production of consumer goods. His goal was to establish steel plants and machinery factories that would be used to build up North Korea's future economy. At the same time this would make his nation less dependent on the Soviet Union and Communist China. Kim Il-Sung's plan proved successful, and North Korean industry grew rapidly, increasing by nearly 36 percent annually by the late

1950s. During the 1950s and 1960s, Kim Il-Sung's propaganda truthfully boasted that North Korea, under communist rule, was industrializing more rapidly than South Korea. However, this relationship began to be reversed by the 1970s.

During the 1970s, more than 80 percent of North Korea's investments were in heavy industry, but the economy's growth rate fell. As the economy grew, central planning by the government became more difficult and inefficient. In addition, the Soviets and Chinese no longer supplied large grants of money. They now gave their economic aid in the form of loans, which had to be repaid. As a result, North Korea was unable to buy the advanced technology it needed to expand its industry. With a population less than half the size of South Korea's, it began to experience a shortage of labor. Moreover, North Korea's huge defense expenditures diverted funds from heavy industry. Kim Il-Sung's policy of *chuch'e* that emphasized a self-sufficient economy proved to be a drawback. It handicapped future development since it prevented North Korea from shifting to the production of the new kinds of export goods that were in increasing demand in the world market. To make matters worse, many of the nation's factories and plants were becoming old and outdated and needed to be replaced.

During the 1970s, North Korea finally turned to Japan and European nations for new technology. It imported entire factories as well as the most up-to-date equipment from these nations. By the mid-1970s, nearly 40 percent of its trade was with non-communist nations. Unfortunately, world prices on many of the minerals that North Korea exported in order to pay for these imports fell sharply. Kim Il-Sung's government then was unable to pay the debt it owed Japan and other nations. North Korea also was handicapped by the sharp rise in the cost of Middle East oil in the 1970s, especially when the Soviet Union stopped selling oil to North Korea at artificially low prices. In addition, North Korea faced continuing problems in producing enough coal and hydroelectric power to fuel its energy-intensive industries. By 1976, North Korea's GNP stood at about $10 billion, less than half the GNP of South Korea.

In the 1980s, North Korea continued to experience difficulties in its industrial development. The government seemed to alternate between the *chuch'e* policy of self-sufficiency and importing needed products and technology from other countries. Its trade with Communist China and the Soviet Union continued to decline, while South Korea's trade with these communist nations outstripped North Korea's. North Korea's imports continued to exceed its exports in many of these years.

250

It also continued to pile up debts with other nations that it could not repay. Meanwhile, it continued to emphasize heavy industry, becoming a major producer and exporter of tanks, artillery, and other weapons. Industrial production dropped off sharply in the 1990s. In 1992, for the first time in its history, the government tried to attract investment from non-communist countries to bolster its sagging economy.

Agriculture in North Korea. Like industry, agriculture in North Korea is controlled by the state. All farming is done on **cooperatives,** or state-owned farms. More than 300 families live and work on each of the cooperatives. Management committees assign jobs, distribute seeds and fertilizers, and supervise work to ensure that the cooperatives meet the quotas set by the government. Rice is the principal crop, but barley, wheat, soybeans, and sweet potatoes also are widely grown. Although rice production doubled between 1949 and 1969, North Korea still had to import rice to meet its people's needs. During the 1970s and 1980s, the government permitted some cooperatives also to raise vegetables and fruit as well as some livestock. However, those crops, like all others, had to be sold to the state. The only crops that are not under government control are garden vegetables that farmers grow on small plots and sell for their own profit.

PROSPECTS FOR REUNIFICATION

Korea's long history as a single nation with a homogeneous people who share a common language and culture has made its division into two separate countries especially tragic. With the deep-seated Confucian tradition, which all Koreans share, of the vital ties of kinship, the division of Korea and the resulting separation of members of many families is profoundly painful. Therefore, the dream of unification persists today.

Early Negotiations. The earliest attempt by North Korea and South Korea to reconcile their differences came in 1972. In that year, high-ranking officials of the two nations met and, after secret talks, announced agreement on several matters. They stated that North Korea and South Korea would seek reunification through peaceful means, without the intrusion of outside powers, and that they would devote their common efforts to achieving a "great national unity." However, the great hopes this stirred among Koreans everywhere quickly disappeared when the effort failed. Though both sides continued to make proposals during the next few years, they soon bogged down in propaganda and name-calling. Little concrete action toward reunification occurred again until the mid-1980s.

In 1984, serious efforts began again, when North Korea offered to send emergency relief supplies to flood victims in South Korea. After the Red Cross handled these deliveries successfully, officials of the two nations met to discuss plans for the 1988 Olympics and other matters. Although North Korea decided to boycott the Olympics, this meeting did have a positive result. It drew up a plan to reunite a small number of Korean families who had been separated since 1948. In September of 1985, 50 members of separated families from the North and another group from the South were reunited in Seoul and in Pyongyang. Millions of Koreans in both nations watched TV broadcasts of these tearful reunions of family members who had not seen each other in 37 years. Yet, these brief reunions only symbolized the far larger problem of the 5 million South Koreans who had come from North Korea. It symbolized not only the deep longing to reunite families but also people's dreams of reunifying their nation.

New Hope for Reunification. When Cuba was the only other communist nation to boycott the 1988 Olympics, North Korea's growing isolation from other nations became clear. It may have encouraged Kim Il-Sung's government to reconsider its need to improve relations with South Korea. In early 1991, North Korea and South Korea were admitted as separate members of the United Nations. Although some experts feared that this might make discourage moves to end the division of Korea, major world events soon led to important new negotiations between the two Koreas. In 1991, after the collapse of the Soviet Union, U.S. President George Bush announced that the United States would remove its nuclear weapons from most nations, including South Korea. In December, President Roh declared South Korea no longer possessed such weapons and invited North Korea to send inspectors to verify this. Roh then asked North Korea to make the same promise and allow international inspection of its weapons arsenal. South Korea and the United States suspected North Korea had secretly begun to develop nuclear weapons on its own. But even before this matter was settled, in December 1991, North and South Korea reached an historic agreement.

In that agreement, which covered many of the long-standing disputes between the two nations, North and South Korea pledged to move rapidly toward solving these problems in order to bring about the peaceful reunification of Korea. Both sides promised to undertake a

252

CASE STUDY:

A Longing for the Homeland

Before the 1985 reunion, no letters or phone calls or visits had ever been allowed between separated family members in North and South Korea. A U.S. journalist talked to an older couple who had fled from North Korea to Seoul and now more than ever longed to see their family again.

Maybe Min Kyung Nam's parents were alive and maybe they died when he was a young man. Lately he had been thinking about his parents. He had nothing from them, except for a photograph taken of his father and his father's friend. . . .

Min had not seen his parents since he left their home for the South to avoid conscription [being drafted] in the North Korean army. "We thought we'd go back and get them," he said. "We didn't know the division would be permanent. . . ."

The Red Cross office was all but empty when Min came to fill out his application to search for his parents. . . .

I asked Min and his wife Kim when they thought most of home and Kim said, "I tend to think about my home during festival time, during a full moon, or the time when we pray to our ancestors. I want to go and see where I lived. But I don't want to live there."

I asked if they could find their homes if they returned. Min said, "Yes, I could find my home. I dream about the roads I used to walk, about the landscape, about the whole place, what it looked like."

Now, however, he was dwelling upon the circumstances of his leaving, about having to run while his parents stayed behind to safeguard the home. "At that time it was a matter of life and death," he said. "Maybe if I had stayed there, it would have been different. I don't know if I did the right thing by leaving. But I couldn't stay. It was a choice where regrets were inevitable."

From Michael Shapiro, *The Shadow in the Sun*. New York: Atlantic Monthly Press, 1990.

1. Why did Min Kyung Nam leave North Korea?
2. What feelings did Kim and his wife express about wanting to return to their hometown?

*Meetings like this of diplomats from North Korea and
South Korea have encouraged Koreans to believe that at
last the two countries may be on the road to unification.*

series of important steps that would end their rivalry and lead to friendship and unity. For example, they pledged to stop all aggressive policies
and propaganda, to promote disarmament, and to allow free travel by
their citizens and the reuniting of divided families.

No one could be certain, of course, of the outcome of this ground-
breaking agreement. Some experts warned that it might not be carried
out at all. They pointed to the possible buildup of nuclear weapons in
North Korea, which stalled on accepting inspection by international
observers. Others worried that when Kim Il-Sung departed his successor
might pursue less peaceful policies that would delay or even destroy
plans for unification of the two Koreas. Yet, despite these uncertainties,
the Korean people in the early 1990s seemed to have more reason than
ever for optimism as they viewed their future.

REVIEWING THE CHAPTER

I. Building Your Vocabulary

Match the definitions with their terms.

authoritarian rule	*chuch'e*
junta	*chaebol*
command economy	totalitarian state
cooperatives	propaganda
infrastructure	

1. a nation in which the ruler has absolute control over the people

2. state-owned farms

3. information used to indoctrinate ideas

4. a government controlled by army officers

5. government that ignores limits on executive power

6. business conglomerates that control large industries in South Korea

7. an economic system that controls all the nation's human and natural resources to serve the state

8. North Korea's policy of stressing self-reliance and independence

9. a nation's roads, communication systems, and other facilities

II. Understanding the Facts

Write the letter of the correct answer to each statement next to its number.

1. President Syngman Rhee of South Korea used authoritarian rule during his four terms in office because:
   a. he had been elected by the majority of the voters.
   b. he had been put in power by army officers.
   c. he believed he must take strong measures to unite South Koreans to prevent North Korea from attacking.
   d. he established a communist government.

2. During the 18 years that Park Chun-Hee headed the government of South Korea:
   a. South Korea built up its economy and strengthened its military power.
   b. North Korea signed agreements with South Korea that helped reduce tensions between the two nations.
   c. South Korea kept the same constitution that had been written during the Rhee regime.
   d. South Korea sent President Rhee into exile.

3. During Kim Il-Sung's rule of North Korea, the government:
   a. won victory in the Korean War with the support of Communist China.
   b. developed a propaganda machine that indoctrinated the people to support Kim as the "Great Leader."
   c. became an ally of Japan and the Soviet Union during the Cold War.
   d. sought to make North Korea more democratic.

4. North Korea's policy of self-reliance and independence caused it to:
   a. reduce its trade with other communist nations and build up its own heavy industry.
   b. support the Soviet Union in its quarrels with Communist China.
   c. shift more toward producing and exporting consumer goods and rice.
   d. ease tensions and open trade with South Korea.

5. The growth of South Korea's economy during the 1970s and 1980s:
   a. changed it from a nation that manufactured products for export to one that produced goods largely for its own people.
   b. was helped by the government's strict regulations on the business conglomerates.
   c. depended largely on its military power.
   d. changed it from a developing agricultural nation into a newly industrialized nation.

III. Thinking It Through

Write the letter of your correct conclusion to each statement next to its number.

1. Strong rule by Presidents Rhee and Park was accepted by South Koreans in part because:
   a. they were the citizens of a totalitarian, communist state.
   b. Confucian tradition taught that the people should respect and honor their rulers.
   c. South Koreans had a strong democratic tradition.
   d. Buddhist tradition taught that enlightenment was brought by strong rulers.

2. Kim Il-Sung spent a large part of his nation's GNP on building up North Korea's military power after the Korean War because:
   a. this was a major part of his policy of seeking alliances with the Soviet Union and Communist China.
   b. the North Korean armed forces provided discipline and training for future members of the Korean Workers party.
   c. he followed a policy that aimed at unifying Korea by force.
   d. he was planning to establish a new North Korean empire.

3. The conglomerates of South Korea's businesses and industries have an important role in the nation's economy because:
   a. they employ half the workforce and produce most of the products manufactured in South Korea.
   b. they hire the most talented workers.
   c. the government's Economic Planning Board established them.
   d. they are monopolies that control South Korea's government.

4. Propaganda in North Korea taught the people to regard Kim Il-Sung as their "Great Leader" because:
   a. Kim wanted to provide the people with a free, open society in which they could enjoy the benefits of communism.
   b. propaganda and indoctrination helped the communist leader to maintain his absolute rule.
   c. both Buddhist and Confucian teachings emphasize the absolute power of rulers.
   d. he brought the people a living standard much higher than that of South Korea.

5. The division of Korea into two nations has been a tragedy for the Korean people because:
   a. each nation has been unable to take advantage of the resources that it lacked but that the other nation had.
   b. both governments have developed the same kind of economic

system but have been unable to agree on how to reunite the nation.

   c. the people were divided, families were separated, and two different ways of life developed among a homogenous people.

   d. the Japanese occupation separated the people and destroyed Korea's culture.

DEVELOPING CRITICAL THINKING SKILLS

1. Explain why the Korean War was such a severe setback for the Korean people.

2. Describe the main features of the totalitarian state established by Kim Il-Sung in North Korea.

3. Explain why South Korea was able to achieve an "economic miracle."

4. Discuss some of the reasons for North Korea's present economic problems.

5. Give three reasons why North and South Korea have found it so difficult to reunify their nation.

ENRICHMENT AND EXPLORATION

1. Make a chart comparing the economies of North Korea and South Korea. Use these headings for each nation: type of economy, the role of government, main features of the economy, natural resources, chief industries, major crops, main imports, main exports.

2. Imagine that you are an adviser to President Roh of South Korea and are helping him prepare for final negotiations with North Korea on reunifying the nation. Draw up a list of the major points that you think he should discuss at the meeting. Then prepare a brief memorandum outlining the terms of the agreement you believe he should propose. One of your classmates should act as an adviser to Premier Kim Il-Sung and prepare the same kind of list and proposal.

Glossary

arable: suitable for farming *(p. 13)*

archipelago: (ahr-kuh-PEL-uh-goh): a chain of islands *(p. 2)*

artificial intelligence: the capability of a machine to imitate intelligent human behavior *(p. 141)*

authoritarian rule: system of government characterized by unlimited executive power *(p. 234)*

balance of trade: the difference in value between a country's imports and exports *(p. 155)*

barter: to trade by exchanging one commodity for another *(p. 48)*

bicameral: a legislature consisting of two chambers or houses *(p. 114)*

bonsai: (bohn-seye): potted plant dwarfed by special methods or the art of growing such a plant *(p. 101)*

Buddhism: a religion of eastern and central Asia based on the teachings of Gautama Buddha *(p. 28)*

bunraku (boon-RAH-koo): Japanese puppet plays *(p. 47)*

burakumin (boo-rah-KOO-min): descendants of people who were butchers and leather tanners in early Japan *(p. 17)*

bureaucracy: the administrative or management system of a government; the officials in such a system *(p. 29)*

bushido (BOO-shee-doh): Japanese code of chivalry that valued honor above life and guided the lives of the samurai *(p. 36)*

calligraphy: beautiful or elegant handwriting or the art of producing such writing *(p. 32)*

centralized: power and authority concentrated in one body or organization *(p. 28)*

ch'usok (choo-sahk): Korean moon festival *(p. 198)*

chaebol (cheh-bohl): business conglomerates that control large industries in South Korea *(p. 244)*

chuch'e (choo-cheh): North Korean nationalist policy *(p. 242)*

clan: a group united by a presumed common ancestor *(p. 207)*

coalition: a temporary alliance between states or parties for the purpose of joint action *(p. 27)*

Cold War: the state of tension and hostility short of actual fighting between the United States and the Soviet Union *(p. 80)*

command economy: economic system in which the state controls all of a nation's human and natural resources *(p. 249)*

cooperatives: in North Korea, state-owned farms *(p. 251)*

cultural adaptation: the process of borrowing aspects of another nation's culture *(p. 15)*

daimyo (DEYE-myoh): a Japanese feudal baron *(p. 39)*

danchi (DAHN-chee): a modern Japanese apartment complex built with government money *(p. 102)*

developing nation: a nation stil largely dependent on farming that is developing its industry *(p. 175)*

dialect: form of a language spoken in a particular region or community *(p. 18)*

Diet: the Japanese national legislature *(p. 65)*

DMZ: the demilitarized zone between North Korea and South Korea *(p. 227)*

economic miracle: term used to describe Japan's spectacular economic growth beginning in the 1950s *(p. 138)*

embargo: a restriction imposed on trade with a country *(p. 73)*

enterprise union: in Japan a labor union formed within a single company (p. 147)

extended family: a family group that includes in one household near relatives in addition to the father and mother and their children (p. 88)

extraterritoriality: the right of foreigners in a country to be subject to their own country's laws rather than the laws of the country in which they live (p. 57)

faction: a special-interest group in a larger unit such as a political party (p. 121)

feudalism: social and political system based on loyalty of vassals to lords (p. 35)

foreign policy: the policy of a nation in its dealings with other nations (p. 167)

fudai (foo-DEYE): hereditary daimyo who owned estates before 1600 (p. 44)

genro (gen-roh): elder Japanese statesmen (p. 58)

Greater East Asia Co-Prosperity Sphere: term applied by Japan to its planned empire in Asia and the Pacific region (p. 74)

gross national product: the amount of goods and services that a nation produces each year; abbreviated as GNP (p. 138)

group identity: people's sense of belonging to the same group (p. 16)

habatsu (hah-BAHT-soo): factions within the Japanese Diet (p. 121)

haiku (heye-koo): poem of 17 syllables in three lines that conveys a mood or paints a scene (p. 47)

han'gul (hahn-gul): the first Korean phonetic alphabet (p. 214)

Hermit Kingdom: Korea during a 200-year period when it isolated itself from other states (p. 216)

hierarchy (HEYE-uhr-ahr-kee): the ranking of people in a society (p. 99)

homogeneous: of the same or similar qualities (p. 14)

House of Councillors: upper house of the Japanese national legislature (p. 114)

House of Representatives: lower house of the Japanese national legislature (p. 114)

hydroelectric power: electricity produced by waterpower (p. 189)

ideology: a body of ideas about some aspect of human life or culture (p. 121)

ikebana (ih-kay-BAH-nah): Japanese art of flower arrangement (p. 101)

inflation: a sharp rise in the price of goods (p. 62)

infrastructure: the basic facilities of a nation such as roads and sewers (p. 246)

internationalize: to become part of the world community (p. 180)

isolationism: policy of withdrawal from contacts with other nations (p. 167)

jimu-jikan (jee-moo-JEE-kahn): in Japan, the vice-ministers who possess the real power in the ministries (p. 119)

juku (joo-koo): Japanese after-hours schools, or "cram schools," that give students additional instruction and prepare them for their tests (p. 94)

junta: military government controlled by army officers; also, the group that controls such a government (p. 237)

kabuki (kuh-BOO-kee): traditional Japanese popular drama performed in a highly stylized manner (p. 47)

kami (kahm-ee): gods of the Shinto religion (p. 27)

kamikazi (kah-mih-KAH-zee): literally, the "divine wind," applied to the typhoon that stopped the Mongol invasion of Japan in 1281 (p. 38)

kana (KAH-nah): writing system by which Japanese syllables are represented by Chinese characters (p. 18)

kanji (KAHN-jee): Chinese characters adopted by the Japanese for their written language (p. 18)

Keidanren (kay-dahn-ren): political organization representing the interests of Japan's businesses and industries (p. 123)

keiretsoo (KAY-ret-soo): large Japanese business firms (p. 143)

kendo: a Japanese form of fencing with bamboo swords (p. 94) *koenkai* (koh-en-keye): Japanese local political support groups *(p. 117)*

kogai (koh-geye): Japanese term for environmental harm *(p. 125)*

kojin-shugi (koh-jeen-SHOO-gee): Japanese term for individualism *(p. 101)*

kokusaika (koh-koo-SEYE-kah): Japanese term for internationalization *(p. 181)*

lobbying: attempt to influence public officials *(p. 123)*

mandate: a commission granted by the League of Nations to one country to administer another region or country *(p. 68)*

March 1 Movement: Korean nationalist demonstration of 1919 *(p. 223)*

maritime: of or relating to the sea or navigation *(p. 6)*

megalopolis: a thickly populated region centering in a city or embracing several cities *(p. 6)*

Meiji Restoration (may-jee): Meiji, meaning "enlightened government," the name the new Japanese emperor took in 1868; the period from then to 1912, a time of vast political, economic, and social changes.*(p. 58)*

monsoon: wind that changes direction with the seasons; especially the winds blowing to and from the Indian Ocean *(p. 7)*

morals classes: courses used to reinforce traditional Japanese values *(p. 64)*

nakodo (nah-KOH-doh): in Japan, a go-between or matchmaker *(p. 99)*

nationalism: a feeling of pride in and devotion to one's country *(p. 66)*

nemawashi (NEH-mah-wah-shee): in Japan, a method of reaching decisions by consulting with members of the group *(p. 99)*

newly industrialized country: a nation that has recently developed its industries and trade and has entered the competition for world markets *(p. 247)*

non-aggression treaty: an agreement under which each of the parties agrees not to attack the other *(p. 73)*

nuclear family: a family consisting of parents and their children *(p. 88)*

omiai (OH-mee-eye): Japanese term for arranged marriages *(p. 89)*

Pacific Ring of Fire: an area of deep trenches beneath the ocean along which Japan lies *(p.3)*

Pacific Rim: the countries that border or are located in the Pacific Ocean *(p. 181)*

parliamentary government: government in which power is centered in a parliament, or legislature *(p. 65)*

paternalistic: fatherly *(p. 96)*

pato (PAH-toh): in Japan, a part-time employee *(p. 91)*

planned economy: an economy in which all economic activity is planned by the state *(p. 240)*

population density: the number of inhabitants in a given area of land *(p. 11)*

prefecture: in Japan, a unit of local government *(p. 60)*

propaganda: ideas spread deliberately to further one's cause, or to damage an opposing cause *(p. 241)*

protectorate: a country ruled by and dependent on another power *(p. 221)*

puppet state: a country such as Manchuria that was under the control of Japan before World War II *(p. 71)*

quality circles: Japanese work-planning teams that meet regularly to discuss ways to improve group performance *(p. 143)*

regent: one who governs in place of a sovereign *(p. 34)*

reverse course: the attempt to return power that had been lost to local governments to the central government in post-occupation Japan *(p. 127)*

ringisei (ring-ee-say): in Japan, the process by which lower-level business executives and managers submit proposals to top management *(p. 144)*

robotics: computer-driven machines that perform tasks formerly done by humans *(p. 149)*

samurai (SAM-uh-reye): warrior knights of Japan during the feudal period (*p. 35*)

sarariiman: a term that comes from the English "salary man" that refers to businesspeople and white-collar workers (*p. 104*)

seppuku (sep-poo-koo): ritual suicide (*p. 37*)

shaman: a priest who uses magic to cure the sick and control events (*p. 197*)

shamanism: a religion characterized by belief in an unseen world of ancestral spirits responsive only to the shamans (*p. 197*)

Shinto: a Japanese religion, meaning literally, "the way of the Gods," that worships many gods that are found in nature (*p. 27*)

shogun (SHOH-gun): one of the military governors who ruled Japan in feudal times (*p. 35*)

shogunate: the government of shoguns (*p. 36*)

sirhak (seer-hahk): practical learning movement in Korea (*p. 217*)

sowon (soo-wun): special Confucian schools in Korea (p. 213)

sphere of influence: area in a country within which another nation claims exclusive trading privileges (*p. 57*)

status: position, rank, or prestige in relation to others (*p. 97*)

subcontractor: business person who supplies parts or other goods for larger industrial corporations (*p. 150*)

subsidies: public money granted by a government to assist enterprises that are thought to be advantageous to the country (*p. 162*)

sumo (SOO-moh): Japanese wrestling (*p. 47*)

Taika Reforms (TEYE-kah): adoption by the Japanese in 645 of Chinese systems of taxation, land ownership, and organization of government (*p. 28*)

tangjaeng (tahng-jeng): factional strife in Korea in the 1500s (*p. 216*)

tariff: a tax on imported goods (*p. 56*)

tatami (TAH-tuh-mee): straw matting used as a floor covering in Japanese homes (*p. 102*)

tax incentive: reduction in taxes to encourage business growth, recovery, or relocation (*p. 141*)

Tonghak (tahng-hahk): a Korean religion based in part on shamanism (*p. 220*)

tozama (toh-ZAH-mah): in Japan, outer warlords; daimyo with weak bonds of loyalty to the shogunate (*p. 44*)

trade surplus: an excess of exports over imports (*p. 156*)

trading partner: a nation that trades with another nation (*p. 155*)

two-tiered system: the economic system in Japan in which there is a sharp division between large corporations and smaller business enterprises (*p. 150*)

typhoon: a violent tropical wind of great destructive force (*p. 7*)

uji (OO-jee): small groups of families, thought to be descended from a common ancestor, with their own priest-ruler (*p. 27*)

universal suffrage: electoral system in which all adult citizens may vote (*p. 114*)

urban: related to cities (*p. 13*)

vassal: a subject of powerful lord (*p. 41*)

yangban (yahng-bahn): Korean aristocracy that dominated the government and the military during the Yi dynasty (*p. 213*)

yen: basic unit of Japanese currency (*p. 61*)

zaibatsu (zeye-baht-SOO): Japanese families who owned the chief industries of the country (*p. 63*)

Zen Buddhism: form of Buddhism emphasizing deep meditation and communion with nature to achieve enlightenment (*p. 40*)

zoku (zoh-koo): groups of Japanese Diet members who interceded on behalf of special-interest factions (*p. 130*)

Bibliography

Chapter 1

Finklestein, Barbara and Anna Imamura, eds. *Transcending Stereotypes: Discovering Japanese Culture and Education.* Yarmouth, ME: Intercultural Press, 1991.

Hall, John W., gen. ed. *The Cambridge History of Japan.* Cambridge, England: Cambridge University Press, 1988.

Hendry, Joy, *Understanding Japanese Society.* London and New York: Croom Helm, 1987.

Mason, R.H.P. *A History of Japan.* New York: Free Press, 1974.

Morton, W. Scott, *Japan: Its History and Culture.* New York: McGraw-Hill, 1984.

Reischauer, Edwin O. *Japan: The Story of a Nation.* 4th ed. New York: McGraw-Hill, 1990.

Chapters 2-3

Allen, Louis, *Japan: The Years of Triumph; From Feudal Isolation to Pacific Empire.* New York: American Heritage Press, 1971.

Beasley, William G. *The Rise of Modern Japan.* London: Weidenfield and Nicholson, 1990.

————— *The Modern History of Japan.* 3rd ed. London: Weidenfield and Nicholson, 1981.

Benedict, Ruth, *The Chrysanthemum and The Sword.* Boston: Houghton Mifflin, 1946.

Hane, Mikiso, *Pre-Modern Japan: A Historical Survey.* Boulder, CO: Westview Press, 1991.

Jansen, Marius B. and Gilbert Rozman, eds. *Japan in Transition: From Tokugawa to Meiji.* Princeton, NJ: Princeton University Press, 1986.

Lifton, Robert Jay, *Death In Life: Survivors of Hiroshima.* Chapel Hill, NC: Chapel Hill, 1991.

Murakami, Hyoe, *Japan: The Years of Trial, 1919-1952.* Tokyo: Japan Culture Institute, distributed by Japan Publications Trading, 1982.

Selden, Kyoko and Mark, eds. *The Atomic Bomb: Voices From Hiroshima and Nagasaki.* Armonk, NY: M.E. Sharpe, 1989.

Smith, Bradley, *Japan: A History in Art.* New York: Simon & Schuster, 1964.

Chapters 4-7

Bingman, Charles F. *Japanese Government, Leadership, and Management.* New York: St. Martin's Press, 1989.

Burks, Ardath W. *Japan: A Post-Industrial Power.* 3rd ed. Boulder, CO: Westview Press, 1991.

Christopher, Robert C. *The Japanese Mind: The Goliath Explained*. New York: Simon & Schuster, 1983.

Cohen, Steven D. *Uneasy Partnership: Competition and Conflict in U.S.-Japan Trade Relations*. Cambridge, MA: Ballinger, 1985.

Crump, Thomas, *The Death of an Emperor: Japan at the Crossroads*. New York: Oxford University Press, 1989.

Curtis, Gerald L., *The Japanese Way of Politics*. New York: Columbia University Press, 1988.

Davis, Winston, *Japanese Religion and Society: Paradigms of Structure and Change*. Purchase, NY: SUNY Press, 1992.

Emerson, John K., *The Eagle and the Rising Sun: America and Japan in the Twentieth Century*. Reading, MA: Addison-Wesley, 1988.

Fukutake, Tadashi, *Japanese Society Today*. 2nd ed. Tokyo: University of Tokyo Press, 1982.

Gibney, Frank, *Japan: The Fragile Superpower*. New York: Meridian, 1985.

Haiducek, Nicholas J., *Japanese Education: Made in the U.S.A.* New York: Praeger, 1991.

Holstein, William J., *The Japanese Power Game: What It Means for America*. New York: Maxwell Macmillan International, 1990.

Ishinomori, Shotaro. *An Introduction to Japanese Economics (The Comic Book)*. Berkeley, CA: University of California Press, 1988.

Lincoln, Edward J. *Japan Facing Economic Maturity*. Washington, DC: The Brookings Institute, 1988.

Morris-Suzuki, Tessa, *A History of Japanese Economic Thought*. London and New York: Nissan Institute for Japanese Studies, Oxford University, 1989.

Murakoshi, Yukio, *The Role of Women: Japanese Society and American Society*. Tokyo: Yumi Press, 1984.

Reischauer, Edwin O. *The Japanese Today: Change and Continuity*. Cambridge, MA: The Belknap Press of Harvard University Press, 1988.

Reischauer, Haru Matsukata, *Samurai and Silk: A Japanese and American Heritage*. Cambridge, MA: The Belknap Press of Harvard University Press, 1986.

Richardson, Bradley M., and Scott C. Flanagan, *Politics in Japan*. Boston: Little Brown, 1984.

Storry, Richard, *A History of Modern Japan*. London: Penguin Books, 1990.

Tasker, Peter, *The Japanese: Portrait of a Nation*. New York: Meridian, 1987.

White, Merry, *The Japanese Educational Challenge: A Commitment to Children*. New York: The Free Press, 1987.

Chapters 8-10

Brandt, Vincent S. *A Korean Village: Between Farm and Sea*. Prospect Heights, IL: Waveland Press, 1990.

Clark, Donald N. *Christianity in Modern Korea*. Lanham, MD: University Press of America, 1986.

Clark, Donald N., ed. *Korea Briefing, 1991*. Boulder, CO: Westview Press, 1991.

Eckert, Carter J., and Ki-baik Lee, *Korea Old and New: A History*. Cambridge, MA: Harvard University Press, 1990.

Handbook of Korea, A. Seoul: Seoul International Publishing House, 1987.

Hastings, Max, *The Korean War*. New York: Simon & Schuster, 1987.

Howe, Russell Warren, *The Koreans*. New York: Harcourt Brace Jovanovich, 1988.

Human Rights in Korea. New York: Asia Watch, 1987.

Hyde, George D. *South Korea: Education, Culture, and Economy*. New York: St. Martin's Press, 1988.

Hyun, Peter, *Koreana*. Seoul: Korea Britannica, 1984.

Kearney, Robert, *The Warrior Worker: The Challenge of the Korean Way of Working*. New York: Henry Holt, 1991.

Kendall, Laurel, *The Life and Hard Times of a Korean Shaman*. Honolulu: University of Hawaii Press, 1988.

Kendall, Laurel, and Mark Peterson, eds. *Korean Women: A View from the Inner Room*. New Haven, CT: East Rock Press, 1983.

Kim, Joungwon Alexander, *Divided Korea: The Politics of Development, 1945-1972*. Cambridge, MA: Harvard University Press, 1975.

Koh, Byung Chul, *The Foreign Policy Systems of North and South Korea*. Berkeley, CA: University of California Press, 1984.

Kwon, Jene K. *Korean Economic Development*. New York: Greenwood Press, 1990.

Lee, Peter H. *Anthology of Korean Literature: From Early Times to the 19th Century*. Honolulu: University of Hawaii Press, 1981.

Lee, Ki-baik, *A New History of Korea*. Cambridge, MA: Harvard University Press, 1985.

Macdonald, Donald Stone, *The Koreans: Contemporary Politics and Society*. Boulder, CO: Westview Press, 1990.

Morse, Ronald A., ed. *Wild Asters: Explorations in Korean Thought, Culture and Society*. Washington, DC: Woodrow Wilson International Center for Scholars, The Smithsonian Institution, 1986.

Nahm, Andrew C. *Korea: Tradition and Transformation: A History of the Korean People*. Elizabeth, NJ; Hollym International Corp., 1988.

Rhee, Yung Whee, Bruce Ross-Larsen, and Gary Pursell, *Korea's Competitive Edge: Managing the Entry into World Markets.* Baltimore, MD: Johns Hopkins University Press, 1984.

Scalapino, Robert A., and Han Sung-Joo, eds. *United States-Korea Relations.* Berkeley, CA: Institute of East Asian Studies, University of California Press, 1986.

Soh, Chung-hee, *The Chosen Women in Korean Politics: An Anthropological Study.* New York: Praeger, 1991.

Steinberg, David I. *The Republic of Korea: Economic Transformation and Social Change.* Boulder, CO: Westview Press, 1989.

Whelan, Richard, *Drawing the Line: The Korean War, 1950-1953.* Boston: Litttle Brown, 1990.

Winchester, Simon, *Korea.* New York: Prentice Hall Press, 1988.

Yoo, Yushin, *The Making of Modern Korea.* Rockville, NY: Golden Pond Press, 1990.

Index

Mutsuhito, Emperor, 58, 69
Myanmar (Burma), 174, 175

Nagasaki, 39, 46, 76, 170
Nagoya, 5, 9, 11, 39
nakodo, 99
Nanjing, 73
Nara, 25
Nara Period, 31-32, 34
National Assembly, South Korean, 234, 238
National Police Reserve, 80, 127
nationalism
    Japanese, 65-66, 179
    Korean, 221-222, 223, 233
    North Korean, 242
natural resources of Japan, 65, 67, 71, 137, 138, 154, 174, 176
natural resources of Korea, 189-190, 222, 243, 249
nemawashi, 99, 122
Netherlands, the, 55, 56, 73
New Zealand, 181
New Community Movement, 200-201, 245
Nissan, company, 150
Nixon, President Richard, 169
Nobi Plain, 5
Nokyo, 124-125
non-aggression treaty, 73
North Korea, 188-201, 224-227, 233, 234, 239-243, 249-254
    five-year plans, 240, 243, 245

occupation of Japan, U. S., 75-80, 136, 143, 165-66, 167, 168
Oda Nobunaga, 41
oil embargo, 73, 74, 170
Okinawa, 76, 169
Olympic Games, 1980, 173; 1988, 233, 253; 1992, 179
omiai, 89
Onin War, 38-39
Opium War, 55
Organization for Economic Cooperation and Development (OECD), 177
Osaka, 5, 6, 9, 11, 31, 39, 47, 48, 61, 136
Osaka Plain, 5
Osaka University, 95

Pacific nations, 174-176
Pacific Ocean, 6
Pacific Rim, 181
Pacific Ring of Fire, 3
Paekche Kingdom, 208
Park Chung Hee, General, 236-238, 243, 244, 245, 246
parliamentary government of Japan, 65, 112-117

pato, 91
Pearl Harbor, 74
Peking, 67, 72
Perry, Commodore Matthew, 48, 55-57, 136
Persian Gulf Crisis, 10, 171
Pescadores islands, 67
Philippines, 46, 174, 175, 181
Pillow Book, The, 32
planned economy, 240
political parties, in Japan
    Communist, 120, 122, 125, 127, 129, 167
    Democratic, 128
    Democratic Socialist, 122, 125
    Komeito, 123
    Liberal Democratic (LDP), 81, 117, 118, 120-122, 124, 125, 126, 128-130
    Liberal, 126-127, 128
    Social-Democratic, 120, 122, 125
    Socialist, 111, 127, 129, 167
political parties in Korea
    Communist, 239, 241
    Democratic Justice, 238
    Democratic Liberal, 238
    Korean Workers, 241, 242
    Liberal, 235
population
    of Japan, 2, 5, 6, 8, 11, 48, 86
    of Korea, 189, 191, 199-200, 218, 243, 244, 250
Port Arthur, 67
Portsmouth, Treaty of, 67
Portuguese traders, 46
Pre-industrial Japan, 8
prefectures, 60, 112
priest-rulers, 30
prime minister, Japanese, 115, 116-117, 121, 122, 130
propaganda, 190, 241-242, 249, 253, 254
protectorate, 221
puppet state, 71
Pusan, 200, 217
Pyongyang, 188, 217, 226, 240, 253

quality circles, 143

railroads, 61
Red Cross, 253
regents, 34
religion
    Buddhism, 15, 18, 25, 28, 30, 31, 39-40, 41, 87, 195, 197, 198, 209, 210-211
    Catholicism, 198, 219
    Christianity, 46, 198
    Confucianism, 15, 47, 87, 190, 193, 197-198, 213-216, 225, 241, 251
    missionaries, 46, 198
    priest-rulers, 30
    shamanism, 197, 209, 220

between Japan and Great Britain, 57
between Japan and the United States,
55-57, 81, 152-158, 172-173, 178
between Korea and China, 209
between Korea and Japan, 209, 222, 248,
250
between Korea and the United States,
246, 247-248
surplus in Japan, 156, 169, 178, 181
treaties, 56-57, 59, 62, 63, 65, 67, 68, 73, 80,
111, 126-127, 128, 167, 169, 220
Truman, Harry S., 226
Tsushima, 67
Twenty-one Demands, 68
two-tiered system, 150
typhoons, 7, 38, 87

uji, 27, 35
unequal treaties, 56-57, 59, 62, 63, 65
United Nations, 10, 176, 181, 224, 226, 253
United States, 136
and the Cold War, 80-81, 126-127, 129,
176, 177
influence on Japan, 63-64, 104
Japanese investment in, 156-158, 178
occupation of Japan, 75-80, 136, 143,
165-66, 167, 168
relations with Korea, 219-220, 224, 226-
227, 234, 237, 240, 243
trade with China, 55
trade with Japan, 55-57, 81, 152-158, 172-
173, 178
trade with Korea, 246, 247-248
treaties with Japan, 56-57, 80, 111, 126-
127, 128, 167
treaties with Korea, 220
and World War II, 71, 73, 74
urban life in Japan, 9-13, 18, 48, 70, 102-
103, 104-105, 129
urban life in Korea, 152, 192, 193, 199-201,
222

vassals, 41, 44

Versailles, Treaty of, 68
Vietnam War, 169, 171, 237, 246
volcanoes, 3,4
voting rights, 78, 90, 114

Wang Kon, 210
Washington Naval Conference, 71
Wataru Hiraizumi, 79, 118
Western influence,
on Japan, 63, 70, 87, 104, 112, 135, 180
on South Korea, 244
Wi Man, 208
women
in Japan, 37, 78, 89-93, 122-123, 126
in Korea, 192-194, 235, 242, 244
workforce, Japanese, 96-100, 111, 140, 143,
152
executives and managers, 144-145
workforce, Korean, 190, 192, 196, 245
World War I, 67-69, 70
World War II, 70-81, 139, 224, 226, 233,
235, 239
World Bank, 177
writing systems, 15, 209, 214

Xavier, Francis, 46

Yalu River, 207, 226
Yamato Period, 27-30
yangban, 213, 215, 216, 217, 219
Yayoi Period, 26-27
Yellow Sea, 189
yen, 61
Yi Dynasty, 212-213, 216, 218
Yi Song-gye, 212
Yi Sun-sin, Admiral, 205, 217
Yokohama, 5, 9, 11, 53, 56, 61, 105
Yonsei University, 195
Yoshida Shigeru, 81

zaibatsu, 62, 63, 69, 70, 81, 126, 142-143
Zen Buddhism, 40
zoku, 130

Picture Acknowledgments: Cover Photo: Gamma Liaison; x, FPG; xi, Fridmar Damm/Leo De Wys; 3, Steve Vidler/Nawrocki; 12, Travelpix/FPG; 15, Steve Vidler/Leo De Wys; 17, Westlight; 26, Granger Collection; 31, Steve Vidler/Nawrocki; 32, Sekai Bunka Photo; 36, Museum of Fine Arts, Boston; 37, 42, Granger Collection; 45, 48, Nawrocki; 56, Granger Collection; 59, Shashinka Photo Library; 60, 66, Sekai Bunka Photo; 72, 75, 77, Shashinka Photo Library; 88, Rick Smolan/Leo De Wys; 92, Steve Vidler/Leo De Wys; 94, Kaku Kurita/New York Times Photo; 95, Courtesy of the Japanese Information Center; 97, Danilo Boschung/Leo De Wys; 100, Henri Cartier-Bresson/Magnum; 114, Bettmann Archive; 115, Courtesy of the Japanese Information Center; 116, Bettmann Archive; 123, Magnum Photos; 125, 128, Bettmann Archive; 140, Steve Vidler/Leo De Wys; 144, Consulate General of Japan; 146, Shashinka Photo Library; 147, Karen Kasmauski/Matrix; 151, Consulate General of Japan; 153, Steve Vidler/Nawrocki; 172, 174, 175, Bettmann Archive; 192, Bill Kaufman/Leo De Wys; 196, 199, Consulate General of the Republic of Korea; 201, Mike Yamashita/Westlight; 210, Korea National Tourism Corp.; 212, Brian Lovell/Nawrocki; 214, Consulate General of the Republic of Korea; 216, Brian Lovell/Nawrocki; 218, Korea National Tourism Corp.; 225, Ed Hoffmann/Bettmann Archive; 227, Consulate General of the Republic of Korea; 235, United Nations; 236, 239, 241, Bettmann Archive; 247, Jean Paul Nacivet/Leo De Wys; 248, Fridmar Damm/Leo De Wys.